About This Book

Why is this topic important?

Continuing education and development lie at the very heart of any successful organization. Time and time again, studies show that the best organizations, those that deliver better-than-average return on investment, also happen to be the ones with the highest commitment to training and development. Moreover, training has become a powerful ally in the war for talent. Job seekers frequently cite a strong commitment to development as one of the principal reasons for joining or remaining with an organization.

What can you achieve with this book?

In your hands is a working toolkit, a valuable source of knowledge for the training professional. Offering entirely new content each year, the Pfeiffer Training *Annual* showcases the latest thinking and cutting-edge approaches to training and development, contributed by practicing training professionals, consultants, academics, and subject-matter experts. Turn to the *Annual* for a rich source of ideas and to try out new methods and approaches that others in your profession have found successful.

How is this book organized?

The book is divided into four sections: Experiential Learning Activities (ELAs); Editor's Choice; Inventories, Questionnaires, and Surveys; and Articles and Discussion Resources. All the material can be freely reproduced for training purposes. The ELAs are the mainstay of the *Annual* and cover a broad range of training topics. The activities are presented as complete and ready-to-use training designs; facilitator instructions and all necessary handouts and participant materials are included. Editor's Choice pieces allow us to select material that doesn't fit the other categories and take advantage of "hot topics." The instrument section introduces reliable survey and assessment tools for gathering and sharing data on aspects of personal or team development. The articles section presents the best current thinking about training and organization development. Use these for your own professional development or as lecture resources.

About Pfeiffer

Pfeiffer serves the professional development and hands-on resource needs of training and human resource practitioners and gives them products to do their jobs better. We deliver proven ideas and solutions from experts in HR development and HR management, and we offer effective and customizable tools to improve workplace performance. From novice to seasoned professional, Pfeiffer is the source you can trust to make yourself and your organization more successful.

Essential Knowledge Pfeiffer produces insightful, practical, and comprehensive materials on topics that matter the most to training and HR professionals. Our Essential Knowledge resources translate the expertise of seasoned professionals into practical, how-to guidance on critical workplace issues and problems. These resources are supported by case studies, worksheets, and job aids and are frequently supplemented with CD-ROMs, websites, and other means of making the content easier to read, understand, and use.

Essential Tools Pfeiffer's Essential Tools resources save time and expense by offering proven, ready-to-use materials—including exercises, activities, games, instruments, and assessments—for use during a training or team-learning event. These resources are frequently offered in looseleaf or CD-ROM format to facilitate copying and customization of the material.

Pfeiffer also recognizes the remarkable power of new technologies in expanding the reach and effectiveness of training. While e-hype has often created whizbang solutions in search of a problem, we are dedicated to bringing convenience and enhancements to proven training solutions. All our e-tools comply with rigorous functionality standards. The most appropriate technology wrapped around essential content yields the perfect solution for today's on-the-go trainers and human resource professionals.

Essential resources for training and HR professionals

The Pfeiffer Annual Series

The Pfeiffer Annuals present each year never-before-published materials contributed by learning professionals and academics and written for trainers, consultants, and human resource and performance-improvement practitioners. As a forum for the sharing of ideas, theories, models, instruments, experiential learning activities, and best and innovative practices, the *Annuals* are unique. Not least because only in the *Pfeiffer Annuals* will you find solutions from professionals like you who work in the field as trainers, consultants, facilitators, educators, and human resource and performance-improvement practitioners and whose contributions have been tried and perfected in real-life settings with actual participants and clients to meet real-world needs.

The Pfeiffer Annual: Consulting
Edited by Elaine Biech

The Pfeiffer Annual: Human Resource Management
Edited by Robert C. Preziosi

The Pfeiffer Annual: Training
Edited by Elaine Biech

Call for Papers

How would you like to be published in the *Pfeiffer Training* or *Consulting Annual*? Possible topics for submissions include group and team building, organization development, leadership, problem solving, presentation and communication skills, consulting and facilitation, and training-the-trainer. Contributions may be in one of the following three formats:

- Experiential Learning Activities
- Inventories, Questionnaires, and Surveys
- Articles and Discussion Resources

To receive a copy of the submission packet, which explains the requirements and will help you determine format, language, and style to use, contact editor Elaine Biech at Pfeifferannual@aol.com or by calling 757-588-3939.

Elaine Biech, EDITOR

The 2005 Pfeiffer Annual

TRAINING

Pfeiffer
A Wiley Imprint
www.pfeiffer.com

Copyright © 2005 by John Wiley & Sons, Inc.
Published by Pfeiffer
An Imprint of Wiley.
989 Market Street, San Francisco, CA 94103-1741 www.pfeiffer.com

Except as specifically noted below, no part of this publication may be reproduced, stored in a retrieval system, or transmitted in any form or by any means, electronic, mechanical, photocopying, recording, scanning, or otherwise, except as permitted under Section 107 or 108 of the 1976 United States Copyright Act, without either the prior written permission of the Publisher, or authorization through payment of the appropriate per-copy fee to the Copyright Clearance Center, Inc., 222 Rosewood Drive, Danvers, MA 01923, 978-750-8400, fax 978-750-4470, or on the web at www.copyright.com. Requests to the Publisher for permission should be addressed to the Permissions Department, John Wiley & Sons, Inc., 111 River Street, Hoboken, NJ 07030, 201-748-6011, fax 201-748-6008, e-mail: permcoordinator@wiley.com.

The Presentation and Discussion Resources, Experiential Learning Activities, Inventories, Questionnaires, and Surveys and their accompanying handouts from this book and the materials on the accompanying CD-ROM are designed for use in a group setting and may be customized and reproduced for educational/training purposes. The reproducible pages are designated by the appearance of the following copyright notice at the foot of each page:

> *The 2005 Pfeiffer Annual: Training.* Copyright © 2005 by John Wiley & Sons, Inc. Reproduced by permission of Pfeiffer, an Imprint of Wiley. www.pfeiffer.com

This notice may not be changed or deleted and it must appear on all reproductions as printed.

This free permission is restricted to limited customization of the CD-ROM materials for your organization and the paper reproduction of the materials for educational/training events. It does not allow for systematic or large-scale reproduction, distribution (more than 100 copies per page, per year), transmission, electronic reproduction or inclusion in any publications offered for sale or used for commercial purposes—none of which may be done without prior written permission of the Publisher.

For additional copies/bulk purchases of this book in the U.S. please contact 800-274-4434.

Pfeiffer books and products are available through most bookstores. To contact Pfeiffer directly call our Customer Care Department within the U.S. at 800-274-4434, outside the U.S. at 317-572-3985 or fax 317-572-4002 or visit www.pfeiffer.com.

Pfeiffer also publishes its books in a variety of electronic formats. Some content that appears in print may not be available in electronic books.

ISBN: 0-7879-6934-6
ISSN: 1046-333-X

Acquiring Editor: Martin Delahoussaye
Director of Development: Kathleen Dolan Davies
Developmental Editor: Susan Rachmeler
Editor: Rebecca Taff
Senior Production Editor: Dawn Kilgore
Manufacturing Supervisor: Bill Matherly
Interior Design: Chris Wallace
Illustrations: Leigh McLellan Design

Printed in the United States of America

Printing 10 9 8 7 6 5 4 3 2 1

658.3124
B586
2005

Contents

Preface   xiii

The Difference Between Training and Consulting: Which Annual to Use?   xvii

Introduction to *The 2005 Pfeiffer Annual: Training*   xxi

Experiential Learning Activities

Introduction to the Experiential Learning Activities Section   1

Experiential Learning Activities Categories   5

Well-Being: Drawing the Bottom Line   11
Teri-E Belf

Rich Traditions: Managing Diversity   19
Edwina Pio

Life Balance: Juggling Priorities   31
Gail Hahn

What's Your Priority? Clarifying Instructions   35
Jean Barbazette

Stand-Up and Sit-Down Talkers: Experiencing Diversity   41
Linda Byars Swindling

What Zoo Animal Would You Be? Giving and Receiving Feedback   47
George E. Krock

The Modern Art Factory: Experiencing Changing Leadership   51
Frank A. Prince

Musical Introductions: Melting the Ice   55
Lenn Millbower

Four Thermometers: Planning for Implementation — 59
Steve Sphar

Learning Charts: Cataloging for Future Planning — 65
Robert C. Preziosi

Role Models: Achieving Long-Term Results — 77
Robert Shaver

Chains: Keeping Lines of Communication Open — 89
Deborah Spring Laurel

The Human Body: Creating a Business Plan — 93
Lois Danis and Donna L. Goldstein

Editor's Choice

Introduction to the Editor's Choice Section — 99

Three Activities: Making Online Courses More Interactive — 101
Ryan Watkins

Far Versus Near Transfer: Planning for Success — 109
Paul L. Garavaglia

Inventories, Questionnaires, and Surveys

Introduction to the Inventories, Questionnaires, and Surveys Section — 115

Developing Trainers: A Self-Assessment and Observer Feedback Process — 117
John Sample

Best People Practices Assessment — 135
Stephen G. Haines

Articles and Discussion Resources

Introduction to the Articles and Discussion Resources Section — 147

Learning from Diversity Training: Outcome Assessment Strategies — 149
Anne M. McMahon and C. Louise Sellaro

Let's Talk — 159
Carolyn Nilson

From Stand Up to Sit Down: Translating Classroom Presentations to Computer-Based Classes — 165
Niki Nichols

Growing Community Online — 175
Zane L. Berge

How You Know What You Know — 183
Herb Kindler

Semi-Structured Online Debate — 189
Chih-Hsiung Tu

Creating the People Edge — 199
Stephen G. Haines

Does Executive Education Improve Business Performance? — 209
Adrian Furnham

Establishing a Stimulating Environment for Communication and Learning — 215
Robert William Lucas

**A Comprehensive, Effective, Proven Model to Develop Leaders — 231
Lois B. Hart and Charlotte S. Waisman

**Management Rhythm — 255
Peter R. Garber

Performance-Management Techniques for Developing Self-Sufficient Workers — 261
Teri Lund and Susan Barksdale

Contributors — 270

Contents of the Companion Volume, *The 2005 Pfeiffer Annual: Consulting* — 274

How to Use the CD-ROM — 277

Pfeiffer Publications Guide — 279

**Topic is "cutting edge."

Preface

Fast, Fresh, and Functional

"How do I stay on top of all the information coming my way?" "How will I find time to create new ideas?" "Where can I find a resource that will provide me with tools that are practical and guaranteed to work?" "How can I live up to my boss's expectations to do my tasks faster than ever?" and "How do I take care of me: learning new things and networking with others?"

If you've been asking yourself more questions lately than you have answers for, join the crowd! I call it the *fast, fresh,* and *functional* dilemma! Everyone in your life wants everything faster than ever. As a trainer or consultant, you are most likely turning projects around at a pace you never dreamed possible. But in addition to fast, your projects must be fresh. Your clients, customers, bosses, and participants want new ideas, new activities, new tools. Yes, and in addition to fast and fresh, all of your projects must be successful—they must be functional!

If this is true for you, you have come to the right place. The content of the *2005 Pfeiffer Annual: Training* is fast, fresh, and functional! Let me share some of the highlights with you.

Gail Hahn helps participants experience how to juggle priorities in a mere 20 minutes. As for fresh, check out Linda Swindling's "Stand-Up and Sit-Down Talkers." She shares an experiential learning activity (ELA) that demonstrates behaviors that may obstruct communication and prevent conflict resolution. Fast? About one-half hour. Fresh? The submission was so entertaining I was laughing out loud while I read it. Functional? You bet! I tried it the very next week. It works!

Also in this *Annual,* John Sample shares a self-assessment for developing trainers. Many new trainers do not have a support system for improving their performance. This instrument provides the feedback required. It's very fast; it's very functional. The Editor's Choice section—my personal selections—includes Ryan Watkins' three activities to make online courses more interactive. Now there's a fresh idea! In the articles section, "Let's Talk" presents a fast, fresh, and functional approach to structured dialogue and ongoing learning. And Bob Lucas presents dozens of ways to establish a stimulating environment in the classroom. Most of Bob's ideas take little time, come from a fresh perspective, and are definitely functional.

So if your job is asking you to do the impossible, the Pfeiffer *Annual* has resources to help you produce—fast, fresh, and functional. What else is happening that you should know about?

What's New to Take Care of You?

What about you? What are you doing to refresh yourself? After being in the middle of the fast, fresh, and functional milieu, you need to be sure that you are finding ways to continue to learn and to network with other professionals. Whether you are a trainer or a consultant, you will be happy to know that there is something new out there for you.

Trainers

The American Society for Training and Development (ASTD) released its 2004 competency study, Mapping the Future. It is the icon for the profession, and its impact on the workplace learning and performance community is expected to be huge. The model provides content required to develop competencies that ensure trainers think more strategically and link learning and performance to results. Even more significantly, however, is that ASTD will launch a certification program for learning and performance professionals in 2005. This provides credibility to the training field that has been sorely lacking.

The best news of all for trainers everywhere is that the certification effort will spawn well-thought-out, practical training for you to do your jobs better, or shall we say, fast, fresh, and functional! More information about the competency study and certification is available on ASTD's website, www.ASTD.org.

Consultants

A new association, Independent Consultants Association (ICA), has formed recently to help consultants be more successful. ICA will offer free listings to consultants in its directory, which will be published online and in a hard-cover library edition. In addition, the Association will feature a newsletter, seminars, interactive web events, a national conference, daily tips, and consultant news on its website. Tom Peters will chair the Advisory Council.

This is great news for all consultants. Finally a fresh new association exists that understands the independent consultant and his or her needs. Get involved on the ground floor, become a member, attend the first national conference, or at least list yourself in the directory. Looking for networking opportunities? This looks like a big one to me! Visit ICA's website at www.ica-assn.org.

What Is the *Annual*?

The 2005 Pfeiffer Annual: Training presents a collection of practical materials written for trainers, consultants, and performance-improvement technologists. This source for experiential learning activities, resource for instruments, and reference for cutting-edge articles has inspired human resource development (HRD) professionals for thirty-three years.

The *Pfeiffer Annual: Training* focuses on skill building and knowledge enhancement and also includes cutting-edge articles that enhance the skills and professional development of trainers.

Whether you are a trainer, a consultant, a facilitator, or a bit of each, you will find tools and resources that provide you with the basics and challenge (and we hope inspire) you to use new techniques and models.

Annual Loyalty

The Pfeiffer *Annual* series has many loyal subscribers. There are several reasons for this loyalty. In addition to the wide variety of topics and implementation levels, the *Annuals* provide materials that are applicable to varying circumstances. You will find instruments for individuals, teams, and organizations; experiential learning activities to round out workshops, team building, or consulting assignments; ideas and contemporary solutions for managing human capital; and articles that increase your own knowledge base, to use as reference materials in your writing, or as a source of ideas for your training or consulting assignments.

Many of our readers have been loyal customers for a dozen or more years. If you are one of them, we thank you. And we thank each of you who provided input about the new features and the improvements we initiated last year. The cover design, the binding style, and the CD-ROM all received rave reviews. The *Annuals* owe most of their success, though, to the fact that they are immediately ready to use. All of the materials may be duplicated for educational and training purposes. If you need to adapt or modify the materials to tailor them for your audience's needs, go right ahead. We only request that the credit statement found on the copyright page (and on each reproducible page) be retained on all copies. Our liberal copyright policy makes it easy and fast for you to use the materials to do your job. However, if you intend to reproduce the materials in publications for sale or if you wish to reproduce more than one hundred copies of any one item, please contact us for prior written permission.

If you are a new *Annual* user, welcome! If you like what you see in the 2005 edition, you may want to consider taking out a standing order. By doing so, you are guaranteed to receive your copy each year straight off the press and receive a discount off the cover price. And if you want to go back and have the entire series for your use, then the *Pfeiffer Library—which contains content from the very first edition to the present day*—is available on CD-ROM. You can find information on the *Pfeiffer Library* at www.pfeiffer.com. I often refer to many of my *Annuals* from the 1980s. They include several classic activities that have become a mainstay in my team-building designs. But most of all, the *Annuals* have been a valuable resource for over thirty years because the materials come from professionals like you who work in the field as trainers, consultants, facilitators, educators, and performance-improvement technologists, whose contributions have been tried and perfected in real-life settings with actual participants and clients to meet real-world needs.

To this end, we encourage you to submit materials to be considered for publication. We are interested in receiving experiential learning activities; inventories, questionnaires, and surveys; and articles and discussion resources. Contact the Pfeiffer Editorial Department at the address listed on the copyright page for copies of our guidelines for contributors or contact me directly at Box 8249, Norfolk, VA 23503, or by email at pfeifferannual@aol.com. We welcome your comments, ideas, and contributions.

Acknowledgments

Thank you to the dedicated, friendly, thoughtful people at Pfeiffer who produced the *2005 Pfeiffer Annual: Training*: Kathleen Dolan Davies, Martin Delahoussaye, Dawn Kilgore, Susan Rachmeler, Laura Reizman, and Rebecca Taff. Thank you to Lorraine Kohart of ebb associates inc, who assisted our authors with all the details of submission and who ensured that we met all the deadlines. Most important, thank you to our contributors, who have once again shared their ideas, techniques, and materials so that trainers and consultants everywhere may benefit.

Elaine Biech
Editor
September 2004

The Difference Between Training and Consulting:
Which Annual to Use?

The two volumes of the *Pfeiffer Annuals*—training and consulting—are resources for two different but closely related professions. Each *Annual* serves as a collection of tools and support materials used by the professionals in their respective arenas. The volumes include activities, articles, and instruments used by individuals in the training and consulting fields. The training volume is written with the trainer in mind, and the consulting volume is written with the consultant in mind.

How can you differentiate between the two volumes? Let's begin by defining each profession. A *trainer* can be defined as anyone who is responsible for designing and delivering knowledge to adult learners and may include an internal HRD professional employed by an organization or an external practitioner who contracts with an organization to design and conduct training programs. Generally, the trainer is a subject-matter expert who is expected to transfer knowledge so that the trainee can know or do something new. A *consultant* is someone who provides unique assistance or advice (based on what the consultant knows or has experienced) to someone else, usually known as "the client." The consultant may not necessarily be a subject-matter expert in all situations. Often the consultant is an expert at using specific tools to extract, coordinate, resolve, organize, expedite, or implement an organizational situation.

The lines between the consulting and training professions have blurred in the past few years. First, the names and titles have blurred. For example, some external trainers call themselves "training consultants" as a way of distinguishing themselves from internal trainers. Some organizations now have internal consultants who usually reside in the training department.

Second, the roles have blurred. While a consultant has always been expected to deliver measurable results, now trainers are expected to do so as well. Both are expected to improve performance; both are expected to contribute to the bottom line.

Facilitation was at one time thought to be a consultant skill; today trainers are expected to use facilitation skills to train. Training one-on-one was a trainer skill; today consultants train executives one-on-one and call it "coaching."

The introduction of the "performance technologist," whose role is one of combined trainer and consultant, is a perfect example of a new profession that has evolved due to the need for trainers to use more "consulting" techniques in their work. The "performance consultant" is a new role supported by the American Society for Training and Development (ASTD). ASTD has shifted its focus from training to performance improvement.

As you can see, the roles and goals of training and consulting are not nearly as specific as they once may have been. However, when you step back and examine the two professions from a big-picture perspective, you can more easily differentiate between the two. Maintaining a big-picture focus will also help you determine which *Pfeiffer Annual* to turn to as your first resource.

Both volumes cover the same general topics: communication, teamwork, problem solving, and leadership. However, depending on your requirement and purpose—a training or consulting need—you will use each in different situations. You will select the *Annual* based on *how you will interact with the topic, not on what the topic might be*. Let's take a topic such as teamwork, for example. If you are searching for a lecturette that teaches the advantages of teamwork, a workshop activity that demonstrates the skill of making decisions in a team, or a handout that discusses team stages, look to the Training *Annual*. On the other hand, if you are conducting a team-building session for a dysfunctional team, helping to form a new team, or trying to understand the dynamics of an executive team, you will look to the Consulting *Annual*.

The Training *Annual*

The materials in the Training volume focus on skill building and knowledge enhancement as well as on the professional development of trainers. They generally focus on controlled events: a training program, a conference presentation, a classroom setting.

Look to the Training *Annual* to find ways to improve a training session for 10 to 1,000 people and anything else that falls in the human resource development category:

- Specific experiential learning activities that can be built into a training program;

- Techniques to improve training: debriefing exercises, conducting role plays, managing time;

- Topical lecturettes;
- Ideas to improve a boring training program;
- Icebreakers and energizers for a training session;
- Surveys that can be used in a classroom;
- Ideas for moving an organization from training to performance; and
- Ways to improve your skills as a trainer.

The Consulting *Annual*

The materials in the Consulting volume focus on intervention techniques and organizational systems as well as the professional development of consultants. They generally focus on "tools" that you can have available just in case: concepts about organizations and their development (or demise) and about more global situations.

Look to the Consulting *Annual* to find ways to improve consulting activities from team building and executive coaching to organization development and strategic planning:

- Skills for working with executives;
- Techniques for solving problems, effecting change, and gathering data;
- Team-building tools, techniques, and tactics;
- Facilitation ideas and methods;
- Processes to examine for improving an organization's effectiveness;
- Surveys that can be used organizationally; and
- Ways to improve your effectiveness as a consultant.

Summary

Even though the professions and the work are closely related and at times interchangeable, there is a difference. Use the following table to help you determine which *Annual* you should scan first for help. Remember, however, there is some blending of the two and either *Annual* may have your answer. It depends . . .

Element	Training	Consulting
Topics	Teams, Communication, Problem Solving	Teams, Communication, Problem Solving
Topic Focus	Individual, Department	Corporate, Global
Purpose	Skill Building, Knowledge Transfer	Coaching, Strategic Planning, Building Teams
Recipient	Individuals, Departments	Usually More Organizational
Organizational Level	All Workforce Members	Usually Closer to the Top
Delivery Profile	Workshops, Presentations	Intervention, Implementation
Atmosphere	Structured	Unstructured
Time Frame	Defined	Undefined
Organizational Cost	Moderate	High
Change Effort	Low to Moderate	Moderate to High
Setting	Usually a Classroom	Anywhere
Professional Experience	Entry Level, Novice	Proficient, Master Level
Risk Level	Low	High
Professional Needs	Activities, Resources	Tools, Theory
Application	Individual Skills	Usually Organizational System

When you get right down to it, we are all trainers and consultants. The skills may cross over. A great trainer is also a skilled consultant. And a great consultant is also a skilled trainer. The topics may be the same, but how you implement them may be vastly different. Which *Annual* to use? Remember to think about your purpose in terms of the big picture: consulting or training.

As you can see, we have both covered.

Introduction

to *The 2005 Pfeiffer Annual: Training*

Getting the Most from This Resource

The 2005 Pfeiffer Annual: Training is the forty-fourth volume in the *Annual* series, a collection of practical and useful materials for professionals in the broad area described as human resource development (HRD). The materials are written by and for professionals, including trainers, organization-development and organization-effectiveness consultants, performance-improvement technologists, facilitators, educators, instructional designers, and others.

Each *Annual* has three main sections: experiential learning activities; inventories, questionnaires, and surveys; and articles and discussion resources. A fourth section, editor's choice, has been reserved for those unique contributions that do not fit neatly into one of the three main sections, but are valuable as identified by the editorial staff. Each published submission is classified in one of the following categories: Individual Development, Communication, Problem Solving, Groups, Teams, Consulting, Facilitating, Leadership, and Organizations. Within each category, pieces are further classified into logical subcategories, which are identified in the introductions to the three sections.

"Cutting edge" topics are identified in each *Annual*. This designation highlights topics that present information, concepts, tools, or perspectives that may be recent additions to the profession or that have not previously appeared in the *Annual* or are currently "hot topics."

The series continues to provide an opportunity for HRD professionals who wish to share their experiences, their viewpoints, and their processes with their colleagues.

To that end, Pfeiffer publishes guidelines for potential authors. These guidelines are available from the Pfeiffer Editorial Department at Jossey-Bass, Inc., in San Francisco, California.

Materials are selected for the *Annuals* based on the quality of the ideas, applicability to real-world concerns, relevance to current HRD issues, clarity of presentation, and ability to enhance our readers' professional development. In addition, we choose experiential learning activities that will create a high degree of enthusiasm among the participants and add enjoyment to the learning process. As in the past several years, the contents of each *Annual* span a wide range of subject matter, reflecting the range of interests of our readers.

Our contributor list includes a wide selection of experts in the field: in-house practitioners, consultants, and academically based professionals. A list of contributors to the *Annual* can be found at the end of the volume, including their names, affiliations, addresses, telephone numbers, facsimile numbers, and email addresses. Readers will find this list useful if they wish to locate the authors of specific pieces for feedback, comments, or questions. Further information on each contributor is presented in a brief biographical sketch that appears at the conclusion of each article. We publish this information to encourage "networking," which continues to be a valuable mainstay in the field of human resource development.

We are pleased with the high quality of material that is submitted for publication each year and often regret that we have page limitations. In addition, just as we cannot publish every manuscript we receive, you may find that not all published works are equally useful to you. Therefore, we encourage and invite ideas, materials, and suggestions that will help us to make subsequent *Annuals* as useful as possible to all of our readers.

Introduction
to the Experiential Learning Activities Section

Experiential learning activities ensure that lasting learning occurs. They should be selected with a specific learning objective in mind. These objectives are based on the participants' needs and the facilitator's skills. Although the experiential learning activities presented here all vary in goals, group size, time required, and process, they all incorporate one important element: questions that ensure learning has occurred. This discussion, led by the facilitator, assists participants to process the activity, to internalize the learning, and to relate it to their day-to-day situations. It is this element that creates the unique experience and learning opportunity that only an experiential learning activity can bring to the group process.

Readers have used the *Annuals'* experiential learning activities for years to enhance their training and consulting events. Each learning experience is complete and includes all lecturettes, handout content, and other written material necessary to facilitate the activity. In addition, many include variations of the design that the facilitator might find useful. If the activity does not fit perfectly with your objective, within your time frame, or to your group size, we encourage you to adapt the activity by adding your own variations. You will find additional experiential learning activities listed in the "Experiential Learning Activities Categories" chart that immediately follows this introduction.

The 2005 Pfeiffer Annual: Training includes thirteen activities, in the following categories:

Individual Development: Sensory Awareness

   Well-Being: Drawing the Bottom Line, by Teri-E Belf

Individual Development: Diversity

   Rich Traditions: Managing Diversity, by Edwina Pio

Individual Development: Life/Career Planning

    Life Balance: Juggling Priorities, by Gail Hahn

Communication: Awareness

    What's Your Priority? Clarifying Instructions, by Jean Barbazette

Communication: Conflict

    Stand-Up and Sit-Down Talkers: Experiencing Diversity, by Linda Byars Swindling

Communication: Styles

    What Zoo Animal Would You Be? Giving and Receiving Feedback, by George E. Krock

Teams: How Groups Work

    The Modern Art Factory: Experiencing Changing Leadership, by Frank A. Prince

Consulting, Training, and Facilitating: Facilitating: Opening

    Musical Introductions: Melting the Ice, by Lenn Millbower

Consulting, Training, and Facilitating: Facilitating: Closing

    Four Thermometers: Planning for Implementation, by Steve Sphar

    Learning Charts: Cataloging for Future Planning, by Robert C. Preziosi

Leadership: Interviewing/Appraisal

    Role Models: Achieving Long-Term Results, by Robert Shaver

Organizations: Communication

    Chains: Keeping Lines of Communication Open, by Deborah Spring Laurel

Organizations: Vision, Mission, Values, Strategy

    The Human Body: Creating a Business Plan, by Lois Danis and Donna L. Goldstein

To further assist you in selecting appropriate ELAs, we provide the following grid that summarizes category, time required, group size, and risk factor for each ELA.

Category	ELA Title	Page	Time Required	Group Size	Risk Factor
Individual Development: Sensory Awareness	Well-Being: Drawing the Bottom Line	11	Approximately 1 hour	4 to 100	Low
Individual Development: Diversity	Rich Traditions: Managing Diversity	19	2 to 2½ hours	10 to 40	Low to Moderate
Individual Development: Life/Career Planning	Life Balance: Juggling Priorities	31	20 to 30 minutes	5 to 12	Low to Moderate
Communication: Awareness	What's Your Priority? Clarifying Instructions	35	50 to 60 minutes	10 or groups of 10	Low to Moderate
Communication: Conflict	Stand-Up and Sit-Down Talkers: Experiencing Diversity	41	25 to 35 minutes	10 to 50	Moderate
Communication: Styles	What Zoo Animal Would You Be? Giving and Receiving Feedback	47	60 to 90 minutes	6 to 10	Moderate
Teams: How Groups Work	The Modern Art Factory: Experiencing Changing Leadership	51	40 to 50 minutes	4 to 5/group, unlimited groups	Moderate
Consulting, Training, and Facilitating: Facilitating: Opening	Musical Introductions: Melting the Ice	55	20 minutes	Any	Low
Consulting, Training, and Facilitating: Facilitating: Closing	Four Thermometers: Planning for Implementation	59	40 to 60 minutes	15 to 30	Low to Moderate
Consulting, Training, and Facilitating: Facilitating: Closing	Learning Charts: Cataloging for Future Planning	65	90 to 120 minutes	12 to 15	Low to Moderate
Leadership: Interviewing/ Appraisal	Role Models: Achieving Long-Term Results	77	1 hour	Up to 20	Moderate
Organizations: Communication	Chains: Keeping Lines of Communication Open	89	Approximately 30 minutes	10 to 50	Low
Organizations: Vision, Mission, Values, Strategy	The Human Body: Creating a Business Plan	93	Approximately 40 minutes	15 to 40	Moderate

Experiential Learning Activities Categories

Range	Volume
1-24	Volume I, Handbook
25-48	Volume II, Handbook
49-74	Volume III, Handbook
75-86	1972 Annual
87-100	1973 Annual
101-124	Volume IV, Handbook
125-136	1974 Annual
137-148	1975 Annual
149-172	Volume V, Handbook
173-184	1976 Annual
185-196	1977 Annual
197-220	Volume VI, Handbook
221-232	1978 Annual
233-244	1979 Annual
245-268	Volume VII, Handbook
269-280	1980 Annual
281-292	1981 Annual
293-316	Volume VIII, Handbook
317-328	1982 Annual
329-340	1983 Annual
341-364	Volume IX, Handbook
365-376	1984 Annual
377-388	1985 Annual
389-412	Volume X, Handbook
413-424	1986 Annual
425-436	1987 Annual
437-448	1988 Annual
449-460	1989 Annual
461-472	1990 Annual
473-484	1991 Annual
485-496	1992 Annual
497-508	1993 Annual
509-520	1994 Annual
521-532	1995 Annual: Volume 1, Training
533-544	1995 Annual: Volume 2, Consulting
545-556	1996 Annual: Volume 1, Training
557-568	1996 Annual: Volume 2, Consulting
569-580	1997 Annual: Volume 1, Training
581-592	1997 Annual: Volume 2, Consulting
593-604	1998 Annual: Volume 1, Training
605-616	1998 Annual: Volume 2, Consulting
617-630	1999 Annual: Volume 1, Training
631-642	1999 Annual: Volume 2, Consulting
643-656	2000 Annual: Volume 1, Training
657-669	2000 Annual: Volume 2, Consulting
670-681	2001 Annual: Volume 1, Training
683-695	2001 Annual: Volume 2, Consulting
696-709	2002 Annual: Volume 1, Training
710-722	2002 Annual: Volume 2, Consulting
723-739	2003 Annual: Volume 1, Training
740-752	2003 Annual: Volume 2, Consulting

Note that numbering system was discontinued beginning with the 2004 Annuals.

INDIVIDUAL DEVELOPMENT

Sensory Awareness

	Vol.	Page
Feelings & Defenses (56)	III	31
Lemons (71)	III	94
Growth & Name Fantasy (85)	'72	59
Group Exploration (119)	IV	92
Relaxation & Perceptual Awareness (136)	'74	84
T'ai Chi Chuan (199)	VI	10
Roles Impact Feelings (214)	VI	102
Projections (300)	VIII	30
Mastering the Deadline Demon (593)	'98-1	9
Learning Shifts (643)	'00-1	11
Secret Sponsors (657)	'00-2	11
Spirituality at Work (670)	'01-1	11
What You See (740)	'03-2	11
Highly Leveraged Moments	'04-T	11
Z Fantasy	'04-C	11
Well-Being	'05-T	11
Picture Yourself	'05-C	11

Self-Disclosure

	Vol.	Page
Johari Window (13)	I	65
Graphics (20)	I	88
Personal Journal (74)	III	109
Make Your Own Bag (90)	'73	13
Growth Cards (109)	IV	30
Expressing Anger (122)	IV	104
Stretching (123)	IV	107
Forced-Choice Identity (129)	'74	20
Boasting (181)	'76	49
The Other You (182)	'76	51
Praise (306)	VIII	61
Introjection (321)	'82	29
Personality Traits (349)	IX	158

	Vol.	Page
Understanding the Need for Approval (438)	'88	21
The Golden Egg Award (448)	'88	89
Adventures at Work (521)	'95-1	9
That's Me (522)	'95-1	17
Knowledge Is Power (631)	'99-2	13
Spirituality at Work (658)	'00-2	15
The Imposter Syndrome (696)	'02-1	11
Internet Impressions (710)	'02-2	11
Purposeful Spot Game (723)	'03-1	11
Quotations	'04-T	19
Take a Risk	'05-C	17

Sex Roles

	Vol.	Page
Polarization (62)	III	57
Sex-Role Stereotyping (95)	'73	26
Sex-Role Attributes (184)	'76	63
Who Gets Hired? (215)	VI	106
Sexual Assessment (226)	'78	36
Alpha II (248)	VII	19
Sexual Values (249)	VII	24
Sex-Role Attitudes (258)	VII	85
Sexual Values in Organizations (268)	VII	146
Sexual Attraction (272)	'80	26
Sexism in Advertisements (305)	VIII	58
The Promotion (362)	IX	152
Raising Elizabeth (415)	'86	21
The Problem with Men/Women Is ... (437)	'88	9
The Girl and the Sailor (450)	'89	17
Tina Carlan (466)	'90	45

Diversity

	Vol.	Page
Status-Interaction Study (41)	II	85
Peer Perceptions (58)	III	41
Discrimination (63)	III	62

	Vol.	Page
Traditional American Values (94)	'73	23
Growth Group Values (113)	IV	45
The In-Group (124)	IV	112
Leadership Characteristics (127)	'74	13
Group Composition (172)	V	139
Headbands (203)	VI	25
Sherlock (213)	VI	92
Negotiating Differences (217)	VI	114
Young/Old Woman (227)	'78	40
Pygmalion (229)	'78	51
Race from Outer Space (239)	'79	38
Prejudice (247)	VII	15
Physical Characteristics (262)	VII	108
Whom to Choose (267)	VII	141
Data Survey (292)	'81	57
Lifeline (298)	VIII	21
Four Cultures (338)	'83	72
All Iowans Are Naive (344)	IX	14
AIRSOPAC (364)	IX	172
Doctor, Lawyer, Indian Chief (427)	'87	21
Life Raft (462)	'90	17
Zenoland (492)	'92	69
First Impressions (509)	'94	9
Parole Board (510)	'94	17
Fourteen Dimensions (557)	'96-2	9
Adoption (569)	'97-1	9
Globalization (570)	'97-1	19
Generational Pyramids (571)	'97-1	33
People with Disabilities (594)	'98-1	15
Expanding the Scope of Diversity Programs (617)	'99-1	13
Tortuga Place and Your Place (644)	'00-1	15
Unearned Privilege (659)	'00-2	25

	Vol.	Page
What's Your Generation X IQ? (683)	'01-2	11
Cultural Triangle (697)	'02-1	19
Other Perspectives (724)	'03-1	23
Early Memories (741)	'03-2	17
Generational Bingo	'04-T	27
Diversity from Within	'04-C	23
Rich Traditions	'05-T	19
At the Movies	'05-C	25

Life/Career Planning

	Vol.	Page
Life Planning (46)	II	101
Banners (233)	'79	9
Wants Bombardment (261)	VII	105
Career Renewal (332)	'83	27
Life Assessment and Planning (378)	'85	15
Work-Needs Assessment (393)	X	31
The Ego-Radius Model (394)	X	41
Dropping Out (414)	'86	15
Roles (416)	'86	27
Creating Ideal Personal Futures (439)	'88	31
Pie in the Sky (461)	'90	9
What's in It for Me? (463)	'90	21
Affirmations (473)	'91	9
Supporting Cast (486)	'92	15
Career Visioning (498)	'93	13
The Hand You're Dealt (523)	'95-1	23
Living Our Values (548)	'96-1	25
Career Roads (549)	'96-1	35
Collaborating for Success (572)	'97-1	45
High Jump (573)	'97-1	57
Issues, Trends, and Goals (595)	'98-1	21
Bouncing Back (596)	'98-1	35
Work Activities (597)	'98-1	43
From Good Intentions to Results (645)	'00-1	27
What Works Best? (671)	'01-1	21
Passion and Purpose (672)	'01-1	35
Career Choice	'04-C	27
Life Balance	'05-T	31

COMMUNICATION

Awareness

	Vol.	Page
One-Way, Two-Way (4)	I	13
Think-Feel (65)	III	70
Ball Game (108)	IV	27
Re-Owning (128)	'74	18
Helping Relationships (152)	V	13
Babel (153)	V	16
Blindfolds (175)	'76	13
Letter Exchange (190)	'77	28
Dominoes (202)	VI	21
Blivet (241)	'79	46
Meanings Are in People (250)	VII	28
Mixed Messages (251)	VII	34
Gestures (286)	'81	28
Maze (307)	VIII	64
Feelings (330)	'83	14
Synonyms (341)	IX	5
In Other Words (396)	X	55
Taking Responsibility (397)	X	62
Pass It On (398)	X	68
Shades of Difference (417)	'86	35
E-Prime (440)	'88	39
Words Apart (464)	'90	29
Supportive Versus Defensive Climates (474)	'91	15
Let Me (511)	'94	31
Bugs (553)	'96-1	73
Red Light/Green Light (598)	'98-1	53
Supreme Court (660)	'00-2	33
Music While You Work (684)	'01-2	23
Speed Up! (698)	'02-1	29
Blind Soccer Game (742)	'03-2	23
Taboo, Do I Know You?	'04-C	35
What's Your Priority?	'05-T	35
All Power Is Relative	'05-C	35

Building Trust

	Vol.	Page
Dyadic Encounter (21)	I	90
Nonverbal Communication I (22)	I	101
Intimacy Program (70)	III	89
Dialog (116)	IV	66
Dimensions of Trust (120)	IV	96
Dyadic Renewal (169)	V	116
Disclosing & Predicting (180)	'76	46
Current Status (196)	'77	57
Dyadic Risk Taking (220)	VI	130
Work Dialogue (524)	'95-1	27
Coal to Diamonds (533)	'95-2	9
Alter Ego (599)	'98-1	59
Building Trust in Pairs (632)	'99-2	19
What to Say (661)	'00-2	37
A Fine Predicament (743)	'03-2	27

Conflict

	Vol.	Page
Frustrations & Tensions (75)	'72	5
Conflict Fantasy (130)	'74	22
Escalation (219)	VI	127
Defensive & Supportive Communication (238)	'79	28
Conflict Management (242)	'79	54
Resistance (309)	VIII	75
Conflict Role Play (340)	'83	80
The Company Task Force (352)	IX	84
The Decent but Pesky Co-Worker (400)	X	80
VMX Productions, Inc. (441)	'88	43
Quality Customer Service (475)	'91	27
The Parking Space (476)	'91	35
Time Flies (499)	'93	19
Alpha/Beta (512)	'94	37
Common Ground (539)	'95-2	51
Thumbs Up, Thumbs Down (574)	'97-1	65
The M&M(r) Game (618)	'99-1	19
Retaliatory Cycle (662)	'00-2	45
Workplace Scenarios (673)	'01-1	43
Choices (725)	'03-1	31
12 Angry Men	'04-T	33
Stand-Up and Sit-Down Talkers	'05-T	41

Feedback

	Vol.	Page
Group-on-Group (6)	I	22
Coins (23)	I	104
Behavior Description Triads (50)	III	6
Psychomat (84)	'72	58
Puzzlement (97)	'73	30
Analyzing & Increasing Open Behavior (99)	'73	38
The Gift of Happiness (104)	IV	15
Sculpturing (106)	IV	21
The Portrait Game (107)	IV	24
Party Conversations (138)	'75	10
Adjectives (168)	V	114
Introspection (209)	V	157
Cards (225)	'78	34
Developing Trust (303)	VIII	45
Giving and Receiving Feedback (315)	VIII	125
Feedback (355)	IX	107
Pin Spotter (377)	'85	11
Feedback on Nonverbal and Verbal Behaviors (379)	'85	35
Gaining Support (380)	'85	39
I Am, Don't You Think? (390)	X	8
Two Bags Full (391)	X	22
Seeing Ourselves as Others See Us (426)	'87	17
The Art of Feedback (449)	'89	9
Feedback Awareness (487)	'92	29
A Note to My Teammate (497)	'93	9
Lines (551)	'96-1	59
Coloring Book (646)	'00-1	37
I Appreciate (674)	'01-1	63
Performance Expectations (726)	'03-1	45

Listening

	Vol.	Page
Listening Triads (8)	I	31
Rumor Clinic (28)	II	12
Not-Listening (52)	III	10
Peter-Paul (87)	'73	7
Active Listening (252)	VII	39
I'm All Ears (395)	X	46
Poor Listening Habits (428)	'87	25
In Reply (465)	'90	35
Needs, Features, and Benefits (513)	'94	47
Levels of Dialogue (525)	'95-1	45
He Who Holds the Pen	'04-T	39
The Association for Community Improvement	'05-C	43

Styles

	Vol.	Page
Building Open & Closed Relationships (93)	'73	20
Submission/Aggression/Assertion (206)	V	136
Organizational TA (310)	VIII	83
The Human Bank Account (399)	X	76
The Candy Bar (457)	'89	73
Stating the Issue (503)	'93	43
Enhancing Communication (550)	'96-1	51
Go Left, Go Right (575)	'97-1	69
Memories (699)	'02-1	51
What Zoo Animal Would You Be?	'05-T	47

Technology

	Vol.	Page
Virtual Scavenger Hunt (619)	'99-1	27
Mediated Message Exchange (647)	'00-1	43
Telephone Conference (648)	'00-1	51

Experiential Learning Activities

	Vol.	Page
PROBLEM SOLVING		
Generating Alternatives		
Broken Squares (7)	I	25
Brainstorming (53)	III	14
Quaker Meeting (76)	'72	11
Nominal Group Technique (141)	'75	35
Poems (185)	'77	13
Package Tour (192)	'77	35
Numbers (221)	'78	9
Puzzle Cards (240)	'79	41
Analytical or Creative? (285)	'81	24
Vacation Schedule (312)	VIII	100
Pebbles (335)	'83	45
Bricks (343)	IX	10
Departmental Dilemma (350)	IX	66
QC Agenda (370)	'84	44
Water Jars (392)	X	26
Marzilli's Fine Italian Foods (454)	'89	55
Cooperative Inventions (467)	'90	61
Greenback Financial Services (470)	'90	83
Puzzling Encounters (481)	'91	97
The Real Meaning (502)	'93	39
PBJ Corporation (568)	'96-2	131
Broken Triangles (576)	'97-1	73
Deck of Cards (663)	'00-2	51
Decision, Decisions (684)	'01-2	33
Ask Everyone (711)	'02-2	21
The Chrysalis Flower	'04-T	43
Odyssey	'04-C	41
Give Brands a Hand	'05-C	55
Information Sharing		
Energy International (80)	'72	25
Pine County (117)	IV	75
Farm E-Z (133)	'74	44
Sales Puzzle (155)	V	34
Room 703 (156)	V	39
Al Kohbari (178)	'76	26
Murder One (212)	VI	75
Farmers (284)	'81	16
The Sales Manager's Journey (359)	IX	125
The Welsh Boothouse (383)	'85	67
Society of Taos (432)	'87	57
Dust Pan Case (482)	'91	107
Diversity Quiz (514)	'94	55
Bean Counters (552)	'96-1	67
Systems Redesign (633)	'99-2	31
Persuasion? No Problem! (727)	'03-1	53
Spotlight Dance	'04-T	51
Consensus/Synergy		
Top Problems (11)	I	49
Residence Halls (15)	I	72
NORC (30)	II	18
Kerner Report (64)	III	64
Supervisory Behavior/Aims of Education (69)	III	84
Shoe Store (102)	IV	5
Consensus-Seeking (115)	IV	51
Hung Jury (134)	'74	64
Kidney Machine (135)	'74	78
Lost at Sea (140)	'75	28
Cash Register (151)	V	10
Letter Occurrence/Health Professions Prestige (157)	V	44
Wilderness Survival (177)	'76	19
Pyramids (187)	'77	20
Admissions Committee (223)	'78	15
Alphabet Names (236)	'79	19
What's Important on My Job? (244)	'79	71
Lists (255)	VII	57
Values for the 1980s (271)	'80	20
Ranking Characteristics (429)	'87	31
People Are Electric (501)	'93	35
The Lottery (526)	'95-1	53
Councils to the President (605)	'98-2	9
New-Member Welcome (606)	'98-2	19
The Affinity Diagram (620)	'99-1	39
Shift Happens (664)	'00-2	55
Electric Company (700)	'02-1	55
Successful Leadership Traits (712)	'02-2	25
Decision Making (744)	'03-2	37
Pass It On	'05-C	59
Action Planning		
Force-Field Analysis (40)	II	79
Wahoo City (73)	III	100
Dhabi Fehru (259)	VII	91
Island Commission (260)	VII	99
Missiles (275)	'80	43
Robbery (334)	'83	40
The Impact Wheel (458)	'89	83
Coping Strategies (485)	'92	9
Wreck Survivors (515)	'94	67
Values, Visions, and Missions (527)	'95-1	59
River of Change (555)	'96-1	93
Ideal Work Place (561)	'96-2	45
Award Ceremony (581)	'97-2	9
Inputs, Process, Outputs (582)	'97-2	17
Diametrically Opposed (649)	'00-1	57
Make a Mark (665)	'00-2	63
New Owners (675)	'01-1	75
GROUPS		
How Groups Work		
Committee Meeting (9)	I	36
Process Observation (10)	I	45
Group Tasks (29)	II	16
Self-Interaction Task (37)	II	68
Towers (54)	III	17
What to Look for in Groups (79)	'72	19
Greeting Cards (82)	'72	44
Cog's Ladder (126)	'74	8
Faculty Meeting (139)	'75	15
Tinkertoy Bridge (160)	V	60
LEGO Bridge (161)	V	73
Word-Letter (200)	VI	15
Spy (218)	VI	117
Homesell (228)	'78	46
Line of Four (237)	'79	21
Slingshots (256)	VII	69
Four-Letter Words (287)	'81	34
Dynasell (290)	'81	50
Structures (308)	VIII	69
Team Planning (351)	IX	74
Group Sell (357)	IX	114
Four Corners (442)	'88	51
Orientations (443)	'88	57
Whirlybird (491)	'92	63
Let's Come to Order (528)	'95-1	73
Airplanes (534)	'95-2	13
Rope Trick (577)	'97-1	81
Lincoln Decision Committee (578)	'97-1	89
Web of Yarn (583)	'97-2	25
Innovative Meetings (607)	'98-2	23
No Strings Attached (608)	'98-2	31
Crime-Fighting Task Force (634)	'99-2	35
Piccadilly Manor (650)	'00-1	65
Logos (676)	'01-1	81
Neutral Corner (686)	'01-2	37
Construction Project (713)	'02-2	31
Rulers (728)	'03-1	59
Art Appreciation (745)	'03-2	41
Competition/Collaboration		
Model Building (32)	II	29
Prisoners' Dilemma (61)	III	52
Decisions (83)	'72	51
Wooden Blocks (105)	IV	18
World Bank (147)	'75	56
Testing (164)	V	91
X-Y (179)	'76	41
Blue/Green (189)	'77	24
Circle in the Square (205)	VI	32
Balance of Power (231)	'78	63
Paper Box (243)	'79	60
Trading Cards (263)	VII	112
War Gaming (264)	VII	117
Move to Newtown (278)	'80	60
High Iron (280)	'80	78
Cross-Group Negotiation and Cooperation (302)	VIII	41
Risk Game (311)	VIII	93
Intertwine (319)	'82	20
Block Buster (320)	'82	24
Stock Exchange (384)	'85	75
Assignment Flexibility (516)	'94	75
Property Game (554)	'96-1	77
Egg Drop (564)	'96-2	77
Allied Circuits (609)	'98-2	39
The Forest vs. the Trees (610)	'98-2	53
Powerful Exercise (666)	'00-2	67
Power Poker (701)	'02-1	69
Team Traps (714)	'02-2	37
Tear It Up (729)	'03-1	65
Paper Chain Company	'04-T	55
Altair the Ant	'05-C	63
Conflict		
Conflict Resolution (14)	I	70
Lindell-Billings Corporation (144)	'75	46
Conflict Styles (186)	'77	15
Controversial Issues (224)	'78	28
Budget Cutting (323)	'82	35
Trouble in Manufacturing (374)	'84	67
Datatrak (375)	'84	74
Winterset High School (435)	'87	79

	Vol.	Page
Negotiating/Bargaining		
Unequal Resources (78)	'72	17
Monetary Investment (265)	VII	124
Creative Products (279)	'80	69
Territory (314)	VIII	120
Bargaining, United Nations Style (471)	'90	95
Merger Mania (584)	'97-2	29
Negotiation Tactics	'04-T	65
Why Don't You Want What I Want?	'04-C	45

TEAMS

How Groups Work

	Vol.	Page
System Problems (111)	IV	38
Top Secret Contract (194)	'77	47
Team Development (208)	VI	54
Slogans (276)	'80	51
Project Colossus (288)	'81	43
Group Identity (299)	VIII	25
Chips (322)	'82	31
Meetings Audit (325)	'82	49
Work-Group Review (327)	'82	60
Healthy or Unhealthy? (404)	X	96
Sticky Wickets (405)	X	99
Bean Bags (419)	'86	45
Instant Survey (434)	'87	75
Team Interventions (558)	'96-2	19
Take Note of Yourself (621)	'99-1	43
Team Troubles (635)	'99-2	49
Share the Load (667)	'00-2	73
When Shall We Meet Again? (677)	'01-1	85
Sweet Tooth (702)	'02-1	85
Teams by Any Other Name (746)	'03-2	45
Get Smart	'04-T	69
The Merry-Go-Round Project	'04-C	51
The Modern Art Factory	'05-T	51

Roles

	Vol.	Page
Role Nominations (38)	II	72
Line-Up & Power Inversion (59)	III	46
Role Clarification (171)	V	136
Baseball Game (270)	'80	14
The Car (326)	'82	55
The Seven Pieces (366)	'84	16
Role Power (368)	'84	26
Kaleidoscope (408)	X	122
Position Power (420)	'86	51
America's Favorite Pastime (455)	'89	61
Symbols (469)	'90	73
Multiple Roles (480)	'91	85
Yours, Mine, and Ours (500)	'93	31
Tasks, Skill, and Commitments (546)	'96-1	15
Risky Business (636)	'99-2	67
Appreciative Introductions (668)	'00-2	85
Island Survival (715)	'02-2	41
Decode (730)	'03-1	71
Group Roles (747)	'03-2	51
The Hats We Wear	'05-C	69

Problem Solving/Decision Making

	Vol.	Page
Lutts & Mipps (31)	II	24
Joe Doodlebug (103)	IV	8
Planning Recommendations or Action (132)	'74	32
The Lawn (337)	'83	65
Threats to the Project (373)	'84	62
Unscrambling the Bank Accounts (431)	'87	51
Control or Surrender (453)	'89	47
Fishing for "Why?" (535)	'95-2	21
Team Checkup (547)	'96-1	19
Turbo Affinity Technique (585)	'97-2	47
Hit the Target Fast (586)	'97-2	53
Scope of Control (600)	'98-1	63
News Room (611)	'98-2	59
Risk Tolerance (678)	'01-1	89
Jet Away (687)	'01-2	45
Puzzles (703)	'02-1	91
Scrambled Words (716)	'02-2	45
Aardvark and Antelope (731)	'03-1	79

Feedback

	Vol.	Page
Leveling (17)	I	79
Dependency-Intimacy (18)	I	82
Group Development (39)	II	76
Group Self-Evaluations (55)	III	22
Nominations (57)	III	33
Dividing the Loot (60)	III	49
Team Building (66)	III	73
Organizational Mirror (67)	III	78
Team Identity (77)	'72	13
Twenty-Five Questions (118)	IV	88
Agenda Setting (166)	V	108
Cups (167)	V	111
Person Perception (170)	V	131
Affirmation of Trust (216)	VI	110
Stones, Bands, & Circle (254)	VII	53
I Hear That You... (291)	'81	54
Group Effectiveness (297)	VIII	18
Group Sociogram (316)	VIII	131
Constructive Criticism (345)	IX	28
Messages (356)	IX	110
Sharing and Supporting Goals (386)	'85	87
Smackers (388)	'85	95
Power and Affection Exchange (402)	X	88
Yearbook (403)	X	92
Group Sociogram II (418)	'86	41
The Advertising Firm (444)	'88	69
Images (445)	'88	73
It's in the Cards (456)	'89	67
The Genie's Wish (468)	'90	67
Bases of Power (477)	'91	43
Group Calendar (489)	'92	47
Strengths and Needs (490)	'92	51
The Helping Hand (529)	'95-1	87
Comfort Zones (536)	'95-2	29
This and That (587)	'97-2	59
TeamScores (588)	'97-2	63
Enablers and Barriers (612)	'98-2	63
Jigsaw Puzzles (622)	'99-1	47
Nicknames (679)	'01-1	97
The Last Team Member	'05-C	73

Conflict and Intergroup Issues

Conflict

	Vol.	Page
Ajax Appliance Corporation (406)	X	106
Sharing Perspectives (409)	X	126
Conflict Management (483)	'91	119
Performance Unlimited (566)	'96-2	113

Intergroup Issues

	Vol.	Page
Win as Much as You Can (36)	II	62
Intergroup Meeting (68)	III	81
Intergroup Model Building (81)	'72	36
Win What, Lose What? (145)	'75	51
Riddles (150)	V	5
Intergroup Clearing (289)	'81	48
The Value Profile (407)	X	118
They Said, We Said (530)	'95-1	91
Group Sculptures (637)	'99-2	75

CONSULTING & FACILITATING

Consulting: Awareness

	Vol.	Page
Strategies of Changing (98)	'73	32
Organization Structures (110)	IV	34
Coloring Book (163)	V	85
Marbles (165)	V	98
Tug O'War (188)	'77	22
MANDOERS (232)	'78	71
Organizational Blasphemies (339)	'83	77
Matrix (360)	IX	136
The Shoe-Distribution Company (372)	'84	55
The People of Trion (410)	X	132
Dos and Don'ts (446)	'88	77
Prairie General Hospital (479)	'91	65
The Hundredth Monkey (505)	'93	75
Hats "R" Us (517)	'94	93
Exploring Our Cultural History (537)	'95-2	41
Straws and Pins (538)	'95-2	45
By the Numbers (589)	'97-2	71
Focus Groups (590)	'97-2	89
System Review (613)	'98-2	69
Koosh(r) Ball Company (623)	'99-1	53
Press Conference (638)	'99-2	81

Consulting: Diagnosing/Skills

	Vol.	Page
Roxboro Electric Company (131)	'74	24
Consulting Triads (183)	'76	53
Tri-State (193)	'77	39
HELPCO (211)	VI	66
Willington (230)	'78	55
Elm Street Community Church (347)	IX	34
Inquiries (348)	IX	48
Measuring Excellence (385)	'85	81
Client Concerns (412)	X	148
The Client-Consultant Questionnaire (424)	'86	79
City of Buffington (460)	'89	101
Metaphors (484)	'91	125
Working at Our Company (493)	'92	79
Help Wanted (494)	'92	87
International Equity Claims Department (506)	'93	85
Operational Definitions (540)	'95-2	63
Wooden Towers (541)	'95-2	69
Walking the Talk (559)	'96-2	27
The MPM Scale (563)	'96-2	67
U.S. National Healthcare Commission (591)	'97-2	95

Experiential Learning Activities

	Vol.	Page
Business Cards (601)	'98-1	71
Collecting Diagnostic Data (639)	'99-2	89
Interrogatories (704)	'02-1	95

Facilitating: Opening

Listening & Inferring (1)	I	3
Two-Four-Eight (2)	I	5
Who Am I? (5)	I	19
Group Conversation (25)	II	3
Jigsaw (27)	II	10
First Names, First Impressions (42)	II	88
"Who Am I?" Variations (49)	III	3
"Cold" Introductions (88)	'73	9
Getting Acquainted (101)	IV	3
Hum-Dinger (125)	'74	7
Energizers (149)	V	3
Limericks (173)	'76	7
Labeling (174)	'76	10
Best Friend (197)	V	13
Choose an Object (198)	V	17
Tea Party (245)	VII	5
Autographs (269)	'80	11
Alliterative Names (281)	'81	9
Birth Signs (282)	'81	11
Name Tags (293)	VIII	5
Learning Exchange (294)	VIII	7
Rebus Names (317)	'82	9
Just the Facts (329)	'83	11
News Bulletin (342)	IX	8
Group Savings Bank (376)	'84	92
Daffodil (387)	'85	91
Getting to Know You (413)	'86	11
I Represent (436)	'87	87
Color Me (507)	'93	93
Parsley, Garlic, Ginger, Pepper (518)	'94	107
Your Book Jacket (531)	'95-1	97
Bingo (545)	'96-1	9
I Have an Opinion (602)	'98-1	75
Openers (624)	'99-1	59
A New Twist (640)	'99-2	101
Alpha "Bets" (651)	'00-1	81
Age Barometer (680)	'01-1	101
Who Says That? (688)	'01-2	49
Me in a Bag (717)	'02-2	51
Let's Get Personal (732)	'03-1	83
Transitions (748)	03-2	59
Zen with a Sense of Humor (**)	'04-T	79
Musical Introductions	'05-T	55
Plunge In	'05-C	77
Want/Give Walkabout	'05-C	81

Facilitating: Blocks to Learning

Gunnysack (89)	'73	11
Perception of Task (91)	'73	15
The "T" Test (112)	IV	41
Communication Analysis (191)	'77	32
Buttermilk (234)	'79	13
Resistance to Learning (301)	VIII	37
Needs, Expectations, and Resources (324)	'82	46
Taking Your Creative Pulse (567)	'96-2	119
Benefits and Barriers (652)	'00-1	87
Crochet Hook (705)	'02-1	99

Facilitating: Skills

	Vol.	Page
Fantasies (16)	I	75
Awareness Expansion (19)	I	86
Assumptions About Human Relations Training (24)	I	107
Miniversity (26)	I	17
Verbal Activities Within Groups (43)	II	91
Nonverbal Communication II (44)	II	94
Helping Pairs (45)	II	97
Microlab (47)	II	113
Process Intervention (48)	II	115
Empty Chair (51)	III	8
Nonverbal Communication III (72)	III	97
Medial Feedback (92)	'73	17
Participant-Staff Expectations (96)	'73	29
Group Leadership Functions (148)	'75	63
Training Philosophies (363)	IX	159
Good Workshops Don't Just Happen (495)	'92	97
Up Close and Personal with Dr. Maslow (496)	'92	111
Zodiac for Trainers (508)	'93	97
Disability Awareness (519)	'94	115
Seaside Towers (532)	'95-1	101
Eight Training Competencies (579)	'97-1	105
Word Game (603)	'98-1	79
Your Voice, Your Self (625)	'99-1	63
Building Blocks (626)	'99-1	69
Continuum (669)	'00-2	89
Trade Fair (681)	'01-1	105
Rotating Facilitators (689)	'01-2	53
What's Next? (718)	'02-2	55
Yo-Yos (733)	'03-1	87
The Skilled Facilitator (749)	'03-2	67
Training Trainers	'04-T	85
Search and Find	'04-C	63

Facilitating: Closing

Symbolic Closing Exercise (86)	'72	61
Closure (114)	IV	49
Payday (146)	'75	54
Symbolic Toast (176)	'76	17
Bread Making (201)	VI	19
Golden Awards (222)	'78	12
Kia Ora (318)	'82	12
Aloha (389)	X	5
Feedback Letters (556)	'96-1	99
Tool Box (627)	'99-1	73
Management Wizards (653)	'00-1	93
Wrap-Up (690)	'01-2	59
Certificates (706)	'02-1	111
Billboard Sentiments (719)	'02-2	59
Inner Child (734)	'03-1	91
Four Thermometers	'05-T	59
Learning Charts	'05-T	65

LEADERSHIP

Ethics

What Do You See? (137)	'75	7
Ideal Cards (143)	'75	43
Who Killed John Doe? (235)	'79	15
Personal Identity (246)	VII	11
Louisa's Problem (283)	'81	13
Values and Decisions (361)	IX	146
The Gold Watch (411)	X	142
Living Ethics (580)	'97-1	127
Global Service Provider (592)	'97-2	105
Ethics in Action (614)	'98-2	75

Interviewing/Appraisal

Live Case (142)	'75	40
Sunglow (257)	VII	73
Assistant Wanted (333)	'83	31
Interviewing (358)	IX	122
Inquiries and Discoveries (365)	'84	9
Constructive Discipline (371)	'84	49
BARS (423)	'86	73
Performance Appraisal (425)	'87	11
What's Legal? (451)	'89	23
Consultant's Report (542)	'95-2	89
Precision Bicycle Components (543)	'95-2	97
Calloway Power Station (562)	'96-2	57
Sign Here (615)	'98-2	81
Apple of Your Eye (628)	'99-1	75
Communication Games (654)	'00-1	97
Selection Interview (707)	'02-1	115
Golf Game (735)	'03-1	97
My Worst Nightmare	'04-T	93
Role Models	'05-T	77

Motivation

Motivation (100)	'73	43
Motivation (204)	VI	28
Darts (210)	VI	61
Penny Pitch (253)	VII	46
People on the Job (295)	VIII	10
The Manager's Guidebook (354)	IX	102
MACE (367)	'84	22
There's Never Time to Do It Right (430)	'87	45
Four Factors (452)	'89	39
Master and Apprentice (544)	'95-2	117
The Flip-It Company (560)	'96-2	39
Managerial Perceptions (616)	'98-2	87
Management-HR Partnering (629)	'99-1	81
If You Think You Can (641)	'99-2	105
Millennium Mobile (655)	'00-1	119
The Stephanie Syndrome (691)	'01-2	63
Intrinsic/Extrinsic Motivators (736)	'03-1	105
The Motivation Grid (750)	'03-2	71
Three Roles of Leaders	'05-C	85

Diversity/Stereotyping

Hollow Square (33)	II	32
Hampshire In-Basket (34)	II	41
Absentee (158)	V	49
When to Delegate (304)	VIII	52
Reviewing Objectives and Strategies (328)	'82	65
Vice President's In-Basket (336)	'83	49

	Vol.	Page
Meeting Management (421)	'86	55
Raises (422)	'86	65
Delegation (447)	'88	81
The Robotics Decision (459)	'89	89
Termination (472)	'90	103
The Employment Case (520)	'94	123
Under Pressure (565)	'96-2	87
Leadership History (691)	'01-2	71
Supervisory Success (720)	'02-2	63

Styles

	Vol.	Page
T-P Leadership Questionnaire (3)	I	7
Choosing a Color (12)	I	56
Auction (35)	II	58
Toothpicks (121)	IV	99
Styles of Leadership (154)	V	19
Fork-Labyrinth (159)	V	53
Pins & Straws (162)	V	78
Executive Pie (195)	'77	54
Staff Meeting (207)	VI	39
Power Personalities (266)	VII	127
Managerial Characteristics (273)	'80	31
Choosing an Apartment (274)	'80	37
Power & Affiliation (277)	'80	54

	Vol.	Page
Boss Wanted (296)	VIII	15
Tangram (313)	VIII	108
Manager's Dilemma (331)	'83	19
Power Caucus (346)	IX	31
Management Skills (353)	IX	93
Follow the Leader (369)	'84	38
Management Perspectives (381)	'85	45
Chipping In (384)	'85	57
Choose Me (401)	X	85
Quantity Versus Quality (433)	'87	69
Rhetoric and Behavior (478)	'91	51
The Good Leader (488)	'92	37
Organizational Structures (504)	'93	63
Today and Tomorrow (604)	'98-1	87
Rope-a-Leader (630)	'99-1	87
Leadership Style (656)	'00-1	125
Show and Tell (682)	'01-1	109
Second to None (708)	'02-1	127
When I Manage, When I Lead (737)	'03-1	117
Meet My Leader (738)	'03-1	125
Hubris	'04-C	69
Mentor	'04-C	83

ORGANIZATIONS

Communication

	Vol.	Page
If We Only Knew (642)	'99-2	121
Story Weaving (693)	'01-2	77
Knowledge Is Good (694)	'01-2	85
Think Up the Organization	'04-C	91
Chains	'05-T	89

Vision, Mission, Values, Strategy

	Vol.	Page
It's in the Bag (695)	'01-2	97
Futures (721)	'02-2	71
Lasso Your Vision, Mission, and Values (739)	'03-1	129
Read All About It! (751)	'03-2	77
"Those Who Matter"	'04-C	97
The Human Body	'05-T	93
To Be the Best	'05-C	91

Change Management

	Vol.	Page
The Alphabet Game (709)	'02-1	137
Pink Slip (722)	'02-2	79
Rubber Bands (752)	'03-2	81

Well-Being:
Drawing the Bottom Line

Activity Summary

Executives, managers, supervisors, and employees will gain perspective about well-being as it relates to the bottom line of performance and achievement.

Goals

- To explore the relationship between doing and being.
- To learn how to shift someone's perspective on achievement and performance to encompass being.
- To learn how to monitor well-being.

Group Size

4 to 100 participants.

Time Required

Approximately 60 minutes.

Materials

None are required, although participants may choose to write down some of their thoughts and reflections.

Physical Setting

Extremely flexible auditorium seating or tables that seat 6, 8, or 10, depending on the number of participants.

Facilitating Risk Rating

Low.

Process

1. Begin by asking participants to pair off and ask one member of each pair to start clapping. Say: "Clap hard, harder, *harder* still." After 10 seconds of clapping, say, "Turn to your partner and describe this experience so that your partner, who never has had the experience of clapping before, could replicate it." To the listeners, the ones who have not clapped before, say, "Follow the instructions your partners give you and see whether you can experience the same thing."
(5 minutes.)

2. Call everyone back to the large group. Allow one moment for the energy in the room to quiet down. Then continue, "How many of those giving the instructions included "being" descriptions as part of the instructions, such as, "Pay attention to your state of being," "Be aware of how you feel while clapping," or "Be aware of your energy increasing"?

3. Observe to the group that most people attend only to the "doing" aspects of life and that the purpose of this training exercise is to heighten awareness of the "being" part.

4. Tell participant to think of a time when they needed to return to the basics of a task or process. Give the following two examples or one of your own when you gained mastery and then returned to the beginner's level:

    Example 1. In competitive swing dancing, advanced dancers return to Swing 101 before entering competition. When revisiting the basics with the eye of a master, details are often learned that were overlooked when attempting to gain competence the first time around.

    Example 2. In the martial arts, after receiving a black belt, the student returns to the basics of the white belt.

5. Invite participants to don their beginner's mind for the next 60 minutes to explore new possibilities for why they desire to achieve and succeed. Ask: "What if your being became more important than your doing?" Pause for discussion.
(5 minutes.)

6. Continue, "Let's identify what state of being you want to experience before we DO anything. Do you wish this next hour to feel Calm? Challenged? Authentic? Engaged? What do you want? Check inside yourself as to how much you are experiencing it right now. Rate yourself on a scale of 1 to 10. 10 is high." Ask for some people to share their ratings. Remind them that they are responsible for creating their own states of well-being.
(5 minutes.)

7. State that, "We tend to over-emphasize the 'doing' part of life and minimize the 'being.' We are a 'do' dominant society. How many of you have a *'to do'* list? How many have a *'to be'* list?" (You can expect almost all participants will have a "to do list" and none or very, very few have a "to be" list.)

    Go on to say, "Our motivation coming to work is not just about doing. We also want the experience of being. Look at the word you selected as the quality of being you wished to experience in this workshop. Would you like more of that in your work life as well?"

8. Now say, "I'd like to ask you to fill in the sentence that begins with, 'I want a. . . .' What do you want? A hefty bonus? Piano lessons? It does not need to be restricted to work. A seaside cottage? Increase in sales by 15 percent? A hot air balloon trip? Better communication with your boss? Mention in the company newsletter? A slimmer physique?" Allow 1 minute for responses.
(5 minutes.)

9. Give these three examples or create some of your own:

    - "Peter wanted a promotion. He answered the question, 'What will that bring me?' by saying, 'More money.' I asked him to ask himself the question again, this time using his answer to the question, 'What will more money bring you, Peter?' 'More freedom.' I stopped there because his answer was a state of being. Freedom is a state of being."

    - "Marianna wanted a bigger office. She answered the question, 'What will that bring me?' by saying, 'More space.' I asked her to ask herself the question again, using her answer. 'What will more space bring you, Marianna?' 'Greater peace of mind.' Peace of mind is a state of being. The bottom line was again a state of being."

    - "Carlos wanted to go back to school and earn a degree. He replied that that would bring him more knowledge. His final answer was that knowledge would enable him to contribute more and be of greater service. Another bottom-line state of being."

Summarize with, "See how we went from the promotion and the bigger office, and the degree to freedom, peace of mind, and being of service?"

10. Read this quote:

    "Goethe said: 'Before you can do something you must first be something.'"

11. Ask, "How much are you experiencing the state of being you wanted to create for our time together? Rate yourself again from 1 to 10, 10 being high."

12. Ask participants to find partners and go back and forth for at least three rounds asking, "What do you want?" followed by "What will that bring you?" until they reach the bottom line of being to the satisfaction of their partners.
    (5 minutes.)

13. Allow a few minutes if anyone wants to share any part of the experience.
    (5 minutes.)

14. To summarize, read this quote from Ralph Waldo Emerson.

    "A painter told me that nobody could draw a tree without in some sort *becoming* a tree."

15. Resume with the following discussion questions:

    - What is the "being" definition of your chosen profession or job? Does your company or business or organization's mission statement include a being word or words?

    - Did you realize that your personal mission statement, your life purpose, includes both a *doing* as well as a *being* component?

    - What percentage of your time do you engage in being conversations with your colleagues?

    - Does your performance review include any measures of well-being?

    - Does anyone rate you on your state of well-being?

    (5 minutes.)

16. If appropriate, mention situations outside of the workplace as well such as, "What is the being definition of the role that you play in the community or at home? In your family? With friends?"

17. Ask participants to turn to those people sitting around them and ask them what state or states of well-being is or are most essential to their success at their job. In their family? Allow about 3 minutes for people to comment.

Experiential Learning Activities   15

18. Give these instructions for this next part of the activity:

    "Find a partner different from any you have already worked with today. Decide who will ask the question and who will give the reply. The person who will ask the question will beam a sourpuss face along with non-supportive, lacking confidence, bored, not paying attention, annoyance-type thoughts to his or her partner and at the same time ask: 'What result do you want in your life and what supports do you have to get it?' You will have 2 minutes to do this part of the exercise and then I will give you the rest of the instructions."

    (3 minutes.)

19. Continue the instructions:

    "Now both of you take a deep breath, maintain the *same* roles, and this time the one with the question switches to beaming thoughts of acceptance, caring, encouragement, confidence, and joy while asking: 'What result do you want in your life and what supports do you have to get it?'"

    (2 minutes.)

20. Allow 5 minutes for discussion around differences between the two experiences. Conclude with this saying from Belf (2002b): "Your actions speak louder than your words; your being speaks louder than your actions."

    (5 minutes.)

21. Check again by asking everyone to rate how much they are experiencing the state of being they wanted to create for their time together, 1 to 10, 10 being high.

22. Say: "Let us look at some applications of this new perspective on being.

    - Imagine if you began each business meeting asking your staff or colleagues: 'What state of well-being do you want to create for our time together?'

    - What if you focused more on well-being with your most challenging client or customer or co-worker? What might be different?

    - In the middle of a meeting if it becomes clear you have reached an impasse, what if you stopped talking and asked everyone present to tune inside and ask 'What state of well-being would most support our effort right now?'"

    (5 minutes.)

23. Ask participants what applications they can see for focusing on well-being. What might happen if they did carry out their applications? What would be different?
   (5 minutes.)

24. Do a final check-in about their experience in creating the state of being they wanted. Ask for a show of hands, "How many maintained or increased that state of being?"

25. Deliver a mini-lecture on brain physiology to explain why most were able to increase their state of being:

    > "Each of us has a brain mechanism, referred to as the Reticular Formation (Re-Form), that functions like a television channel selector. Imagine a large screen in the front of the room. We hit Channel 4 on the remote. We see Channel 4. We all know that Channel 5 is out there somewhere, yet we don't see it because we are on Channel 4. When we select a channel we put something in the foreground and relegate everything else to the background. We have the innate ability to choose our own channels, and it is very easy to program them. So when we intentionally program our Re-Form on what we want, we are more likely to get it. If you put *calm* on your channel, that is what you will get. The Re-Form is preprogrammed at birth to screen out threats to our survival. Other than that, it is available for us to program as we choose. Today you have been putting your Re-Form on your state of being and you have selected a channel, your specific state of well-being, as your foreground. Check into that well-being quality you indicated you wanted for this hour when we began. How are you doing? or should I say 'How are you being?'"

    (5 minutes.)

26. Summarize the teaching points.

    - Remember to identify what well-being you want when you create results or goals. For example, instead of, "I want to increase my salary by 10 percent," say, "I want to enthusiastically, with diligence, increase my salary by 10 percent."

    - You alone are responsible for your state of well-being.

    - Well-being can be monitored as simply as rating yourself on a 1 to 10 scale.

    - Whatever you put your awareness on is what you get.

    - What if one of the real reasons we all are in business is about being, not doing?

    (5 minutes.)

27. Conclude with this final statement: "'To be or not to be' is no longer the question; it has become the answer."

References

Belf, T., & Ward, C. (1997). *Simply live it UP: Brief solutions.* Bethesda, MD: Purposeful Press.

Belf, T. (2002a). *Facilitating life purpose: A manual for coaches.* Bethesda, MD: Purposeful Press.

Belf, T. (2002b). *Coaching with spirit: Allowing success to emerge.* San Francisco, CA: Pfeiffer.

Submitted by Teri-E Belf

Teri-E Belf, *M.A., C.A.G.S., M.C.C., is a purposeful, inspired coaching leader and trainer, author, and speaker, cited in the International Who's Who of Entrepreneurs. Her passions include sharing her 35,000 hours of coaching experience and eighteen years of HRD and T&D management experience through presentations, articles, and books. She is the founder and director of Success Unlimited Network®, an international coaching community and an accredited coach training school.*

Rich Traditions:
Managing Diversity

Activity Summary

This is an interactive experience using mental imagery and cognitive group processes to facilitate an awareness, understanding, and appreciation of participants' ethnic/cultural backgrounds as an initial step toward diversity management.

Goals

- To provide an atmosphere for appreciation of ethnic/cultural diversity.
- To assist in the process of diversity management for the organization.

Group Size

10 to 40 participants from the same organization.

Time Required

Approximately 2 to 2½ hours, depending on the group size and the depth of discussion.

Materials

- One copy of the Rich Traditions Lecturette for the facilitator.
- One copy of the Rich Traditions Worksheet for each participant.
- One copy of the Rich Traditions Checklist for each participant.
- One copy of the Rich Traditions Take Aways for each participant.

- One copy of the Rich Traditions Suggested Reading List for each participant.
- Blank paper and pens or pencils for participants.
- Flip-chart easel with paper OR a whiteboard or blackboard.
- Colored felt-tipped markers, whiteboard markers, or chalk.

Physical Setting

A room large enough to accommodate the group for individual as well as small group work, with tables and chairs that can be moved into various configurations.

Facilitating Risk Rating

Low to moderate.

Process

1. Introduce the concept of diversity by giving the Rich Traditions Lecturette, with a focus on diversity management as necessary for sustainability, kaleidoscopic perspectives, and a competitive edge in an increasingly international market. Tell participants that if they have questions, they may note them now to be answered at the end of the session, if they have not already been answered by the experiences that they will go through in the course of this exercise.
   (12 to 15 minutes.)

2. Announce the goals of the activity.
   (1 minute.)

3. Hand out paper and pens or pencils. Give the following instructions to the participants:

   "Think of your country/state of origin, where you were born and brought up. You may wish to close your eyes as you bring to mind the scenery that you remember from those times. Try to recall the flora/fauna, the architecture, and landscape/cityscape from those times. You may also wish to include the modes of dress and some of the day-to-day customs and traditions people use in your country/state of origin. You will have approximately 5 minutes to do this individually in silence. If you require any clarifications at this stage about what you are to do, I would be happy to respond."

   (2 minutes.)

4. Move among the participants and be available to them should any further clarifications arise.
   (5 minutes.)

5. Call time after 5 minutes. Now ask each participant to call out his or her country/state of origin, and form groups based on the same country/state/continent. For example: China, Mexico, and Spain. If all participants are from one particular country, grouping can be done based on states or regions. For example: Tasmania and Western Australia, Maryland and California, or Gujarat, Punjab, and Bengal. Write the different geographic groupings on the flip chart.
   (5 minutes.)

6. Invite participants to share their imagery one at a time for approximately 2 minutes each. All members of a group must finish sharing before moving on to the next geographic group. Jot down on the flip chart some of the main points that each group comes up with.
   (20 to 30 minutes.)

7. Distribute the Rich Traditions Worksheet and tell participants they will have 5 minutes to write their responses.
   (5 minutes.)

8. Form new groups by having participants within groups call out numbers (for example, 1 through 7), and then group by those numbers. Ensure that there is a mix of people from different geographic locations in each group. Tell participants to discuss their responses to the Rich Traditions Worksheet within their new groups.
   (10 minutes.)

9. Instruct participants to wrap up their discussions.

10. Reassemble the original groups and give each group 3 minutes to share their summaries with one another and then share with the total group. Participants may use the flip chart.
    (10 to 15 minutes.)

11. Distribute the Rich Traditions Checklist and ask participants to complete them individually.
    (5 minutes.)

12. Have participants stay in their groups based on geographic origin and ask them to discuss their responses to the Rich Traditions Checklist. Group size should not exceed 8, so large groups may be subdivided. Request that each

group summarize their members' responses for sharing with the larger group. Give each group 2 minutes to share their summary with the total group, and answer questions from the participants.
(20 minutes.)

13. Ask participants what they have learned from this session and what they will be able to implement in their lives. Summarize their comments on the flip chart.
(10 minutes.)

14. Distribute the Rich Traditions Take Aways and encourage participants to write three things that they will give top priority to implementing when working with their colleagues back on the job.
(3 minutes.)

15. Distribute copies of the Rich Traditions Suggested Reading List and encourage participants to continue to learn as much as they can about diversity, particularly as it affects them in the workplace.
(1 minute.)

Variations

- This activity can be done across departments in one organization, across divisions of the same organization in different locations, or with management students.

- If the group size is small, then each of the steps can be done individually with a general sharing after Steps 6, 10, and 12.

- Depending on the group composition, you may wish to stop after Step 10.

- Depending on the group composition, you may wish to spend more time on the Rich Traditions Checklist.

- After Step 15, the group can come up with norms/suggestions they would implement at work or a credo for the organization on diversity management.

- This activity can commence with "Hello" in various languages. For example: Bonjour [French], Kia Ora [Maori], Namaskar [Hindi], Malo lelai [Tongan], Ni Hao [Mandarin].

- The "Goodbye" as closure can be in the languages of the participants. For example: Au Revoir [French], Auf Wiedersehen [German], Arrivederci [Italian], Adieus [Portuguese], Adios [Spanish].

Submitted by Edwina Pio.

Edwina Pio, *Ph.D., specializes in the area of diversity management research and implementation. Traveling to Asia, America, Europe, and Oceania, her study, research, and practice emanate from the intersections of management, psychology, and spirituality. She now lives in New Zealand and is a member of the Faculty of Business at the Auckland University of Technology. She has previously contributed to the* Annuals.

Rich Traditions Lecturette

Diversity management is a dynamic process for an organization as it seeks to put into place policies, strategies, and behaviors to elicit the maximum potential from its people and link these to its business goals and organizational outcomes. Diversity management can be seen as respect for an individual's uniqueness, along with an understanding of and, one hopes, appreciation of, the cultural characteristics and experiences that individuals bring to the organization.

In today's international scenario more than seventy million people work for companies based in other nations, and a multicultural workforce is an emerging reality across nations. Diversity management views the extensive talent pool available globally and seeks to increasingly develop sophisticated methodologies for sourcing people who excel in the world of work.

Recent reports from the United Nations (*United Nations Chronicle*, online edition, issue 1, 2003) note that there are currently 175 million people residing in countries where they were not born, with most of these people being in Europe (56 million), Asia (50 million), and North America (41 million). These astonishing figures underscore the significance of diversity management.

In responding to these realities, organizations can seek out a number of routes. These range from cultural accommodation (lip service, tokenism), to cultural compromise (tolerance), to cultural synergy (valuing). Building bridges between the insider and outsider is another way of looking at diversity management. The challenge is to help all members of the organization feel alike and to be perceived as "insiders."

While diversity has the great advantage of increasing creativity and encourages a kaleidoscopic perspective with new insights to many issues, the flip side is that it could result in low team cohesiveness, communication blockades, insecurity, fear, threat, and conflict. As in many situations when the status quo starts changing with a diverse profile of the workforce, the dominant culture often seeks to hold onto its power and resists change. Diversity management explores avenues for a smooth transition, while nurturing and utilizing the psychological capital available in the organization. It seeks to reinforce the subtle cultural dynamics that make for valued employees.

Corporate globalization has ensured diversity within organizations and among clients in the marketplace. As cultural cocoons are dismantled for current and future enhanced performance, there is an urgency to understand the local and global environment and capitalize on networking opportunities. Cap Gemini (IT consultancy), The Cheesecake Factory (desserts), Disney (entertainment), IBM (computers), L.J. Hooker (real estate), Microsoft (software), Nestle (foodstuff), Mercedes-Benz (automobiles), Qantas (airways), and Swatch (watches) are some companies that utilize diversity management. Much has also been written on the success of businesses in the Silicon Valley, where diversity is a core organizational strategy.

From a practical point of view the organization can ask itself the following questions:

1. What are some of the critical diversity issues we face?
2. What do we want to do about them?
3. What is the time frame within which we want to make changes?
4. What steps will we follow?
5. How will we involve our people?

Bear in mind that the leadership vision and rationale for a diverse workforce are *the* lynchpin for the promise of diversity management to be fulfilled.

Tapping into diversity means:

- Incorporating employees' perspectives into the rhythm of daily work life;
- Creating a dynamic ambience conducive to knowledge sharing, novel linkages, and interpretations;
- Composing, implementing, monitoring, and reviewing a diversity management checklist;
- Redesigning and, if necessary, redrawing how the business operates; and
- Having a future orientation toward building and sustaining organizational capability and commitment, sometimes at the expense of short-term cost-cutting and quarterly financial results.

As businesses spread their international wings and employ a less homogenized workforce, there will be more opportunities to leverage and internalize cultural differences, to learn, and to grow. Organizations must remain alert to choices or fall into the trap of all men being created equal, yet some being more equal than others. Diversity management is an invitation to cherish and embrace the rich traditions of a diverse workforce in an endeavor to control one's destiny, rather than being swept along as a prisoner of one's heritage.

Take a gentle walk into the rich traditions for diversity management.

Rich Traditions Worksheet

1. What have you learned about the other participants in this room?

2. In what way might this learning affect how you see them in the workplace?

3. Is there anything that you might want to do differently based on this learning?

Rich Traditions Checklist

Instructions: This checklist will help you to explore diversity management in your organization. Read each sentence, and if it is applicable to your organization, put a check mark on the rule beside the item number. After every sentence, space is provided for your constructive suggestions.

_____ 1. Our induction programs are geared toward the various ethnicities we have in this organization.

_____ 2. Our promotion policies are relevant to the job profile.

_____ 3. We provide feedback to unsuccessful candidates in promotion rounds.

_____ 4. Potential supervisors of various ethnicities are provided with mentors.

_____ 5. Collaboration and consultation with all ethnicities are done on a fairly regular basis.

_____ 6. Diversity management audits are carried out every year.

_____ 7. Cultural practices in the workplace encourage and accept all ethnicities.

_____ 8. The HR department is aware of immigration entrance requirements.

_____ 9. Health and safety classes are customized for different ethnicities.

_____ 10. Interpreters are available in the organization.

_____ 11. Classes in the dominant language of the country are easily available.

_____ 12. Retirement policies take into account the needs of different ethnicities.

Rich Traditions Take Aways

1. Respect, understanding, appreciation for the cultural characteristics, experiences, and uniqueness of individuals.

2. Multicultural workforce an emerging reality.

3. Valuing and embracing diversity by reinforcing subtle cultural dynamics for making employees feel valued.

4. Understanding the local and global environment and capitalizing on networking.

5. Building bridges between the insider and outsider.

6. Leadership vision as the lynchpin for fulfilling diversity's promise.

7. Incorporating employees' perspectives into the rhythm of daily work life.

8. Creating a dynamic environment conducive to knowledge sharing, novel linkages, and interpretations.

9. Composing, implementing, monitoring, and reviewing a diversity management checklist.

10. Redesigning and, if necessary, redrawing how the business operates.

11. Having a future orientation toward building and sustaining organizational capability and commitment, sometimes at the expense of short-term cost-cutting and quarterly financial results.

12. Take a gentle walk into the rich traditions of diversity management.

My top priority implementation areas:

Rich Traditions Suggested Reading List

Bartlett, C.A., & Ghoshal, S. (1989). *Managing across borders: The transnational solution.* Cambridge, MA: Harvard Business School Press.

Deal, T.E., & Kennedy, A.A. (1999). *The new corporate cultures.* Reading, MA: Perseus.

Esty, K., Griffin, R., & Hirsch, M.S. (1995). *Workplace diversity.* Holbrook, MA: Adams Media Corporation.

Hofstede, G. (1991). *Cultures and organizations: Software of the mind.* New York: McGraw-Hill.

Morrison, A.M. (1996). *The new leaders: Guidelines on leadership diversity in America.* San Francisco, CA: Jossey-Bass.

Patrickson, M., & O'Brien, P. (Eds.). (2001). *Managing diversity: An Asian and Pacific focus.* Queensland, Australia: John Wiley & Sons.

Pio, E. (2004). Z biz: The art of wealth: Stepping stones for spirituality in organizations. *The 2004 Pfeiffer annual: Training* (pp. 227–239). San Francisco, CA: Pfeiffer.

Thomas, D., & Ely, R. (1996, September/October). Making differences matter: A new paradigm for managing diversity. *Harvard Business Review,* pp. 79–90.

Trompenaars, A. (1994). *Riding the waves of culture.* Burr Ridge, IL: Irwin.

www.ipma-hr.org
www.the-hrnet.com
www.workindex.com

Life Balance:
Juggling Priorities

Activity Summary

Use this activity to introduce the concept of balancing personal and professional priorities in life while introducing team members to each other as an icebreaker. It is mildly active and humorous to build connections, laughter, and shared experience.

Goals

- To allow team members to get to know the names of their teammates.

- To experience what it feels like to be able to handle one or several priorities with success and while in balance.

- To demonstrate how each individual operates under the stress of many priorities and how the group members support one another (or not) while juggling many priorities.

Group Size

5 to 12 people per small group.

Time Required

20 to 30 minutes.

Materials

- Five or six different soft objects per small group that are heavy enough to throw and soft enough so they won't injure teeth or faces when thrown across a circle. Objects should be differing weight and size and should not be round. Examples are Koosh® balls, a small ball of yarn, rubber spiders, plastic animals, plastic cookies, or children's toys.

- A small container that will hold all the objects from view.
- A watch.

Physical Setting

A space large enough for each group to stand in a circle with about one to two feet between people. Groups can stand around a round table, but make sure there are no open beverage containers on the table.

Facilitating Risk Rating

Low to moderate.

Process

1. Form groups of 5 to 12 participants each and ask the group members to stand in a circle with about the distance of one outstretched arm between them. Explain that there will be three rounds to this game and that Round 1 will involve juggling one priority. Explain the rules below while keeping all of the objects except the first one hidden in a small container of some sort.

   - The person who has the object says another person's name first, and then throws the object (the priority) to that person (Catcher 1). The catcher is to say, "Thank you, [name of thrower]" to the thrower, then say a new person's name and throw the object to the new person (Catcher 2).

   - Once a person has caught an object, he or she is to fold his or her arms across the chest to demonstrate that he or she has already had a turn.

   - This continues until all participants have caught that object, and the last person to catch it then throws the object back to the leader.

2. Give the first object to one of the group members and let the game begin.

3. After one round of juggling one priority, explain to them that they will do the exact same thing in Round 2, except that they must stand on one leg if they are physically capable of doing so. They must throw the object to the same person they threw it to in Round 1.

4. For Round 3, do not explain anything else and just start by throwing the first object to the same person as before while still standing on one leg. As soon as the catcher has thrown Object 1 to the next person, say the catcher's first name again and throw Object 2 to that person. As soon as the catcher throws Object 2 to the next person, continue by throwing Object 3 to him or her.

5. Continue until the first object you threw returns to you and then collect all the objects as they are thrown back to you.

6. Have everybody sit down and debrief the exercise. Bring closure with the following questions:

   - What just happened when you tried to juggle all the priorities?

   - Who stood on only one leg the whole time?

   - How did you compensate for not being able to hold your leg up? Did you use your teammates for support or other sources?

   - Did you practice self-policing? Did you decide that you could be more productive doing this activity your own way instead of how you were told to do it? Did you notice that you could focus better on your mission—your work—when you were better balanced? Do you notice this at work or in your life at home or school?

   - Was anybody "cheating," in your opinion? How? How we play is typically how we work; our authentic selves come out in play.

   - Were you more or less productive when balanced? When unbalanced? Did you find yourself dropping the ball when more priorities were called into play?

   - What happened to the names and the thank you's when things got hectic and stressful? Does this happen at work?

   - What happened when you threw an object to people without calling their names first? How could this be a metaphor for your on-the-job performance?

   - What happened if the ball was dropped? Did it lie there being ignored; did other people pitch in to pick it up; or did the person who dropped it pick it up?

   - What happened to the volume level in the room or the laughter level? Sometimes things get so tough, we have to laugh or we cry.

- How did you handle all the priorities flying at you at once? What happened with the ball of yarn? (It usually unravels.) How did you handle it?
- How else can you compare this activity with things at work?

(10 minutes.)

Variations

- If the task seems easy with only three objects, add a fourth, fifth, or sixth.
- Allow groups to repeat the exercise after discussing the experience and making any adjustments they wish to the process. Debrief this new attempt and compare it with their on-the-job experiences.

Submitted by Gail Hahn.

Gail Hahn, *MA, CSP, CPRP, CLL, is the CEO (Chief Energizing Officer) of Fun*cilitators and author of* Hit Any Key to Energize Your Life *as well as contributing author of over sixteen other books. She is an international keynote speaker, corporate trainer, and an award-winning team-building facilitator.*

What's Your Priority?
Clarifying Instructions

Activity Summary

Supervisors do not always give complete instructions or directions. Participants experience the need to ask questions to get the job done according to the unspoken expectations.

Goals

- To learn the importance of time efficiency (use correct techniques) versus time effectiveness (select correct priorities).
- To identify elements of teamwork that help or hinder task accomplishment.
- To learn how to respond appropriately to incomplete instructions or directions.

Group Size

Groups of 10.

Time Required

50 to 60 minutes.

Materials

- 30 poker chips for each group of 10 people (10 blue, 10 red, 10 white).
- A glass, cup, or container for each set of chips.
- A stopwatch.
- A flip chart and markers.

- One copy of the What's Your Priority? Discussion Questions for each person.
- Pens or pencils for participants.

Physical Setting

Most classroom settings with tables and chairs can be used. Some groups may choose to stand around a table for the activity. Clearing tables for a free workspace is helpful.

Facilitating Risk Rating

Low to moderate.

Process

1. Divide the group into teams of 10 people per team. Appoint an observer for each group.

2. Give each team blue, red, and white poker chips, 10 of each color. If your purpose for this activity is working on priorities, provide an additional 10 white chips to each group's supply.

3. Explain the rules and post them on a flip chart if desired:

    - The group must pass each chip through all hands into its cup within 30 seconds.
    - The starter must pick up each chip with one hand, move it to his or her other hand, and then pass it to the next person in the group.
    - Participants may not slide the chips on the table.
    - Any participants may have only 1 chip in each hand at a time.
    - No more chips may be placed in the cup after time is called.

4. Allow groups to choose team names, practice, strategize, and move chairs, clear tables, and so on. Be unavailable to participants during their practice time. Pull the observers into the hallway outside of the room and ask them to observe their groups' techniques (what helps the process, what hinders the process, examples of teamwork, and so on). Give the observers each a copy of the What's Your Priority? Discussion Questions.

5. Conduct the first 30-second drill and have each group count the number of chips that completed the circuit and ended up in the cup. Have them record their scores on the easel next to their team names.
(5 minutes.)

6. Reveal the point values (10 = blue, 5 = red, 1 = white). Many in the group will say "No fair. You didn't tell us that!" That's one of the learning points. (If someone asks before this point whether the chips have value, avoid answering the question.)

7. Have them record the point values on their easels next to the chip count for each group from the first round. At this point most groups want another opportunity to improve their scores. Conduct the drill a second time and say that the objective is to improve their point scores. Groups may want a few moments to strategize in light of the information about point values. Ask the participants whether they have questions. The same point values apply to Round 2. Have them record their chip counts and scores for the new round.
(5 minutes.)

8. Hand out the What's Your Priority? Discussion Questions to all participants. Explain that people sometimes need time to gather their thoughts before a group discussion. Give them pens or pencils and allow time for them to write down their answers before discussing the questions as a group.
(5 minutes.)

9. In large groups, ask the observers to facilitate small-group discussions of the questions from the handout.
(10 minutes.)

10. Lead a large group discussion, covering the topics of knowing one's priorities, roles different group members played, not knowing all the rules, and so forth. Include the following questions:.

    - What do the numbers say about the results of your efforts?

    - What helped or hindered the process (include feedback from observers). (For groups with a teamwork purpose, it may be helpful for each team member to rate on a scale of 1 to 5 the helpfulness of each group member.)

    - What generalizations can be made about group productivity and teamwork from what happened?

    (10 minutes.)

11. If the concept you want the participants to discover is about teamwork, time management, or listening to directions, ask questions that will help participants find the relevant concept.
   (10 minutes)

12. Finally, ask participants how they can apply this experience to their teams and their jobs. Make a list and perhaps form pairs who will commit to helping one another keep the learning fresh when they go back to the job.

Submitted by Jean Barbazette.

Jean Barbazette, *MA, is president of The Training Clinic, a training consulting firm she founded in 1977 that specializes in train-the-trainer, new employee orientation, and enhancing the quality of training and instruction for major national and international clients. She holds a master's degree in education from Stanford University. Her published works include* Successful New Employee Orientation *(2nd ed.; Pfeiffer, 2001),* The Trainer's Support Handbook *(McGraw-Hill, 2001), and* Instant Case Studies *(Pfeiffer, 2003).*

Experiential Learning Activities

What's Your Priority? Discussion Questions

Instructions: After playing the Poker Chip Game, write the answers to the following questions:

1. What did you do that helped the process?

2. What did you do that hindered the process?

3. What did other team members do that helped?

4. What did other team members do that hindered?

5. What could have been done differently that would have helped your group get better results?

6. What are some general concepts about teams, time management, or listening to directions that you learned from this activity? For example, "It is better to . . . , than to . . . ."

7. What can you do to be a more effective team member in the future?

8. How can you apply what you learned from this experience to your team? To your job?

Stand-Up and Sit-Down Talkers:
Experiencing Diversity

Activity Summary

This is a mildly physical activity that allows participants to experience diversity and resolve disputes through communication.

Goals

- To demonstrate diversity through an artificial distinction.
- To demonstrate the potential of reacting instead of strategizing.
- To develop participants' awareness of behaviors that may obstruct or undermine effective communication.

Group Size

10 to 50 participants.

Time Required

25 to 35 minutes.

Materials

- Chairs for all participants.
- Copies of the Stand-Up Talkers' Confidential Information Sheet for half the group.
- Copies of the Sit-Down Talkers' Confidential Information Sheet (copied on a different color of paper) for half the group.

Physical Setting

A room large enough for groups of partners to move about and move chairs into various settings.

Facilitating Risk Rating

Moderate.

Process

1. Explain to the group that they are going to work on a communication activity while pretending to be co-workers for ThoughtStream Technology.

2. Have members of the group number off 1 and 2. Give the Number 1's copies of the Stand-Up Talkers' Confidential Information Sheet and the Number 2's copies of the Sit-Down Talkers' Confidential Information Sheet.

3. Say to the group:

   "You are co-workers for ThoughtStream Technology. Recently, your computer system has had several crashes. Number 1's, you work in customer relations and sales. You are known as Stand-Up Talkers, which means that you cannot speak unless you are standing. Number 2's, you work in programming and troubleshooting for the company's computer system. You are known as Sit-Down Talkers, which means that you cannot speak unless you are sitting. Please read through your Confidential Information Sheets. Each Stand-Up Talker must find a Sit-Down Talker with whom to discuss the problem described on your sheets."

   (5 minutes.)

4. Tell the group that they will have between 5 and 7 minutes to speak with their partners. (*Note:* You may have to help partners pair up as they finish reading their Confidential Information Sheets.)

5. While partners are attempting to negotiate/communicate with one another, watch the body language of the participants. Pay special attention to whether the participants move from standing to sitting positions, how the participants speak to one another, and whether one partner is silent so that the other can state his or her position.

6. Be sure to walk among the pairs to ensure that they are moving toward a solution. End the activity after 10 minutes to prevent frustration.

Experiential Learning Activities

7. Bring closure with the following questions:
   - At the beginning of the process, what did you think of your partner's situation?
   - What did you discover about the other person's challenges?
   - What, if any, resolution did you reach?
   - Did your approach to resolving the issue change? If so how?
   - When could this type of situation arise at work?
   - When have you experienced something similar?
   - What managerial behaviors encourage diverse communication? Discourage them?

   (10 minutes.)

8. Review your observations from the process with the group.

Trainer's Note

Participants may arrive at their own solutions to the diverse situations. This is positive. Two of many possibilities follow:

- Parties take turns standing and sitting in order for each person to speak. However, it is amazing how some partners refuse to compromise in this manner. Many times one talker will be unwilling to "yield the floor" by being silent and going to the other party's position to speak.

- Partners come up with some sort of leaning where a Stand-Up Talker leans or steps down a stair in order to be more at eye level.

Submitted by Linda Byars Swindling.

Linda Byars Swindling, *JD, CSP, is a recognized expert on workplace issues and negotiations. Author of the popular* Passports to Success *series, she is co-author of* The Consultant's Legal Guide, What Smart Trainers Know, *and* The Productivity Path. *Her clients include the American Heart Association, Crowne Plaza Hotels, Holt, Reinhart and Winston, and Global Marketing Services, in association with IBM. She currently serves on the national board of directors for the National Speakers Association and is the editor of* Professional Speaker *magazine.*

Stand-Up Talkers' Confidential Information Sheet

You are a Stand-Up Talker. You come from a distinguished family of Stand-Up Talkers. You are employed with ThoughtStream Technology and take pride in your work, much of which is customer relations and sales. Recently, your system has had several crashes. Had the information not been backed up, ThoughtStream would have been destroyed. As it was, you have had to spend countless hours waiting for the technology people to restore information while you calmed down aggravated clients.

Your boss hired you to generate income and handle the people issues. When the system crashes, you can't do either. Thank goodness your boss is a Stand-Up Talker and you have such a good relationship. You told him you would explain the importance of fixing the problem to the technology department. He told you to find a solution to this problem by the end of next week. You also know you will have to give a false deadline to the technology people or it will never be done.

A solution has to exist to stop these crashes. A friend of yours told you that his company fixed a similar problem with a piece of software known as Save-It. Unfortunately, that software is in the possession of a Sit-Down Talker.

You don't know why, but you have never been able to get along with Sit-Down Talkers. You can't understand how they are able to succeed in life with their challenges. For instance, there is no way a Sit-Down Talker could ever have a conversation while walking. When they speak to a group, no one can see them in the back because they are sitting when they lecture.

You dread going to this particular Sit-Down Talker, who has an attitude and likes people to beg for help before finding solutions. It's not your fault that this Sit-Down Talker was born with the sitting and talking challenge. Some people just have bad luck. However, you have to have an answer to this system problem. The Sit-Down Talker has the Save-It software and you need it. Now, go talk!

Sit-Down Talkers' Confidential Information Sheet

You are a Sit-Down Talker. Your people have battled discrimination all of their lives. Despite that, Sit-Down Talkers are famous inventors, were incredible pilots in the nation's wars, and are well-respected in almost every field.

You are employed with ThoughtStream Technology and take pride in your work, much of which is programming and troubleshooting. Recently, ThoughtStream's system has had several crashes. Had the information not been backed up, ThoughtStream would have been destroyed. Although no one remembers it, you were the one who created the back-up protocol. You systemized the method that allowed ThoughtStream to store and recapture information in the event crashes occurred. Due to your recapture system, you and the technology people were able to restore information in hours instead of months.

You take a lot of pride in your work and you are embarrassed that what you know to be a great system has crashed on a few occasions. You have spent nights and weekends trying to figure out what the problem is. What is really irritating is that you have people, especially Stand-Up Talkers, coming to you with their own solutions. They don't even understand the system, so how could they understand how to fix it? Also, the company's bosses are Stand-Up Talkers. You like your job, so you give respect to them and their suggestions. However, their suggestions usually take you away from really important work.

At first, you thought some software wasn't properly installed, and then you thought that a new software program called Save-It would be a solution. However, it appears that Save-It is just a temporary fix and may cause even more problems. You now believe that the current software programs are not reading each other correctly. You just need people to leave you alone and let you spend two uninterrupted days working on this problem. Unfortunately, the company is run by Stand-Up Talkers. They don't like having Sit-Down Talkers telling them they aren't doing anything new for two days.

Stand-Up Talkers always act superior or as if they pity you. You think there are many great things about being a Sit-Down Talker, and you don't know how you would do your job if you were a Stand-Up Talker. They certainly couldn't sit down at a computer and have the conversations needed to be successful. You are getting a little tired of this second-class treatment. Some Sit-Down Talkers have been speaking with you about forming their own company and want you to be a part of it.

You have just heard that a Stand-Up Talker from sales is coming to speak with you about the crashes. If this person doesn't look you in the eye and listen to what you have to say, you'll keep quiet about the real solution and just do what you're told.

What Zoo Animal Would You Be?
Giving and Receiving Feedback

Activity Summary

This is a brief and fun activity in which participants describe one another as zoo animals and share feedback with one another.

Goals

- To get to know one another in a light-hearted way.
- To give feedback in a non-threatening way.

Group Size

6 to 10 participants who work together often.

Time Required

60 to 90 minutes.

Materials

- One copy of the What Zoo Animal Would You Be? handout for each participant.
- Flip chart and markers.
- Pens or pencils for participants.

Physical Setting

Any meeting room.

Facilitating Risk Rating

Moderate.

Process

1. Explain the goals of the activity. Set the expectation that the feedback provided should be positive and helpful and explain that the intention is not to hurt anyone's feelings or be insulting in any manner.

2. Distribute one copy of the What Zoo Animal Would You Be? handout and a pen or pencil to each participant.

3. Go over the instructions with the group, reminding them that they are to describe each other in terms of the characteristics of a zoo animal, such as personality, style, qualities, and so on, *without describing any physical characteristics.*

4. Encourage participants to be creative in their comparisons, thinking of unique ways to describe the other participants. Emphasize that the purpose is to give each person unique perspectives on how he or she is perceived by the other members of the group. Allow at least 2 minutes per person being described for the task.
   (15 to 20 minutes.)

5. Once everyone has completed the form for all the other people, assign a scribe to capture all of the comparisons presented for each individual on a flip chart, one sheet of flip-chart paper per person. Ask the scribe to include the zoo animal as well as the characteristics of that animal/person that are given (or you may wish to give everyone a break while you do this yourself).

6. Have participants take turns providing feedback for everyone else in the group so that each person hears all his or her feedback at once. Allow 4 or 5 minutes per participant to hear and process the feedback.
   (25 to 50 minutes.)

7. After all team members have shared their feedback about a person, give him or her the flip-chart page for future reference.

8. Debrief with these questions:
   - What have we learned about each other?
   - What did you learn about yourself?
   - What have we learned about our team?
   - How can we use this information to be a better team?

   (10 minutes.)

9. Thank participants for their imaginative ways of providing feedback to one another. Ask the group to use the unique descriptions of the members of their group to help them better understand one another and to work more effectively as a team in the future.

Trainer's Note

This activity is designed to provide participants with unique personal feedback from peers, subordinates, supervisors, or others who know them well. It is a creative and easy method of providing an alternative to the 360-degree feedback tools that are much more complicated, expensive, and time-consuming. This exercise provides participants with candid and useful feedback in a pleasant manner and can provide them with a personal perspective not otherwise available.

It is ideal to help a department or group of people who work closely together build stronger interpersonal relationships. The feedback that each person receives can be extremely useful in helping the group better understand all their personal characteristics and styles. The exercise is also unique in that it provides individualized feedback as part of a group exercise.

Variations

- The feedback could be given privately by having participants complete one copy of the handout for each person and give it to that person. In this case, provide each person with enough handouts.

- If there is an *artist* in the group, pictures of the zoo animals could be created and posted in the meeting room as a reminder of the analogies made during the exercise. This would provide an entertaining and useful reminder of the exercise during the remainder of the meeting or in the future.

- Arrange to have the meeting at a local zoo to build on the theme and to create an interesting sidelight to the day. As a diversion, go on a tour of the zoo or have animals brought into your meeting room.

Submitted by George E. Krock.

George E. Krock has been working in the human resources field for PPG Industries for over thirty-five years. He is currently the director of HR Planning & Development. His portfolio over the years has included labor and employee relations, wages and benefits, selection and staffing, equal employment, and diversity. He led the team that developed and installed PPG's Performance & Learning Process and Rounded Feedback.

What Zoo Animal Would You Be?

Instructions: Describe each of the other participants in the room in terms of a zoo animal that person reminds you of in terms of personality, style, qualities, etc.

On the chart below, list that person's name, the animal, and the characteristics of that animal that remind you of that particular person, *without describing any physical characteristics.*

Take your time and make your answers thoughtful and precise. Be creative, but do not attempt to be humorous at the expense of anyone else.

Name	Animal	Why? (Style, Qualities, Characteristics)

The Modern Art Factory:
Experiencing Changing Leadership

Activity Summary

This is a nonverbal group activity that allows participants to experience the changing role of leadership while in the process of co-creating.

Goals

- To demonstrate the effect of control on the leadership role.
- To demonstrate the power of nonverbal communication in leading others.
- To develop participants' awareness of the adaptability and flexibility required in the process of co-creating.

Group Size

4 to 5 participants per group in an unlimited number of groups.

Time Required

45 to 50 minutes.

Materials

- One sheet of flip-chart paper on a large sheet of poster board or an easel for each group.
- One marker for each group.
- Masking tape.

Physical Setting

An area large enough for each group to gather around the sheet of paper (either on a table or on the floor). This activity can also be conducted outdoors in good weather.

Facilitating Risk Rating

Moderate.

Process

1. Divide participants into groups of four or five. Give each group one piece of flip-chart paper mounted on poster board (or on an easel) and one marker.

2. Explain to the participants that they are teams of artists who have decided to collaborate on creating a modern art masterpiece. Say that each group will create a piece of artwork.

3. Say to the groups, "Sit down around your 'canvas' (the flip-chart paper). Only one artist will be working at a time while you create your masterpiece."

4. Then give the participants the rules. Say, "Everyone will be given 20 minutes to work. The activity is to be done in complete silence. There will be no talking within your group or with anyone in another group. You are to take turns working on the masterpiece within your own small group. Your turn starts when you touch the pen to the paper. Your turn ends when you lift the pen from the paper. The next person must begin drawing at the exact spot where you stopped."

5. Tell the groups to begin. Note the time in order to end the activity in 20 minutes. Walk around the groups to observe the no-talking and drawing rules. *(20 minutes.)*

6. After 20 minutes elapses, stop the groups. Allow the participants to debrief the activity in their small groups. Direct the small group discussions with the following questions:

    - How did not being able to talk affect your process of co-creating?
    - In what ways did leadership emerge and change hands?
    - How did your group's drawing evolve and why?

- What part of the process was challenging or even frustrating?

- What work situations require this type of leadership?

(10 minutes.)

7. Have all the groups post their masterpieces on a wall and have an "art gallery viewing" by all the participants.

8. Conclude the session with open sharing of key learning in the large group.
(10 minutes.)

Variation

- Follow the same rules except give each team member a different color marker. At the end they can see what each member created during the process.

Submitted by Frank A. Prince.

Frank A. Prince *is president and founder of Unleash Your Mind LLC, a consulting firm focused on applied innovation within corporations. He is the author of* C and the Box: A Paradigm Parable, *published by Pfeiffer. He is also the voice of and inventor of* Speed Sleep, *an innovative audio CD that accelerates sleep and creativity at a subconscious level.*

Musical Introductions:
Melting the Ice

Activity Summary

This activity turns the traditional icebreaker into an "ice melter," engaging the participants emotionally while broaching the subject to be taught holistically.

Goals

- To entice participants to begin thinking about the training subject holistically.
- To introduce participants to one another.
- To establish the differences and commonalities among participants.

Group Size

Workable with any group size, but a smaller group (4 to 10 participants) allows time for each participant to share. With groups larger than 10, divide participants into subgroups of 3 to 7 and ask them to share their selections within their groups.

Time Required

Approximately 20 minutes.

Materials

- A CD or audiotape player.
- Appropriate musical selections.
- Easel stand, newsprint pads, and felt-tipped markers.
- (Optional) A list of musical selections for participants to choose from.

Physical Setting

Any training environment where music CDs can be played and heard by all the participants.

Facilitating Risk Rating

Low.

Process

1. Welcome participants to the training. Introduce the topics: a desire to get to know the participants while also beginning to explore the training subject. To that end, ask the participants a music-related question. Two examples of training subjects follow:

    - Diversity/Cultural Awareness: What's your favorite song?

    - Communication: What was the most popular song during your senior year in high school?

2. Provide the participants a minute to think about their answers and play music themed to the subject at hand. Two examples follow:

    - Diversity/Cultural Awareness: "Respect" by Aretha Franklin.

    - Communication: "I Heard It Through the Grapevine" by Marvin Gaye.*

3. Call the participants back to attention and instruct them to, one by one, share their answers. Write the names of their musical selections for the two topics (getting to know one another and the theme for the session) on the flip chart. *(5 minutes.)*

4. Once the list is complete, ask the following questions and make the following points for the two topics. Create your own questions related to the topic you will facilitate. The discussion should be limited to about 15 minutes.

    Diversity/Cultural Awareness

    - "What do you notice about these selections?" (Most of them come from the broad category of popular music.)

---

*NOTE: Be sure to abide by any copyright laws pertaining to using music in your training.

- "What is the origin of popular music?" (It is a result of the combination of two cultures: the chord and tonal structure of European music and the rhythm of African music.)

- "Can you imagine a world without that music?" (It is fortunate for us that the two cultures did combine to create the wonderful auditory palate we enjoy.)

- "How does this information relate to today's subject?" (Diversity is a tool for creating new inspirations. But to do that, we must be open to the new and different possibilities diversity offers.)

Communication

- "What do you notice about the selections?" (They vary widely.)

- "What can you infer about people who select such different music?" (Their influences, history, and culture are different.)

- "How do you think those differences would affect communication?" (Communication may be more difficult when people come from differing backgrounds or may be easier when people share commonalities.)

- "How can you use this fact to become a more effective communicator?" (The more you understand another person, the easier communication becomes.)

Trainer's Note

In my 2000 work *Training with a Beat,* I noted the application of music in the learning environment. I stated that people are often uncomfortable entering the learning environment. "Learning requires admitting knowledge gaps, in front of strangers, in an unfamiliar room, to facilitators not yet met."

In addition, some people remember negative school experiences. Others, especially older learners, doubt their own learning abilities. Professionals often see themselves as too busy to learn. Still other participants are suspicious of the motives behind the training. The traditional icebreaker, presented as a way to begin the learning, does little to surmount these anxieties. It too can generate participant hostility.

Fortunately, none of these difficulties is insurmountable. Music familiar to the learners transcends intellectual learning blocks by reaching deeper into the brain, into the limbic system and the emotions, disarming anti-learning defenses.

Variations

- Career Development/Life Skills: "Identify the song that would be most played on the sound track if a movie was being made of your life."

- Change: "What song best describes the situation in your work environment?"

- Leadership Development: "If you had to choose a song to become your leadership motto, what song would you choose?"

- Musical Introductions questions can also be assigned as pre-work by instructing the participants to bring CDs of their chosen songs to the class. In that scenario, provide each participant the opportunity to play his or her selection for the other participants.

Reference

Millbower, L. (2000). *Training with a beat.* Sterling, VA: Stylus Publishing.

Submitted by Lenn Millbower.

Lenn Millbower *is an expert in the use of show biz techniques to enhance learning. He is the author of* Show Biz Training, Cartoons for Trainers, Training with a Beat *and* Game Show Themes for Trainers; *an instructional designer and facilitator; a musical composer; a magician and comedian; a professional speaker; and the chief Learnertainer™ at Offbeat Training®, where he helps organizations reinvent their training through show biz techniques that increase retention and decrease expense.*

Four Thermometers:
Planning for Implementation

Activity Summary

This is an end-of-training activity to help promote learning transfer.

Goals

- To allow participants to reflect together on what they have learned in the training session.
- To give participants ideas on how they can use what they have learned back on the job.

Group Size

15 to 30 people.

Time Required

40 to 60 minutes, depending on the size of the group.

Materials

- Four posters, prepared in advance, each with *one* of the four questions from the Four Thermometers Worksheet and a thermometer, laid out as on the worksheet.
- One Four Thermometers Worksheet for each participant.
- Four different types of stickers, enough to give one sticker to each participant. The stickers can be four different colors of dots, four types of animals, four types of cartoon characters, or other distinction.

- Four flip-chart easels with paper and marking pens.
- Pens or pencils for participants.
- Masking tape.

Physical Setting

A room in which four groups can work without disturbing one another.

Facilitating Risk Rating

Low to moderate.

Preparation

Near the end of a training session, hang the four prepared posters in separate corners of the room, or an adequate distance from each other to allow subgroups to talk without disturbing one another. Provide an easel and marking pens by each poster.

Process

1. Begin by explaining the goals of the exercise. Give each participant one copy of the Four Thermometers Worksheet and a pen or pencil.

2. Ask the participants to reflect on the questions and jot down their answers individually.
   (10 minutes.)

3. Divide the group into four subgroups by randomly handing out the four types of stickers. Make sure that there are equal amounts of each sticker so that the groups will be equally divided. Tell the participants that everyone with the same type of sticker forms a subgroup.

4. Assign each subgroup to one of the posters.
   (1 to 2 minutes.)

5. In their subgroups, tell participants to begin by placing their stickers on the thermometer at the appropriate place along the continuum to indicate their opinions with respect to the question on that poster. Participants should place their stickers first and then discuss their answers among themselves.
   (2 to 3 minutes.)

Experiential Learning Activities

6. Give subgroups 15 to 20 minutes for discussion. Tell each subgroup to elect a scribe to record the high points of their discussion on their flip chart.
   (15 to 20 minutes.)

7. Reconvene the whole group and ask each subgroup to report out their answers and insights on their assigned question. Invite the entire group to ask questions or add comments.
   (10 to 20 minutes.)

8. Close the activity by asking all participants to write down at least one idea from the discussion that they feel they can act on back at work.
   (1 to 2 minutes.)

Submitted by Steve Sphar.

Steve Sphar, *J.D., is an internal organization development consultant for the California State Teachers' Retirement System. He has counseled managers and employees in both the private and public sectors for over fifteen years. He is a frequent contributor to professional publications, including the* Pfeiffer Annual *and the* McGraw-Hill Training and Performance SourceBook.

Four Thermometers Worksheet

Instructions: Review each of the following questions and jot down your initial responses to the question, using the thermometer as a continuum.

- What opportunities do you see for implementing the ideas of this course back on the job?

- What aspects of your work culture make it easy or difficult to use what you've learned in this course?

Lots of Opportunities

Easy Culture to Implement

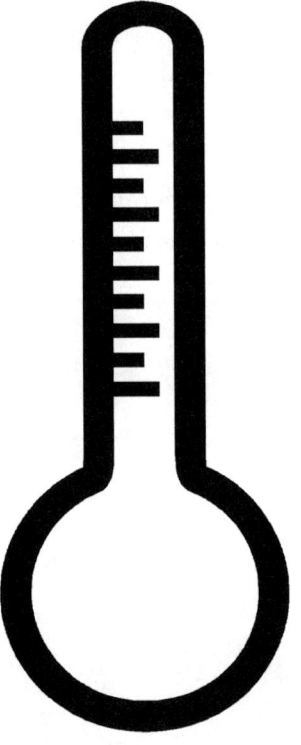

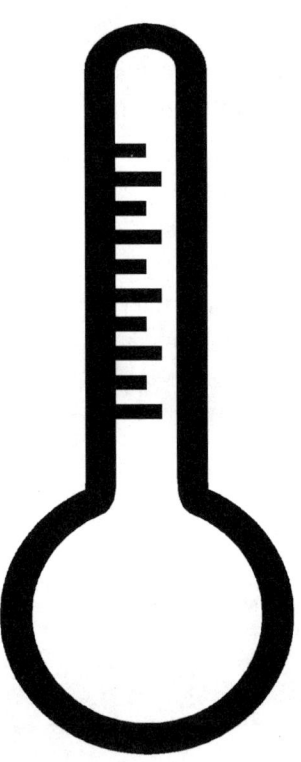

Not Many Opportunities

Hard Culture to Implement

- Has this course been worth the time invested? What changes at work would make it more worthwhile?

- What specific things could you do differently at work to implement what you have learned in this course?

Very Worthwhile

Lots of Things

Not Very Worthwhile

Not Many Things

Learning Charts:
Cataloging for Future Planning

Activity Summary

This activity involves cataloging the learning events that have influenced a person's professional and/or personal life, conducted at the conclusion of a leadership or management development program.

Goals

- To examine previous learning activities to determine whether learning needs have been met.
- To use reflective thinking to increase the value of past learning events.
- To place a value on the development of learning plans for future learning.

Group Size

12 to 15 participants (a number divisible by 3 for triads) who are attending a leadership or management program.

Time Required

90 to 120 minutes.

Materials

- One set of Learning Charts Handouts A, B, C, and D for each participant.
- Pens or pencils for participants.
- Flip-chart stands and plenty of paper.

- Felt-tipped markers.
- Masking tape.

Physical Setting

A room large enough for 5 triads to work without disturbing one another with enough wall space for hanging flip-chart paper.

Facilitating Risk Taking

Low to moderate.

Process

1. As an introduction, tell participants the importance of assessing and discussing learnings gained from their work lives with others. Be sure to point out that assessing their learning at the end of a program is useful because it serves as a review and a springboard for planning future learning.

2. Give out copies of Learning Charts Handout A: Needs and pens or pencils and have participants read the first section and provide written responses to the Questions to Ask Yourself. Also tell them to fill out the chart at the bottom of the handout.
(5 minutes.)

3. Have participants share their responses to the handout in triads. Facilitate a total group discussion. List key points on the flip chart.
(10 minutes.)

4. Give out and ask participants to read Learning Charts Handout B: Events, and have them provide written responses to the Questions to Ask Yourself section. Also tell them to complete the chart at the end.
(10 minutes.)

5. Again, have participants share their responses from the handout in triads. Facilitate a total group discussion of their insights. List key points on a flip chart.
(10 minutes.)

6. Hand out and ask participants to read Learning Charts Handout C: Applications, and have them provide written responses to the questions. Also have them fill out the chart at the end.
(10 minutes.)

7. Again have participants share their responses to the handout in triads and facilitate a total group discussion. List key points on a flip chart.
   (10 minutes.)

8. Hand out and ask participants to read Learning Charts Handout D: Reflections, and have them provide written responses to the questions and fill out the chart.
   (10 minutes.)

9. Have participants share their answers to the questions in triads and share their charts with one another. Facilitate a total group discussion, listing key points on a flip chart.
   (10 minutes.)

10. Conduct a total group discussion using the following questions:
    - What is your overall level of satisfaction with what you've learned so far to help you perform as a leader or manager?
    - Are there any obstacles to your future learning?
    - What are they, and how would you overcome them?
    - What do you need to learn during the next three years in order to advance your leadership capabilities?
    - How will you go about learning this information?

    (15 minutes.)

Variations

- This activity can be modified for an electronic format using chat rooms and bulletin boards.
- This activity could serve as the tool for a one-on-one discussion between a mentor and a protégé.

Submitted by Robert C. Preziosi.

Robert C. Preziosi, *D.P.A., is a professor of management at the Huizenga School of Business and Entrepreneurship at Nova Southeastern University in Fort Lauderdale, Florida. He is the faculty chair for the master's in HRM and master's in Leadership programs. He has received numerous awards, including Excellence in Teaching, Professor of the Decade, and Faculty Member of the Year. He is also president of Preziosi Partners, Inc., a consulting firm. ASTD has bestowed the Outstanding Contribution to HRD award and two Torch Awards. He is also the editor of the* 2005 Pfeiffer Annual: Human Resource Management, *recently added to the Pfeiffer line.*

Learning Charts Handout A: Needs

People grow and develop as individuals with personal aspirations and as performers working in organizations to earn a living. It is necessary to learn skills, knowledge, and behavior to fulfill aspirations and/or meet performance expectations. Normally, there is a gap between one's current state and one's aspirations and/or expectations. Thus, a person has learning needs. Satisfying the needs results in eliminating the gap. As aspirations and/or expectations change, new gaps are born and new needs appear. Learning events lead to met needs.

Questions to Ask Yourself

1. How did these learning needs surface for you?

2. What key people helped you identify those needs?

3. Did you ever overlook any of your learning needs?

4. Were most of your learning needs focused on skill, knowledge, or attitude?

5. How do you expect to identify your learning needs in the future?

Learning Needs That Have Been Identified by/for Me
Start of personal/career growth stages:
Next phase of growth:
Ongoing growth:
Most recent growth stage:
Current needs to prepare for future growth:

Learning Charts Handout B: Events

Each of us has been involved in a variety of formal and informal learning events. The formal include classroom and training room experiences conducted by a professional learning facilitator. Informal learning takes place when we read something or talk with a boss, colleague, or mentor. In all these instances, what we learn has the potential to be taken to heart and change our behavior. We may choose to attend these events or may be sent to them by a boss or strongly encouraged to attend by a well-intentioned colleague.

These events launch or inject energy into a person's long-term and/or short-term learning plan. Our plans may be well-thought-through and sketched out or simply responses to an opportunity that seems to come out of nowhere. The bottom line is that they have the potential to have some learning impact.

Questions to Ask Yourself

1. Generally speaking, did the learning events you engaged in meet your learning needs?

2. Who provided the most significant learning events in your life?

3. Where did most of your learning events take place?

4. What made learning events memorable?

5. What learning events do you need to focus on in the future?

Learning Events That Met Learning Needs
High School:
College:
During your first job (post high school and/or college):
During your next job(s):
During your current job:

Learning Charts Handout C: Applications

Learning needs cause us to participate in learning events so that gaps in knowledge, skill, and/or attitude can be eliminated. The final phase in this process is application. Individuals use their new knowledge, skills, and/or attitudes in appropriate personal and/or work situations.

The result is partial or total fulfillment of aspirations or a successful effort at meeting performance expectations. If the result is only partially fulfilling or not fully successful, a person will continue the effort until a comfortable level of fulfillment or success is attained. This sustained effort can be short-term or long-term and may even require a "refresher" learning event.

The key is arriving at a point where one becomes a "better" person and/or shows improvement in individual contribution. Personal satisfaction is the key benchmark.

Questions to Ask Yourself

1. Were most gaps in your knowledge, skills, or abilities aspiration-driven or expectations-driven?

2. What learning situations were conducive to appropriate application of what you learned?

3. Did someone add value to applications by providing feedback and/or offering advice? Who? In what way?

Experiential Learning Activities

4. Would you have done anything differently as far as learning opportunities go?

5. Did you ever leave any gaps in your knowledge unresponded to? Why? What were the consequences?

Learning Applications That Eliminated Gaps				
What Training	Where Conducted	By Whom	Gaps Eliminated	Comments

Learning Charts Handout D: Reflections

Some learning psychologists believe that reflective thinking is a powerful component of adult learning and that this kind of thinking is essential if learning is going to have any real impact on a person's behavior. However, when asked about reflective thinking many adult learners aren't sure what it includes or how to do it.

It helps to consider reflective thinking as (1) an assessment, (2) a reinforcer, and (3) a predictor. First, as an assessment tool, reflective thinking requires an analysis of the positive and negative impacts of the learning on aspirations and/or expectations in the context of one's daily activities. It also requires one to review the extent to which learning gaps have been eliminated.

Second, as a reinforcement tool, this kind of thinking leads us to conclusions about our behavior. It helps us see the value of actions we've taken and provides a kind of "intellectual" reinforcement for them.

The third aspect of reflective thinking as an applied tool has to do with helping us feed forward about our behavior. Assessment and reinforcement serve as building blocks for future desired behavior. This is the predictive aspect of reflective thinking. It invites us to, as necessary, work toward exhibiting the appropriate behavior that we desire.

Reflective thinking is, thus, a very essential tool for learning. It takes place within an individual as personal reflection. While it may include things that have been fed back, it is not driven by a coach, mentor, colleague, or boss, but by the individual as a continuous adaptation to personal and/or work situations.

Questions to Ask Yourself

1. Do I take time for reflective thinking?

2. Have I used reflective thinking more for assessment, reinforcement, or feeding forward? In what ways?

3. How would I characterize the results of my reflective thinking?

4. How can I ensure that my future reflective thinking adds value to my overall learning?

Actions That Added Impact to My Learning			
What I Learned	My Thoughts	How Used	Impact

Role Models:
Achieving Long-Term Results

Activity Summary

This is an exercise to encourage participants to reflect on what they have learned from role models they have encountered.

Goals

- To discuss what differentiates good leaders from poor leaders.
- To reflect on the qualities of role models.
- To share insights about leadership.

Group Size

Up to 20 participants who are studying the topic of leadership.

Time Required

60 minutes.

Matcrials

- One copy of the two-part Role Models Survey for each participant.
- A whiteboard and markers or several flip-chart-sized sheets of paper and felt-tipped markers.
- Two small Post-it® Notes in two different colors per participant.
- Pens or pencils for participants.
- Masking tape.

The 2005 Pfeiffer Annual: Training.
Copyright © 2005 by John Wiley & Sons, Inc. Reproduced by permission of Pfeiffer, an Imprint of Wiley. www.pfeiffer.com

Physical Setting

Any room in which the group can meet comfortably.

Facilitating Risk

Moderate.

Process

1. Introduce the activity with the following comments:

    "Recently, there has been a shift in leadership training from an emphasis on leadership behaviors to an emphasis on the results that leaders are responsible for creating. In addition, every year, authors publish yet other lists of the 'top ten essential leadership behaviors.' I don't think we need another list. Few of us memorize the lists for any reason other than to take a test. This exercise will help you make the link between leadership behaviors and results.

    "It will encourage you to reflect on, and learn from, the role models you have encountered during your work life. Role models, both the 'Best' and the 'Worst,' are powerful, emotion-laden memories that can be tapped for wisdom now and in the future.

    "The thirty questions included in the survey you will take were developed from a search of the leadership literature (Magretta, 2002; Ulrich, Longs, & Smallwood, 1999) and several large-scale employee surveys."

2. Distribute copies of the complete Role Models Survey and pens or pencils to participants. Instruct the participants to note that the survey has thirty questions for the "Best" leader and exactly the same thirty questions for the "Worst" leader. Note also that the scale is negatively worded for some of the questions (strongly disagree = 5 points because these are negative behaviors). The minimum score is 30 and the maximum score is 150.
    (10 minutes.)

3. Ask them to begin. On the whiteboard or flip-chart pages taped to the wall, create a 9-foot to 12-foot line numbered from 1 to 150, with markers at 25, 50, 75, and so on. Do this while participants complete their surveys.
    (10 minutes.)

4. When it is clear that everyone has completed both parts of the survey, ask them to write the score they gave each leader on a single Post-it Note and place that note on the whiteboard or flip-chart sheet in the place that corresponds with the score they gave that leader.
    (10 minutes.)

5. When all participants have posted both of their scores, draw attention to the two or three highest scores. Ask these participants to briefly describe what it was like working with these leaders. Then do the same with the two or three lowest scores. Ask about their results and outcomes.
   (10 minutes.)

6. Note that the group tendency may be to discuss leadership behaviors; thus it is important that you direct the group to focus on the *outcomes* of leadership behaviors, instead of the behaviors themselves. Use the following discussion statements to help them focus.

   - Describe the work environment and results created by the leaders you rated. Consider such things as creativity and innovation; customer service behavior; employee morale, development, and retention; health and safety; productivity; profitability; quality; and teamwork.

7. Typical group results include the following:

   Employees with Best Leaders

   Employees felt confident, empowered, included, trusted and valued; enhanced employee commitment, development, morale, retention, safety and teamwork; employees took ownership of their jobs and focused on the "want to" part of the job.

   Employees with Worst Leaders

   Employees felt used and abused; low attendance, morale, self-esteem; lot of passive-aggressive behavior; no trust, high interpersonal conflict and cynicism; high employee turnover among key talent; lot of self-protection and turf protection; little or no initiative or risk taking; employees focused on the "must do" part of the job.

   Customers with Best Leaders

   Improved customer satisfaction and service.

   Customers with Worst Leaders

   Not served; poor quality products and services; lost key customers.

   Organizations with Best Leaders

   More efficient, effective, productive and profitable; we became an employer of choice, we attracted and retained better employees; more flexible and ready to change; employees spoke with pride about working at this company.

Organizations with Worst Leaders

Three times the effort and one-third the results; lot of scrap and re-work; low productivity and profitability; no loyalty to the organization; disrespect for other leaders; unsafe work environment; increase in number of sick days and length of lunch breaks; favoritism; company went out of business.

(10 minutes.)

8. Debrief the experience. Briefly summarize the group discussion. Note that these are some of the ways the best leaders create long-term results for an organization. In addition, these are some of the ways that the worst leaders undermine an organization and destroy employees and shareholder value.

   - What are great leaders worth to their organizations?
   - Where do they want their organizations to be five years from now?
   - What steps are they prepared to take to create long-term results for their work groups and organizations?
   - Where do you think you would be on the graph as a leader?
   - How do you feel about that?
   - What will you do differently as a result of this discussion?

Trainer's Note

About 5 percent of the time, scores for the "best" leader will be less than 100. Draw attention to this when it occurs. Unfortunately, some people have never had a great leader as a role model.

About 5 percent of the time, scores for the "worst" leader will be greater than 100. Draw attention to this when it occurs. Some people have never experienced a poor leader; they have much to be grateful for.

Variations

- A little preparation can enhance this exercise. For example, ask the participants to briefly discuss the behaviors of great leaders they have known personally. Or use short video clips from recent movies to share examples of great and poor leadership behaviors. Examples of abusive leaders include Kevin Spacey from *Swimming with Sharks* and one of the coaches in *Bad News Bears*.

- After the group discussion, remind them how good it felt when they talked about the "best" leaders and how painful it was when they discussed their "worst" leaders. Suggest that there is a way to take advantage of these memories. The next time they are faced with a difficult leadership decision, ask them to imagine placing their best leader on one shoulder and their worst leader on the other shoulder. Ask both for advice.

- Most leaders fall between the best and the worst. Ask the participants to reflect on three or four other leaders they have known well. Don't take time to complete the survey; just estimate where they would be between their best and worst leaders. Post these scores on the flip chart. The result is usually something that resembles a normal distribution curve. Ask the group, "What can we learn from this?" No one is asking them to be perfect. All leaders are human. But we do have a right to expect our leaders to learn from their mistakes.

- This exercise was originally developed to teach leadership, but the outcomes can also be used to initiate a discussion of coaching, motivation, managing change, and emotional intelligence.

References

Magretta, J. 2002. *What management is: How it works and why it's everyone's business.* New York: The Free Press.

Ulrich, D., Zenger, J., & Smallwood, N. 1999. *Results-based leadership.* Boston, MA: Harvard Business School Press.

Submitted by Robert Shaver.

Robert Shaver *is a faculty associate with Executive Education, a continuing education unit of the University of Wisconsin-Madison School of Business. As the director of the Basic Management Certificate Series program, he is responsible for development, marketing, staffing, and management. He works with companies throughout the Midwest, designing and delivering custom, in-house training programs. He received his bachelor's degree in communication, economics, and business administration from the University of Wisconsin-Stevens Point and his M.B.A. from the University of Wisconsin-Madison.*

Role Models Survey, Best Leader

Instructions: For this section of the survey, think of a person you have known and consider to be the best leader ever (a team leader, supervisor, manager, or other leader). The questions are designed to identify "blind spots," the personal and interpersonal behaviors that destroy workplace motivation and organizational commitment and create dead ends in aspiring managerial careers.

Use the following scale as you answer each question, keeping your "BEST" leader in mind. Note that some scales have been reversed for you below.

Strongly Disagree	Disagree	Neither Agree Nor Disagree	Agree	Strongly Agree	Don't Know
1	2	3	4	5	N/A

1. This person knows the business. 1 2 3 4 5 N/A

2. This person does not compromise safety for short-term results. 1 2 3 4 5 N/A

3. This person does not compromise quality for short-term results. 1 2 3 4 5 N/A

4. This person demonstrates a strong commitment to ethical behavior. 1 2 3 4 5 N/A

5. I can rely on this person to follow through on commitments made to me. 1 2 3 4 5 N/A

6. I know what this person expects of me. 1 2 3 4 5 N/A

7. This person recognizes people who make an extra effort. 1 2 3 4 5 N/A

8. This person understands when personal or family obligations occasionally take an employee away from work. 1 2 3 4 5 N/A

9. This person is always looking for better ways to do things. 1 2 3 4 5 N/A

10. This person is an effective communicator. 1 2 3 4 5 N/A

11. This person listens to me. 1 2 3 4 5 N/A

Strongly Disagree	Disagree	Neither Agree Nor Disagree	Agree	Strongly Agree	Don't Know
1	2	3	4	5	N/A

12.	This person has a "can do" attitude.	1	2	3	4	5	N/A
13.	This person seems to care about me as a person.	1	2	3	4	5	N/A
14.	This person helps others "save face" in difficult situations.	1	2	3	4	5	N/A
15.	Work is fun for this person.	1	2	3	4	5	N/A
16.	This person does not effectively manage the pressures/stresses of the job.	5	4	3	2	1	N/A
17.	This person is overly ambitious, ready to get ahead at the expense of others.	5	4	3	2	1	N/A
18.	This person pushes others too hard.	5	4	3	2	1	N/A
19.	This person takes credit for the work of others.	5	4	3	2	1	N/A
20.	This person usually blames others for his/her mistakes.	5	4	3	2	1	N/A
21.	This person is often moody.	5	4	3	2	1	N/A
22.	This person is too harsh/critical in his/her feedback to others.	5	4	3	2	1	N/A
23.	This person has a reputation for angry outbursts.	5	4	3	2	1	N/A
24.	This person is boastful/arrogant.	5	4	3	2	1	N/A
25.	This person is often abusive/insensitive to others.	5	4	3	2	1	N/A
26.	This person is very defensive when others give feedback to him/her.	5	4	3	2	1	N/A
27.	This person tends to see others as allies or enemies.	5	4	3	2	1	N/A

Strongly Disagree	Disagree	Neither Agree Nor Disagree	Agree	Strongly Agree	Don't Know
1	2	3	4	5	N/A

28. This person seeks power for his/her own interests.   5   4   3   2   1   N/A

29. This person is very rigid, unwilling to adapt his/her management style to the people or the situation.   5   4   3   2   1   N/A

30. This person has to win, or appear "right," at all costs.   5   4   3   2   1   N/A

Totals   ___ ___ ___ ___ ___ ___

Role Models Survey, Worst Leader

Instructions: For this section of the survey, think of a person you have known and consider to be the worst leader ever (a team leader, supervisor, manager, or other leader). The questions are designed to identify "blind spots," the personal and interpersonal behaviors that destroy workplace motivation and organizational commitment and create dead ends in aspiring managerial careers.

Use the following scale as you answer each question, keeping your "WORST" leader in mind. Note that the scale has been reversed for some items below.

Strongly Disagree 1	Disagree 2	Neither Agree Nor Disagree 3	Agree 4	Strongly Agree 5	Don't Know N/A

1. This person knows the business.   1 2 3 4 5 N/A
2. This person does not compromise safety for short-term results.   1 2 3 4 5 N/A
3. This person does not compromise quality for short-term results.   1 2 3 4 5 N/A
4. This person demonstrates a strong commitment to ethical behavior.   1 2 3 4 5 N/A
5. I can rely on this person to follow through on commitments made to me.   1 2 3 4 5 N/A
6. I know what this person expects of me.   1 2 3 4 5 N/A
7. This person recognizes people who make an extra effort.   1 2 3 4 5 N/A
8. This person understands when personal or family obligations occasionally take an employee away from work.   1 2 3 4 5 N/A
9. This person is always looking for better ways to do things.   1 2 3 4 5 N/A
10. This person is an effective communicator.   1 2 3 4 5 N/A
11. This person listens to me.   1 2 3 4 5 N/A

The 2005 Pfeiffer Annual: Training.
Copyright © 2005 by John Wiley & Sons, Inc. Reproduced by permission of Pfeiffer, an Imprint of Wiley. www.pfeiffer.com

Strongly Disagree	Disagree	Neither Agree Nor Disagree	Agree	Strongly Agree	Don't Know
1	2	3	4	5	N/A

12.	This person has a "can do" attitude.	1	2	3	4	5	N/A
13.	This person seems to care about me as a person.	1	2	3	4	5	N/A
14.	This person helps others "save face" in difficult situations.	1	2	3	4	5	N/A
15.	Work is fun for this person.	1	2	3	4	5	N/A
16.	This person does not effectively manage the pressures/stresses of the job.	5	4	3	2	1	N/A
17.	This person is overly ambitious, ready to get ahead at the expense of others.	5	4	3	2	1	N/A
18.	This person pushes others too hard.	5	4	3	2	1	N/A
19.	This person takes credit for the work of others.	5	4	3	2	1	N/A
20.	This person usually blames others for his/her mistakes.	5	4	3	2	1	N/A
21.	This person is often moody.	5	4	3	2	1	N/A
22.	This person is too harsh/critical in his/her feedback to others.	5	4	3	2	1	N/A
23.	This person has a reputation for angry outbursts.	5	4	3	2	1	N/A
24.	This person is boastful/arrogant.	5	4	3	2	1	N/A
25.	This person is often abusive/insensitive to others.	5	4	3	2	1	N/A
26.	This person is very defensive when others give feedback to him/her.	5	4	3	2	1	N/A
27.	This person tends to see others as allies or enemies.	5	4	3	2	1	N/A

Strongly Disagree	Disagree	Neither Agree Nor Disagree	Agree	Strongly Agree	Don't Know
1	2	3	4	5	N/A

28. This person seeks power for his/her own interests. 5 4 3 2 1 N/A

29. This person is very rigid, unwilling to adapt his/her management style to the people or the situation. 5 4 3 2 1 N/A

30. This person has to win, or appear "right," at all costs. 5 4 3 2 1 N/A

Totals ___ ___ ___ ___ ___ ___

Chains:
Keeping Lines of Communication Open

Activity Summary

This is a mildly physical activity that allows participants to experience the impact of every link in a communication chain.

Goals

- To demonstrate the importance of clear and ongoing communication and follow-up.
- To reinforce the idea that the effectiveness of organizational communication can be measured if outcomes have been clearly defined.

Group Size

10 to 50 participants, ideally in groups of 5.

Time Required

Approximately 30 minutes.

Materials

- Blank index cards, one for each participant.
- Pens or pencils for participants.
- A flip chart and felt-tipped markers or overhead projector, blank transparencies, and markers.

Physical Setting

A room that provides a writing surface for the participants.

Facilitating Risk Rating

Low.

Process

1. Ask participants to choose a legal three-digit number that is not a palindrome. Explain that a palindrome is a number that reads the same forward and backward because it begins and ends with the same number. Just as the words mom and dad are palindromes, because they read the same way both forward and backward, so are 909 or 353.

2. Demonstrate what the participants should do, placing the legal, non-palindrome, number "917" at the top of a flip chart or overhead transparency.

3. Have participants write their own legal, non-palindrome, three-digit numbers on their index cards.

4. Instruct the participants to pass their cards to the "customers" on their right.

5. Once participants have received the index cards, ask them to review the number on the card they received from the "supplier" on their left to ensure that it is a legal three-digit number. If it is not, they are to give that feedback to their "supplier" and return the card so that the "supplier" can correct it.

6. Once there is a legal number on the card, have participants create a new three-digit number by reversing the legal number and then subtracting the smaller number from the larger number. Demonstrate how to perform the computation on the flip chart or overhead projector, as shown in the sample below:

    917 is the legal number

    –719 is the reversed number

    198 is the remainder

7. Indicate that the remainder must be written as a three-digit number. Therefore, if the remainder is only two digits (such as 75), the participants should place a "0" in front of the two-digit remainder to create a three-digit number (075).

8. When the participants have completed their computations, remind them to be sure their remainder is written as a three-digit number. Then tell them to "pass the card to the 'customer' on your right."

9. Ask participants to once again review the work of their "suppliers" and check the math. If there is a problem, they should give feedback to their "suppliers" and return the card so that the "supplier" can fix it.

10. When the math is correct on all cards, instruct the participants to "create a new three-digit number by reversing the remainder and then adding that new number to the remainder." Demonstrate how to perform the computation on the flip chart or overhead transparency, as shown in the sample below:

    198 is the remainder

    +891 is the reversed number

    1089 is the sum

11. Once again, ask each participant to pass his or her card to the "customer" on his or her right. When everyone has a new card, ask them to review the work of their "suppliers" and check the math.

12. If all mathematical computations have been done correctly, the sum on every card should be 1089.

13. Debrief the exercise by discussing the following questions with the participants:

    - How frequently do you have organizational communications that are intended to achieve clearly defined results?

    - What are some examples of those communications? What do they concern and how are they handled (face-to-face, by email, by written note, by phone)?

    - How often do these communications fail to achieve the desired results?

    - What are the consequences if those communications are not successful?

    - Based on what you learned during this activity, what could you or others in the communication chain do to increase the probability that the desired results will be accomplished?

    (20 minutes.)

Submitted by Deborah Spring Laurel.

Deborah Spring Laurel, *president of Laurel and Associates, Ltd., is an international management training consultant who specializes in the design and presentation of skill-building, participant-centered workshops in personnel management, interpersonal relations, leadership, organization development, and train-the-trainer. She is also a Certified Professional Consultant to Management, with expertise in human resource management, organization development, and performance consulting. She has her master's degree from the University of Wisconsin-Madison.*

The Human Body:
Creating a Business Plan

Activity Summary

This is an interactive group exercise that allows participants to relate the various parts of a business plan to associated parts of the human body.

Goals

- To recognize the various elements of a business plan.
- To develop participants' awareness of the interconnectedness of the elements of a business plan.

Group Size

15 to 40 participants.

Time Required

Approximately 40 minutes.

Materials

- One The Human Body: Seven Components of a Business Plan handout for each participant.
- A simple outline diagram of a human body with major organs drawn on it in their correct locations for posting on the wall (include brain, eyes, ears, mouth, heart, hands, and feet).
- Index cards with the names of various elements of an effective business plan with sticky tape on the back of each card, at least one card per small group.

- Pencils for participants.
- Masking tape.

Physical Setting

A room with tables large enough to accommodate teams of 4 to 6 members.

Facilitating Risk Taking

Moderate.

Process

1. Arrange participants in groups of 4 to 6 at tables and explain the goals of the activity.

2. Start by giving each participant a copy of The Human Body: Seven Components of a Business Plan and a pencil.

3. Discuss each component on the handout and ask for examples from participants' organizations.
   (10 minutes.)

4. Post the body diagram on the wall for all to see. Distribute the cards with names of business plan elements, one or two to each group.

5. Explain that each body part on the diagram is a metaphor for one element of an effective business plan. Tell the groups to discuss among themselves and decide where on the human form they think each of the cards should go. For example, which body part would be the best metaphor for Human Resources?
   (10 minutes.)

6. Bring the total group back together and select volunteers from each group one at a time to come to the flip chart and to stick their cards next to the most appropriate body parts. (More than one card may initially be placed for each body part.)

7. Once all seven cards have been placed on the body outline, lead a discussion to select the most appropriate body part for each part of the business plan. Encourage participants to justify their choices based on the definitions of the plan elements discussed earlier. The authors' preferred choices are as follows:

Strategic Planning = eyes

Leadership = mouth

Human Resources = heart

Process Management = hands

Business Results = feet

Measurement/Analysis = brain

Customers = ears

The answers may vary depending on the organization's culture.
(10 minutes.)

8. Bring closure with the following questions:

   - How is a business plan like a human body? (Possible answers may be: it has varying parts, each part has a specific function, it is a "living," dynamic process.)

   - A human body and an effective business plan are healthy when all systems work. . . . (Possible answers may be together, in concert, linked, reinforcing.)

   - Which organ of the body that is not illustrated on the diagram ties the elements together? (Possible answers: blood, skin, lymphatic system, lungs.)

   - What can happen when an organization's business plan elements are not linked? (Possible answers: lack of focus or continuity, divisiveness, duplication of efforts.)

   (10 minutes.)

Variations

- With a group that is experienced in the strategic planning process, this activity can be used to emphasize the need for a comprehensive plan that includes all elements. In this case both the words and a smaller version of the body diagram would be given out for the participants to draw lines to match the words to the appropriate parts.

- Give groups cards with all seven terms and have them decide how to arrange the terms on the body diagram. Have the groups then compare and process their answers and come to a consensus about the best arrangement for their organization.

- Each group could receive one or more cards with body part diagrams to be matched to a list of business plan elements posted on the wall.

Submitted by Lois Danis and Donna L. Goldstein.

Lois Danis *is the performance manager for District IV of the Florida Department of Transportation in Ft. Lauderdale. Prior to her current position, she worked in the banking and education fields. She holds a master's degree in educational administration. She has produced courses in how to implement the Sterling Business Model, career development, and employee reward and recognition.*

Donna L. Goldstein, *Ed.D, is the managing director of Development Associates International, a human resource, consulting, and training group. She has contributed to nineteen books and has written dozens of articles on contemporary HR issues. Over the past twenty-five years, she has trained over 10,000 individuals and has provided team building, training, and consulting services to more than three hundred organizations worldwide.*

The Human Body:
Seven Components of a Business Plan

1. *Leadership* is how senior leaders address values, organizational direction, and performance expectations. It also includes focus on customers and partners, empowerment, innovation, learning, systems for management accountability, and public community responsibilities.

2. *Strategic Planning* is how units develop strategic objectives and action plans and how these plans are deployed and measured.

3. *Customer and Market Focus* is how customers' requirements, expectations, and preferences are determined. Also included are how relationships are built with customers and factors that lead to customer acquisition, satisfaction, loyalty, and retention.

4. *Measurement, Analysis, and Knowledge Management* are how data and information are selected, collected, analyzed, and used.

5. *Human Resource Focus* is how systems are used to assure employee learning and motivation that align with the organization's business results. It also includes development of a work environment that supports personal and organizational growth.

6. *Process Management* identifies key business and support processes that create organizational value by assuring quality, timeliness, and efficiency to the customer.

7. *Business Results* are the key outcomes derived from the organization's mission and may be expressed in terms of customer satisfaction, financial and operational performance, management accountability, and human resource results.

Introduction
to the Editor's Choice Section

Unfortunately, in the past we have had to reject exceptional ideas that did not meet the criteria of one of the sections or did not fit in one of our categories. So we recently created an Editor's Choice Section that allows us to publish unique items that are useful to the profession rather than turn them down. This collection of contributions simply does not fit in one of the other three sections: Experiential Learning Activities; Inventories, Questionnaires, and Surveys; or Articles and Discussion Resources.

Based on the reason for creating this section, it is difficult to predict what you may find. You may anticipate a potpourri of topics, a variety of formats, and an assortment of categories. Some may be directly related to the training and consulting fields, and others may be related tangentially. Some may be obvious additions, and others may not. What you are sure to find is something you may not have expected but that will contribute to your growth and stretch your thinking. Suffice it to say that this section will provide you with a variety of useful ideas, practical strategies, and creative ways to look at the world. The material will add innovation to your training and consulting knowledge and skills. The contributions will challenge you to think differently, consider a new perspective, and add information you may not have considered before. The section will stretch your view of training and consulting topics.

The 2005 Pfeiffer Annual: Training includes two editor's choice items. Both are activities this year. Keep in mind the purpose for this section—good ideas that don't fit in the other sections. This year two activities were submitted as ELAs. Both have great potential but simply do not fit the strict ELA process. Both provide tools that trainers can use to enhance participants' learning. Both are activity designs and both solve problems that most trainers face. But this is where the similarity ends.

Activities

Three Activities: Making Online Courses More Interactive, by Ryan Watkins

This set of activities introduces "old" ways to look at a "new" challenge: how to increase interaction in online courses. There are in fact, three different activities: an icebreaker, a scavenger hunt, and a role play. It almost sounds like a typical classroom session! The three online activities have clear directions and each has enough variations to satisfy most of our designs. Have fun with this one!

Far Versus Near Transfer: Planning for Success, by Paul L. Garavaglia

This activity introduces a "new" way to look at the "age old" challenge of transfer of knowledge from the classroom to the workplace. This activity will create much discussion as a part of a train-the-trainer workshop. It provides a unique way for trainers to consider activities that are included in a workshop design.

Three Activities:
Making Online Courses More Interactive

Pre-Course Activity: Resources Scavenger Hunt

Activity Summary

A pre-course web-based scavenger hunt that encourages learners to explore the various online resources that will be available to them during the course.

Goals

- To identify and locate available online resources.
- To answer specific questions about the available resources.
- To be more effective users of online resources.

Group Size

Online groups of 20 to 25 participants are ideal. Providing feedback on the accuracy of responses from learners is an important role for the instructor, so group sizes much larger can be challenging.

Time Required

The time required depends on the number of items you include. Typical scavenger hunts would include 10 to 15 items; expect the average learner to spend 30 to 40 minutes locating the appropriate information.

Materials

- Instructor and learner access to the World Wide Web.
- Instructor access to web-page development software and skills in creating basic HTML web pages.
- Instructor access to services for hosting web pages.

Process

1. Start by identifying the online resources that will be useful to learners throughout the course. This could include technical support websites, resources for online articles on topics related to the course, professional associations that provide online resources for practitioners, course-specific websites that detail the processes and procedures for completing the course, or other resources related to the specific topic of the course.

2. Identify at least one specific fact within each online resource that you believe would be beneficial for the learners to utilize in the course. For example, the service hours for the online technical support staff on weekends and holidays; the website location (URL) with a listing of full-text online articles in the XYZ journal or in the syllabus.

3. Construct a questionnaire that includes a statement for each specific fact that has been identified that will serve as the instructions for the learners in their search for the necessary information. Examples could include:

   - For the third assignment of this online course you are to submit a complete process diagram for a needs assessment within your organization. How is that assignment to be submitted to the instructor?
   - The technical support staff for our company provides a variety of services to online learners. List three of the primary services they provide.
   - In order to access your email for this course you must sign up for an account. What email address do you write to when requesting your account?
   - Who is the current president of the XYZ professional association?
   - On which web page will you find the login screen to access the online database of articles published in the XYZ magazine? Please provide the web page address (URL).

4. (Optional) Depending on the complexity of the online scavenger hunt items, it can sometimes be useful to provide clues or starting places for learners to begin their search. For example, you may want to provide the basic web server location for participants to begin their search for technical support services (e.g., "Begin at www.ourcompany.com"). Whether or not clues are necessary or desirable typically depends on the difficulty of the search and the desired amount of time required for learners to complete the activity.

5. When instructions have been provided on what facts the learners should locate within each online resource identified, these can be added to a worksheet that can be emailed to learners prior to the start of the course. These instructions can also be included in a web page form that can be automatically emailed to you when the learners have completed the activity. (The online forms version of the scavenger hunt requires additional technical skills of the instructor that the email version of the activity does not.)

6. When learners complete the scavenger hunt, assess their performance and provide them with specific feedback. If they have not identified the correct information, then guided feedback should be used to direct them to the appropriate resource for finding the information.

Variations

- Learners can also develop online scavenger hunts for other learners to complete when the goal of the instructional activity is to provide learners with a variety of online resources for completing a task. For example, in assigning the activity you could require each student to create an online scavenger hunt related to a given topic. Learners would then develop an individual scavenger hunt that they would ask other learners in the course to complete. After finishing the scavenger hunt, the developers would provide feedback to those learners who had completed their hunt.

- Instructors with more advanced technical skills may want to create web pages with email forms for learners to directly email the facilitator with their results.

Icebreaker Activity: Find Someone Who . . .

Activity Summary

As an icebreaker, this variation on a common training or classroom activity motivates learners to actively seek out and meet other individuals in the course.

Goals

- To provide an opportunity to meet other learners in the course.
- To create comfort with other learners throughout the remainder of the course.

Group Size

Groups of 10 to 15.

Time Required

Anywhere from one to five days, depending on the length of the course, how much time is given for learners to introduce themselves to other learners, and how much time individual learners are expected to be online each day.

Materials

- Instructor and learner access to an online asynchronous discussion board (online bulletin board system or BBS).

Process

1. Identify a general characteristic, experience, or possession that is likely to be found among the learners in the course. For example, a bachelor's degree in business, a red sports car, three children, more than three computers at home, administers his or her own web page, and so forth.

2. Establish in the course's asynchronous discussion board a topic area for learners to use in completing the activity.

3. Assign each learner a characteristic, experience, or possession that he or she is to locate among the other learners. For example, Learner A may be required to identify another learner in the course who has a child who is in college, while Learner B is required to identify another learner in the course who has a wireless network at home.

4. Learners cannot, however, reveal to other learners the characteristic, experience, or possession they are searching for in the activity. That is to say, Learner A cannot post a question to the discussion board asking for the names of learners who have children in college. Learners must ask related questions that would provide them with clues about those individuals who meet the requirements of their search. For example, Learner A may ask on the discussion board which learners have children who recently moved away from home. This restriction on the questions learners can pose provides the challenge to the activity.

5. Email learners the search topics and the rules for the activity.

6. Monitor the discussion board to ensure that learners are not asking questions that give away the characteristic, experience, or possession they are searching for.

7. At the end of the allotted time period, have learners post the names of all the learners in the course they believe meet the requirements of their assignment (other learners who have the characteristic, experience, or possession that was assigned). For example, Learner A may state that he/she believes Learners F and G have children in college.

8. Allow learners to review the final posting to check whether they were accurately selected as having the characteristic, experience, or possession assigned to other students.

Variation

- Learners can search for a variety of interesting information among their fellow learners using similar interactive activities. For example, learners can search for previous training experiences to improve the sharing of information related to skills learners possess. This could be done through asking for learners who know how to create the HTML tags for a basic web page, thereby leading learners to identify others in the course who have completed training XYZ within the organization.

Group Activity: Playing Roles in Group Discussions

Activity Summary

This group activity is intended to challenge learners to take on roles within a group discussion (e.g., idea proposer, disagreer, devil's advocate) that may otherwise not have been characterized by online group members.

Goals

- To discuss a topic from a viewpoint that may or may not be held by group members.
- To discuss alternative viewpoints with other learners who have different roles.

Group Size

At least 10 or 12, but fewer than 20 learners per group. Multiple groups can be created within a single online course.

Time Required

Varies depending on the instructional objectives, length of the course, how much time is given for learners to complete the objectives, and how much time individual learners are expected to be online each day. After five to seven days, learners will often start to lose interest.

Materials

- Access to an online asynchronous discussion board (online bulletin board system or BBS) or synchronous chat (Internet Relay Chat or IRC) room is required.

Process

1. Depending on the number of learners in the course and the number of group discussions you want to have going at one time, form groups of learners. If

you are using online course management software (e.g., Blackboard, WebCT), then the online software can facilitate this process.

2. Identify an interesting and broad topic related to the course for learners to discuss, and establish a time limit for the length of the group discussion. Any related reports or assignments based on the group discussion should also be clarified before developing and assigning roles.

3. Assign each learner in each group a role to play in the topic discussion. More than one learner can have the same role, although there should be enough variety in roles to ensure that the group discussion will be engaging to all learners. Examples of roles that you may assign learners include: idea proposer, supporter, questioner, agreer, naysayer, example giver, disagreer, big picture framer, small picture framer, clarifier, tension reliever, and others (see Variation below for additional roles).

4. Facilitate the discussion by reminding group members of their specified roles and the importance of their participation in the discussion.

Variation

- Any number of roles can be created for individuals within the groups. For example, learners can be assigned roles such as discussion leader, devil's advocate, discussion tracker or note taker, online resource finder, conflict negotiator, theme summarizer, moderator, monitor, idea generator, fact supplier, clarifier, and so forth.

Submitted by Ryan Watkins.

Ryan Watkins *is an assistant professor at The George Washington University in Washington, D.C. He teaches both on-campus and online courses in instructional design, needs assessment, research methods, and educational technology. He is an author of the popular book,* E-learning Companion: A student's guide to online success *(2004, Houghton-Mifflin), and he is currently writing* 75 E-learning Activities: Making Online Learning Interactive *(2005, Pfeiffer).*

Far Versus Near Transfer:
Planning for Success

Activity Summary

The purpose of this activity is to distinguish between activities that have the potential for either near or far transfer of learning.

Goals

- To discuss different types of transfer.
- To determine whether an activity is suitable for near or far transfer of learning.

Group Size

5 to 200 participants, in groups of 5 to 7.

Time Required

30 to 40 minutes.

Materials

- One copy of the Far Versus Near Transfer Handout for each participant.
- One copy of the Far Versus Near Transfer Worksheet for each participant.
- A prepared overhead transparency or flip chart of the directions from the Worksheet.
- One copy of the Far Versus Near Transfer Answer Sheet for each participant.
- Pens or pencils for participants.

Physical Setting

A room large enough to accommodate all participants and that allows them to see any projected overhead transparency or flip chart.

Facilitating Risk Rating

Low.

Process

1. Explain to the group that they are going to learn the differences and similarities among several types of transfer of learning and that the primary focus will be on near and far transfer.

2. Say to the group:
   "Becoming familiar with the most common types of learning transfer is important because it will assist you in putting some parameters around the problem of learning not transferring back to the job."

3. Distribute the Far Versus Near Transfer Handout, review the types of transfer and their definitions, and ask for more examples of each.
   (15 to 20 minutes.)

4. Say to the group:
   "Near and far transfer are the two most common transfer types, and in order to gauge our understanding of each, you will complete the Far Versus Near Transfer Worksheet."

5. Distribute the Far Versus Near Transfer Worksheet and pens or pencils.

6. Display the prepared overhead transparency or flip chart of the directions. Read the directions aloud and instruct participants to form pairs and begin.
   (10 minutes.)

7. When everyone has finished, use the Far Versus Near Transfer Answer Sheet to review. Ask for volunteers to provide responses and then lead a discussion of each question in turn.
   (10 minutes.)

Submitted by Paul L. Garavaglia.

Paul L. Garavaglia, *Ed.D., is the founder of OpMot, a small company specializing in human resource and training effectiveness. He specializes in assessment and evaluation of people, processes, and procedures.*

Far Versus Near Transfer Handout

Type of Transfer	Definition	Example
Far	Trainees apply skills in contexts that are different from those encountered in training. For example, skills needed to negotiate a supplier contract are not the same as those needed for a union negotiation. These skills are not specific nor generalizable.	Negotiating a union contract
Near	Trainees apply skills in contexts that are the same as those encountered in training and thus are easily seen as related to the learning.	Logging onto a computer
Positive	Trainees' prior knowledge aids performance on a given task.	A baseball player sees the similarities between practicing again and again to hit a baseball and the same type of practice to hit a golf ball; this facilitates a smooth learning process.
Negative	Trainees' prior knowledge interferes with or hinders performance on a given task.	A baseball player's experience swinging a bat (short, compact swing) distorts his perception of how to hit a golf ball (wide arc swing, relax the right elbow) and he has difficulty learning to use his body in a new way.

Type of Transfer	Definition	Example
Zero	Trainees' prior knowledge has no influence on performance of a given task in the way that roller skating and skate boarding, although both require athletic ability and balance, require different skills.	A basketball player does not see the relationship between making free throws and hitting a baseball or hitting a golf ball.
General	Trainees apply basic skills and knowledge to the performance of a broad range of tasks or situations.	Communication skills are equally useful for meetings, presentations, or training sessions.
Specific	Trainees apply specific skills to performance of a given task.	A bank teller is trained in making cash deposits and makes a cash deposit for a customer or a nurse takes a patient's blood pressure.
Horizontal	Trainees apply what has been learned in the training environment to a similar work situation.	Once trained in using the keyboard, one can type memos, type meeting minutes, or use a word processor.
Vertical	Trainees apply what has been learned in the training environment to a higher level and more complex work situation.	After being trained in using spreadsheet software, a clerk becomes proficient at managing the entire general ledger.

Far Versus Near Transfer Worksheet

Instructions:

1. Work in pairs.
2. Review the ten learning activities.
3. Determine whether each of the activities is likely to result in near of far transfer of learning.
4. Use N to represent near; F for far.
5. Take 5 minutes to complete the worksheet.
6. Rejoin the large group for a discussion.

N/F	Transfer Type
_____	Using a video recorder
_____	Baking a cake
_____	Doing a needs analysis
_____	Making a sale
_____	Teaching a course
_____	Handling an employee with personal problems
_____	Changing a tire
_____	Diagnosing a disease
_____	Communicating effectively with customers
_____	Filling out a shipping request

Far Versus Near Transfer Answer Sheet

N/F	Transfer Type
N	Using a video recorder
N	Baking a cake
N/F	Doing a needs analysis
F	Making a sale
F	Teaching a course
F	Handling an employee with personal problems
N	Changing a tire
F	Diagnosing a disease
F	Communicating effectively with customers
N	Filling out a shipping request

Introduction
to the Inventories, Questionnaires, and Surveys Section

Inventories, questionnaires, and surveys are valuable tools for the HRD professional. These feedback tools help respondents take an objective look at themselves and at their organizations. These tools also help to explain how a particular theory applies to them or to their situations.

Inventories, questionnaires, and surveys are useful in a number of training and consulting situations: privately for self-diagnosis; one-on-one to plan individual development; in a small group to open discussion; in a work team to help the team to focus on its highest priorities; or in an organization to gather data to achieve progress. You will find that the use of inventories, questionnaires, and surveys enriches, personalizes, and deepens training, development, and intervention designs. Many can be combined with other experiential learning activities or articles in this or other *Annuals* to design an exciting, involving, practical, and well-rounded intervention. Each instrument includes the background necessary for understanding, presenting, and using it. Interpretive information, scales, and scoring sheets are also provided. In addition, we include the reliability and validity data contributed by the authors. If you wish additional information on any of these instruments, contact the authors directly. You will find their addresses and telephone numbers in the "Contributors" listing near the end of this volume.

The 2005 Pfeiffer Annual: Training includes two assessment tools in the following categories:

Consulting, Training, and Facilitating

Developing Trainers: A Self-Assessment and Observer Feedback Process, by John Sample

Organizations

Best People Practices Assessment, by Stephen G. Haines

Developing Trainers:
A Self-Assessment and Observer Feedback Process
John Sample

Summary

Novice and developing trainers often do not have support systems useful for improving their performance. Recent research has identified twelve of the most common mistakes made by novice and developing trainers. The Facilitator Self-Assessment Survey and the Observer Feedback Form use this research as the foundation for improving the performance of developing trainers. Combined with videotaping actual training sessions, this survey process provides a method to help beginning trainers overcome some of the most vexing problems they face.

Theory Underlying the Feedback Process

Novice and developing trainers often lack opportunities for honing their craft. If they are not careful, they can fall victim to gimmicks and other crutches deemed necessary to survive in a climate driven by a demand for high participant ratings.

Creditable research on the development of trainers is scarce. A recent exception is the work of Swanson and Falkman (1997) that is focused on the problems faced by novice trainers. The authors identified twelve common training delivery problems: fear, credibility, personal experiences, difficult learners, participation, timing, adjusting instruction, questions, feedback, opening and closing techniques, dependency on notes, and media, materials, and facilities. Expert trainers were interviewed for their advice, feedback, and coaching, which is presented in a handout at the end of the survey.

Description of the Instrument

The Facilitator Self-Assessment Survey and the Observer Feedback Form are based on the twelve factors identified by Swanson and Falkman (1997).

The Facilitator Self-Assessment Survey consists of questions that assess a facilitator's ease with the twelve factors, each of which is measured twice, for a total of twenty-four items. Prior to conducting a training session, the facilitator completes a *pre-assessment* survey. After completing the training session, he or she completes a *post-assessment* after privately reviewing a videotape of the training session. Facilitators assess themselves using a five-point scale (disagree, somewhat disagree, neither agree nor disagree, somewhat agree, and agree). This scale is converted during the scoring process to a Likert scale (1 = disagree to 5 = agree).

The Observer Feedback Form consists of twelve statements that are also keyed to the research by Swanson and Falkman (1997). Observers are asked to capture and record descriptive examples of the facilitator's behavior. They then also complete the observer form using a "disagree-agree" scale like the one on the survey itself. This provides qualitative data that support the scale data, which are then transferred to a Composite Scoring Form. New facilitators receive their own evaluations, as well as those of the observers. They also receive a sheet of Expert Solutions to the problems which they can then study and incorporate in future sessions.

Reliability and Validity of the Instrument

The two instruments are content valid. The items were drawn directly from the twelve factors established by Swanson and Falkman (1997). Research efforts are underway to determine Chronbach's alpha and test-retest reliability and inter-rater reliability. Preliminary anecdotal evidence indicates that the Observer Feedback Form has acceptable inter-rater reliability when observers are coached to capture behaviorally descriptive examples for as many of the twelve factors as possible before completing the "disagree–agree" scale.

History of the Instruments

These two instruments were developed for use in a graduate course in staff training and development at Florida State University. In addition to developing a learning module as a group project, class members also facilitated an exercise during one of the regularly scheduled classes. Exercises were selected from Silberman's (2003) *The Active Manager's Toolkit*.

Each student's exercise was videotaped, including the feedback session that followed.

The video technician was a class member in charge of setting up the equipment, monitoring the taping, and giving the facilitator his or her copy of the videotape. The only person to view the videotape was the class member who conducted the exercise.

Each student completed the pre-assessment version of the Facilitator Self-Assessment Survey prior to conducting the exercise. About 20 minutes was scheduled for each exercise, followed by a structured feedback session of 10 to 15 minutes. The feedback session was initially facilitated by the instructor early in the semester; however, this role was quickly adopted by class members who led the feedback sessions.

The person generating the feedback and the facilitator sat in chairs in the front of the class, and the feedback began with "What went well for you in this exercise? Give us some examples." After having probed for several examples, the next question the leader asked was, "What might you do differently the next time you facilitate this exercise?"

The observers were used next to provide feedback. A minimum of two observers were used each week. Working primarily from their examples, observers provided descriptive feedback; however, they did not publicly discuss their ratings. After the feedback sessions, the observer gave the facilitator his or her Observer Feedback Form.

The participants at the session were the last group to provide feedback. All feedback followed a formula of "Something that I liked was. . . ." "Something that you might consider doing differently next time is. . . ." "Another thing that I liked was. . . ." The person receiving the feedback was encouraged to seek clarifying feedback by saying something like, "Tell me more about what you mean by . . ." or "Help me understand with a specific example."

At the end of the feedback session, the facilitator was given the two Observer Feedback Forms and the videotape of the exercise and the feedback session. The facilitator used the post-assessment version of the Facilitator Self-Assessment Survey to critique his or her performance from the video. The Composite Scoring Form was used to summarize and integrate the feedback from the Self-Assessment and the Observer Feedback Form. The class member had a week to view the videotape of his or her exercise and to write a two- to three-page reflective paper that integrated all of the feedback. David Kolb's (1988) model of experiential learning was used to frame the written reflection.

A sequence of the events is shown in Figure 1.

Variations on the Process

I encourage experimentation with the process described above. Multiple tapings of facilitated exercises over time with reliable and accurate feedback will be superior to "one-shot" opportunities. Involving as many people in the production of the feedback as possible is also encouraged. Some people are especially nervous about being videotaped, so setting up and manipulating the video camera serves to reduce some

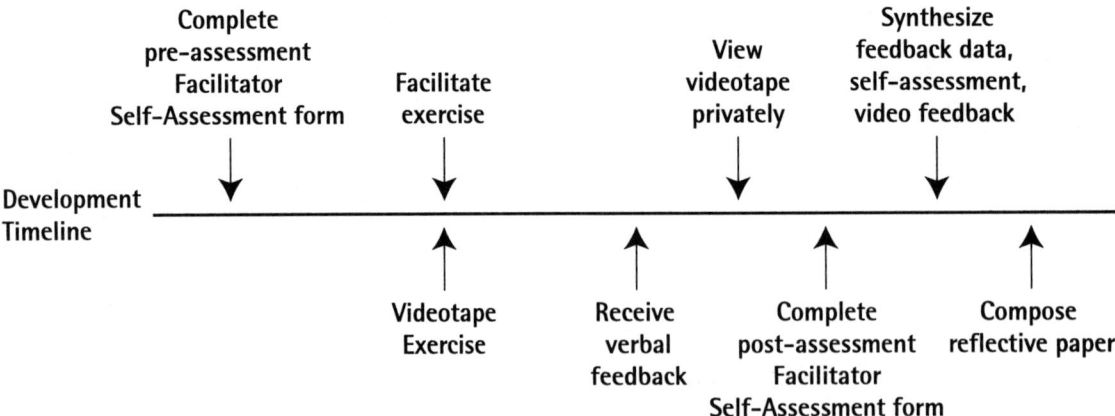

Figure 1. Sequence of Events for Performance Improvement

of the anxiety. Having only the person who was taped view the video also reduces the potential for shame and embarrassment. It is conceivable that the observers could view the video along with the facilitator for the purpose of linking observed behavior to the twelve factors identified by Swanson and Falkman (1997). However, this option would make the process more time- and labor-intensive.

The Observer Feedback Form can be used to track improvements over time for trainers in development. The rating scale becomes a useful metric in a time-series evaluation schema (Yin, 2003).

Consider using the Observer Feedback Form as an alternative to typical Level 1 reaction evaluations. Having an experienced trainer use this form may provide more meaningful information than the "smile sheets" typically used.

References

Kolb, D. (1988). *Experiential learning.* New York: Simon & Schuster.

Silberman, M.(2003). *The active manager's toolkit.* New York: McGraw-Hill.

Swanson, R.A., & Falkman, S.K. (1997). Training delivery problems and solutions: Identification of novice trainer problems and expert trainer solutions. *Human Resource Development Quarterly, 8*(4), 305–314.

Yin, R.K. (2003). *Case study research design and methods.* Thousand Oaks, CA: Sage.

John Sample, *Ph.D. SPHR, is an associate in the Adult Education/HRD program at Florida State University. He coordinated the development of the Internet distance learning master of science degree in human resource development (www.fsu.edu/~adult-ed/), and he also teaches graduate-level courses in adult education and human resource development. Dr. Sample is a recognized authority on legal liability and the HRD function and a frequent contributor to the* Pfeiffer Annual.

Facilitator Self-Assessment Survey

John Sample

Name: _____ Date: _____

Check One: ☐ Pre-Assessment   ☐ Post-Assessment

Instructions: You use this survey to obtain feedback on two different occasions—before and after you have facilitated a training session.

- The PRE-ASSESSMENT should be completed just prior to conducting the training session.
- The POST-ASSESSMENT is to be completed after conducting the training session.

When I am a training session, I am likely to . . .

Disagree	Somewhat Disagree	Neither Agree Nor Disagree	Somewhat Agree	Agree		
_____	_____	_____	_____	_____	1.	ask questions to promote learning.
_____	_____	_____	_____	_____	2.	find creative ways to engage trainees who do not participate.
_____	_____	_____	_____	_____	3.	be anxious while facilitating a training session.
_____	_____	_____	_____	_____	4.	believe that my audience knows more about the subject matter than I do.
_____	_____	_____	_____	_____	5.	rely on my personal experiences as a trainer.
_____	_____	_____	_____	_____	6.	be intimidated by a trainee who becomes angry.

Disagree	Somewhat Disagree	Neither Agree Nor Disagree	Somewhat Agree	Agree		
_____	_____	_____	_____	_____	7.	believe that I do not have enough time to effectively deliver my material.
_____	_____	_____	_____	_____	8.	be frustrated when trainees do not participate.
_____	_____	_____	_____	_____	9.	recall personal stories that relate to the content of the training or the context of the organization.
_____	_____	_____	_____	_____	10.	panic when I have to adjust my design while delivering the training.
_____	_____	_____	_____	_____	11.	panic if I don't have my notes or note cards.
_____	_____	_____	_____	_____	12.	maintain effective timing and pacing of my instructional material.
_____	_____	_____	_____	_____	13.	have a backup plan in case my planned technology becomes unavailable (flip chart, overhead projector, etc.).
_____	_____	_____	_____	_____	14.	make adjustments by anticipating the needs and expectations of the trainees.
_____	_____	_____	_____	_____	15.	be manipulated by a passive or domineering trainee.
_____	_____	_____	_____	_____	16.	summarize and bring to closure a training session.
_____	_____	_____	_____	_____	17.	be frustrated when I cannot answer a trainee's question.

Disagree	Somewhat Disagree	Neither Agree Nor Disagree	Somewhat Agree	Agree		
_____	_____	_____	_____	_____	18.	lack confidence in my training skills.
_____	_____	_____	_____	_____	19.	"read" the ongoing behaviors and attitudes of trainees.
_____	_____	_____	_____	_____	20.	believe that I have sufficient credibility with my audience.
_____	_____	_____	_____	_____	21.	panic if there is a breakdown of equipment (computers, LCD, or VHS).
_____	_____	_____	_____	_____	22.	engage trainees at the beginning of a training session (icebreaker, group intermix).
_____	_____	_____	_____	_____	23.	over-rely on notes throughout a training session.
_____	_____	_____	_____	_____	24.	be irritated if some of the trainees want to modify the training to meet their personal or business needs.

Observer Feedback Form

Name of Trainer: _____ Name of Observer: _____

Training Session Topic: _____ Date: _____

Tips for Observers

- Review and become familiar with the factors listed on the survey the facilitator will fill out on him/herself. They are listed in order below.
- Look for examples of trainer behaviors for each factor and make notes in the spaces provided.
- Wait until the end of the session before you use the agree-disagree continuum from the Scoring sheet to rate each of the twelve dimensions below.
- Add comments at the bottom of the page, in the margins, or on other available space on the survey.
- Give the Feedback Form to the practicing facilitator after you have delivered your verbal and descriptive feedback and given your level of agreement.

The facilitator I was observing . . .

1. appeared anxious while facilitating the training session; lacked confidence.

    Example:

2. appeared comfortable with the audience and subject-matter content.

    Example:

3. used personal stories and/or past experiences to relate to the audience or context of the organization.

    Example:

4. appeared intimidated by a trainee who became angry; was manipulated by a passive or domineering trainee.

   Example:

5. used creative ways that engaged trainees who were not participating.

   Example:

6. managed time effectively; maintained effective timing and pacing of the instructional material.

   Example:

7. appeared irritated when someone wanted to modify the training design.

   Example:

8. asked questions to promote learning.

   Example:

9. made adjustments in facilitation; anticipated the needs and expectations of the trainees; used smooth transitions.

   Example:

10. used instructional equipment that was properly positioned and worked as planned (flip chart, etc.).

    Example:

11. engaged trainees at the beginning of the session; summarized main points and brought closure to the session.

    Example:

12. overly relied on notes or read during the session.

    Example:

    Comments:

Scoring

Instructions: Use the following key to calculate your pre- and post-assessment scores from the Facilitator Self-Assessment Survey:

Disagree = 1

Somewhat Disagree = 2

Neither Agree nor Disagree = 0

Somewhat Agree = 3

Agree = 4

Transfer your self-assessment numbers for the pre- and post-surveys to the Composite Scoring Form. For example, if for item 1 you selected Somewhat Agree, enter a 2 for the item number, and so on. Once you have entered all the numbers for the items, calculate the average for each factor by dividing the total for each item set by 2.

Using the same score key, enter the score from each of your observers for each of the twelve factors. Calculate an average for the observer scores by adding the factor scores for each item together and dividing by the number of observers. Place this number in the Observer Average box.

Composite Scoring Form

Factor	Facilitator Self-Assessment				Observer Feedback					
	Pre-Training Assessment		Post-Training Assessment							
	Items/Score	Average = Total ÷ 2	Items/Score	Average = Total ÷ 2	Observer #	Observer Score	Observer #	Observer Score	Observer Average	Composite Average
Fear, Anxiety	1 + 18		1 + 18		1		1			
Credibility, Confidence	4 + 20		4 + 20		2		2			
Personal Experience	5 + 9		5 + 9		3		3			
Difficult Learners	6 + 15		6 + 15		4		4			
Participation, Involvement	2 + 8		2 + 8		5		5			
Timing, Pacing	7 + 12		7 + 12		6		6			
Adjust Instruction	10 + 24		10 + 24		7		7			
Asking Questions	3 + 17		3 + 17		8		8			
Soliciting Feedback	14 + 19		14 + 19		9		9			
Opening and Closing	16 + 22		16 + 22		10		10			
Dependency on Notes	11 + 23		11 + 23		11		11			
Media, Materials, Facility	13 + 21		13 + 21		12		12			

Experts' Solutions to Problems*

Fear

Novice trainers lack confidence and feel anxious during the delivery of training. Some solutions follow:

- *Be well-prepared.* Expert trainers have a detailed lesson plan, understand the material, and practice their presentation.

- *Use icebreakers.* Experts use icebreakers and begin with an activity that relaxes participants and gets them to talk and be involved.

- *Acknowledge the fear.* Experts understand that fear is normal, confront what makes them afraid, and use positive self-talk or relaxation exercises prior to the presentation.

Credibility

Novice trainers perceive that they lack credibility as subject-matter experts with the learners. Here are some solutions:

- *Don't apologize.* Experts are honest about their knowledge of the subject matter and explain that they are either experts or conduits.

- *Have the attitude of an expert.* Experts are well-prepared and well-organized. They listen, observe, and apply what they know to what the participants know.

- *Share personal background.* Experts talk about their areas of expertise and the variety of experiences they have had.

Personal Experiences

Novice trainers perceive that they lack credibility as subject-matter experts with the learners. Some solutions follow:

- *Relate personal experiences.* Experts tell their personal experiences, sometimes asking themselves probing questions to uncover them.

- *Report experiences of others.* Experts collect pertinent stories and incidents from other people and/or have participants share their experiences.

- *Use analogies; refer to movies or famous people.* Experts use familiar incidents and situations to relate to the subject.

---

*Adopted and modified from R.A. Swanson & S.K. Falkman (1997). Training delivery problems and solutions: Identification of novice trainer problems and expert trainer solutions. *Human Resource Development Quarterly, 8*(4), 305–314.

Difficult Learners

Novice trainers have trouble knowing how to handle a trainee who presents a behavior problem. This kind of trainee may be angry, passive, or dominating. Some solutions from experts follow:

- *Confront the problem learner.* Experts use humor. They may also talk to the individual during a break to determine the problem or to ask the person to leave.

- *Circumvent dominating behavior.* Experts use nonverbal behavior, such as breaking eye contact or standing with their backs to the person and inviting others to participate.

- *Use small groups to overcome timid behavior.* Experts find that quiet people feel more comfortable talking in small groups or dyads and so structure exercises where a wide range of participation is encouraged.

Participation

Novice trainers may have trouble getting people to participate. Some solutions are

- *Ask open-ended questions.* Experts incorporate questions into the lesson plans and provide positive feedback when people do participate.

- *Plan small-group activities.* Experts use dyads, case studies, and role plays to allow people to feel comfortable, to reduce fears, and to increase participation.

- *Invite participation.* Experts structure activities that allow people to share at an early time in the presentation.

Timing

Novice trainers have trouble with timing or pacing the training and may rush through the material. They also worry about having too much or too little material to present. Here's what the experts do:

- *Plan well.* Experts plan for too much material, and some parts of the material are expendable. They prioritize activities so that parts may be omitted, if necessary.

- *Practice, practice, practice.* Experts practice the material many times so they know where they should be at 15-minute intervals. They make sure that there is a clock in the training room.

Adjusting Instructions

Beginning trainers find it difficult to adjust the training to the needs of the learners or to redesign the presentation during delivery. Experts do the following:

- *Know group needs.* Experts determine the needs of the group at an early time in the training and structure activities and processes based on those needs.

- *Request feedback.* Experts watch for signs of boredom and ask participants how they feel about the training, either during breaks or periodically during the session.

- *Redesign during breaks.* Experts find it helpful to have contingency plans and, if necessary, to redesign the program during the break. (Redesigning during delivery is not advocated.)

Questions

Beginning trainers have difficulty using the questioning technique effectively as well as responding to difficult or unanswerable questions. Experts do the following:

- *Anticipate questions.* Experts prepare by putting themselves in the participant's place and by writing out key questions learners might have.

- *Paraphrase learners' questions.* Experts repeat and paraphrase participants' questions to ensure that everyone has heard the questions and understands them.

- *"I don't know" is okay.* Experts redirect questions they can't answer back to the group's expertise. They try to locate answers during breaks.

- *Ask concise questions.* Questions are a great tool for experts. They ask concise, simple questions and provide enough time for participants to answer.

Feedback

Beginning trainers are unable to read the trainees in order to make adjustments and use formative evaluations effectively. Experts, on the other hand, do the following:

- *Solicit informal feedback.* Experts ask participants, either during class or at a break, if the training is meeting their needs and expectations. They also watch for nonverbal cues.

- *Do summative evaluations.* Experts have participants fill out forms at the conclusion of training to determine whether the objectives and the needs of the group were met.

Opening and Closing Techniques

Novice trainers need techniques to use both as icebreakers and introductions as well as effective summaries and closings. Experts use the following:

Openings

- *Develop an "openings" file.* Experts rely on many sources for icebreaker ideas. Through observation and experimentation, they develop ideas and keep a file on them.
- *Memorize.* Experts develop a great opening and memorize it.
- *Relax trainees.* Experts greet people as they enter, take time for introductions, and create a relaxed atmosphere.

Closings

- *Summarize concisely.* Experts simply and concisely summarize the contents of the course, using objectives or the initial model.

Dependence on Notes

Beginning trainers feel too dependent on notes and have trouble determining ways to present information without them. Experts know or use the following ideas:

- *Notes are necessary.* Experts recognize that no one completely outgrows the need for notes.
- *Use cards.* Experts scale down their presentations to an outline or key words, which they write down on note cards to use as prompts.
- *Use visuals.* Experts make notes on frames of transparencies and on copies of handouts.
- *Practice.* Experts learn the script well so that they can deliver it from the key word note cards.

Media, Materials, and Facilities

New trainers are concerned about how to use media and materials effectively, as well as how to take care of the breakdowns that occur in these areas. Here are some suggestions from experts:

Media

- *Know equipment.* Experts know how to operate every piece of equipment that they use.

- *Have backups.* Experts carry a survival kit of extra bulbs, extension cords, markers, tape, and so on. They also bring the information they are presenting in another medium.

- *Enlist assistance.* Experts are honest with the group if there is a breakdown and ask if anyone can be of assistance.

Materials

- *Be prepared.* Experts have all the materials ready and placed at each participant's workplace or stacked for distribution.

Facilities

- *Visit facility beforehand.* Experts visit a new facility ahead of time, if possible, to see the layout of the room and to get an idea of where things are located and how to set up.

- *Arrive early.* Experts arrive at least one hour in advance to ensure enough time for setting up and handling problems.

Best People Practices Assessment

Stephen G. Haines

Summary

This instrument can be used to assess the business importance and status of your organization against research results on six areas of other organizations' best people practices. The results can then be used as key inputs for creating a strategic people plan for your organization (see "Creating the People Edge" in this *Annual*). The results can be used to take specific actions and list priorities to improve your organization's people as a competitive advantage.

Your organization can use this survey to assess its human resources (people) and help it remain competitive in the marketplace.

Administration

Administration is not difficult. Simply follow the steps below:

1. Define the entity to be assessed, whether the whole organization or a unit of the organization. All respondents need not be members of the same organization or unit, but they must fill out the Assessment about the same entity.

2. Fill in the blanks at the beginning of the Assessment saying where to send the completed form if you will not be collecting the data yourself.

3. Select respondents from among management, professional (exempt) employees, or, if appropriate, non-exempt blue-collar workers. A team outside the organization, such as consultants who are experts in the Systems Thinking Approach[SM], could also be asked to assess the organization by completing the survey.

4. As prework, distribute "Creating the People Edge" from page 203 in this *Annual*, both to those who will be completing the Assessment and to the senior management of the organization. Ask that everyone read the article,

which should serve as an executive briefing on the principles involved. If this is not possible, hold a short briefing session for those who will be taking the Assessment.

5. Bring the people who will be responding and senior management together to complete the Assessment simultaneously. Although it has been field-tested to ensure that it can be used generically, there may be those who do not understand certain items, so be prepared to answer questions.

6. Give everyone a copy of the Assessment and a pencil. Be sure everyone understands which entity is being assessed and that they are evaluating the entity's *current* practices. Ask respondents to fill out the survey by giving their initial response in each case, rather than trying to read anything into the questions. Have everyone begin. Allow about 30 minutes.

7. When everyone has finished, ask them to total and average their scores for each section and for the survey as a whole. This usually takes 5 more minutes.

8. Have the completed Assessments returned to you for data collation and report preparation.

9. Set up a meeting with senior management to review the results and report back to the respondents on their organization's strengths and weaknesses against the People Edge Best Practices.

10. Build an action plan to leverage improvement in the areas that require it. An Action Planning Sheet is provided.

The Scoring Process

The instrument is self-scoring. Respondents add and average their scores within each of nine sections, place those numbers in the spaces provided, and then transfer the numbers to the Scoring Sheet. Here they rank order their scores and see how they have rated the overall organization compared with the People Edge Best Practices.

(*Note:* If you have too many employees filling out the Assessment to manually tabulate all the scores, the Centre has this online and can help you quickly tabulate all the scores.)

Stephen G. Haines, *CEO, entrepreneur, and strategist, is a premier systems thinker, facilitator, and author, recognized internationally as a leader in strategic management and in leading strategic and people planning and enterprise-wide change efforts. He has over twenty-five years of working closely with over two hundred CEOs on strategy and positioning of different companies and organizations. He is a U.S. Naval Academy graduate and has a master's degree in OD from The George Washington University. He is president and founder of both the Centre for Strategic Management and its sister company, Systems Thinking Press.*

Best People Practices Assessment

Stephen G. Haines

Fill in the blanks below before turning the page:

Today's date: _____

Organization or unit being assessed: _____

Return confidentially and anonymously to: _____

Name: _____

Address or unit: _____

By (date): _____

Demographic Data. Please circle the appropriate level below:

　　Senior Management　　Middle Management　　First-Line Management

　　Non-management (exempt)　　Non-exempt　　Not in the organization

Your scores will be averaged together with those of others taking this Assessment at this time. You will not be identified by name. However, if you want this Assessment to be returned to you for any future discussion, either put your name or some other code only you know here:

Instructions: Do not ponder over the answers, but use your first instinct. Fill out both parts of each question (1 and 2) for each Best Practice Area before going on to the next one.

Answer BOTH of the following questions about each item.

1. How important to your organization are the following best people practices? Circle the number that applies.

2. What is your organization's current performance in these best people practices? Circle the number that applies.

Then complete the Scoring Sheet and rank the items in each area by importance, according to the scores.

Best People Practices	1. Business Importance					2. Current Performance				
	Not Relevant	Not Important	Some Importance	Very Important	Critical	Poor	Below Average	Average	Above Average	Outstanding
I. The Throughput Processes Area 1—Acquiring the Desired Workforce 1. Identifying core organizational competencies and individual capability requirements.	1	2	3	4	5	1	2	3	4	5
2. Developing alternative workforce arrangements (diverse, flexible, safe).	1	2	3	4	5	1	2	3	4	5
3. Conducting workforce, succession, and retention planning.	1	2	3	4	5	1	2	3	4	5
4. Installing career development programs that assist employees in managing their own careers and lives.	1	2	3	4	5	1	2	3	4	5
5. Implementing recruitment, selection, and hiring methods to assimilate desired employees.	1	2	3	4	5	1	2	3	4	5
	Area 1 Average (total score/5) =					Area 1 Average (total score/5) =				
	COMMENTS:					COMMENTS:				

The 2005 Pfeiffer Annual: Training.
Copyright © 2005 by John Wiley & Sons, Inc. Reproduced by permission of Pfeiffer, an Imprint of Wiley. www.pfeiffer.com

Best People Practices	1. Business Importance					2. Current Performance				
	Not Relevant	Not Important	Some Importance	Very Important	Critical	Poor	Below Average	Average	Above Average	Outstanding
I. The Throughput Processes, *cont.* **Area 2—Engaging the Workforce**										
6. Installing performance management systems that align individual and team behavior with strategic direction and core values.	1	2	3	4	5	1	2	3	4	5
7. Linking compensation systems to individual performance.	1	2	3	4	5	1	2	3	4	5
8. Creating recognition systems that reinforce strategic direction and core values.	1	2	3	4	5	1	2	3	4	5
9. Providing flexible benefit programs to meet changing employee and employer needs.	1	2	3	4	5	1	2	3	4	5
10. Dealing effectively with poor or inadequate performance, discipline problems, and grievances.	1	2	3	4	5	1	2	3	4	5
	Area 2 Average (total score/5) =					Area 2 Average (total score/5) =				
	COMMENTS:					COMMENTS:				
Area 3—Organizing High-Performance Teams										
11. Understanding, designing, and developing teams, task forces, and team skills.	1	2	3	4	5	1	2	3	4	5
12. Developing small unit team leaders/supervisors.	1	2	3	4	5	1	2	3	4	5
13. Developing empowered, self-directed work teams and accountability.	1	2	3	4	5	1	2	3	4	5
14. Establishing participative management skills for management to lead teams in conducting operations.	1	2	3	4	5	1	2	3	4	5

Best People Practices	1. Business Importance					2. Current Performance				
	Not Relevant	Not Important	Some Importance	Very Important	Critical	Poor	Below Average	Average	Above Average	Outstanding
I. The Throughput Processes, *cont.* Area 3—Organizing High-Performance Teams, *cont.*										
15. Developing programs that reward and reinforce teamwork.	1	2	3	4	5	1	2	3	4	5
Area 3 Average (total	Area 3 Average (total score/5) =					score/5) =				
	COMMENTS:					COMMENTS:				
Area 4—Creating a Learning Organization										
16. Developing and sharing learning across the organization.	1	2	3	4	5	1	2	3	4	5
17. Institutionalizing Systems Thinking.	1	2	3	4	5	1	2	3	4	5
18. Developing human resource measurements and information to help the sharing of learning.	1	2	3	4	5	1	2	3	4	5
19. Promoting the value of debriefing and learning from our experiences, mistakes, and successes.	1	2	3	4	5	1	2	3	4	5
20. Creating ways to encourage creative thinking and innovation.	1	2	3	4	5	1	2	3	4	5
	Area 4 Average (total score/5) =					Area 4 Average (total score/5) =				
	COMMENTS:					COMMENTS:				
Area 5—Facilitating Cultural Change										
21. Engaging in a continuous process of communications and dialogue to deepen shared understanding of the organization's vision and desired culture.	1	2	3	4	5	1	2	3	4	5

Best People Practices	1. Business Importance					2. Current Performance				
	Not Relevant	Not Important	Some Importance	Very Important	Critical	Poor	Below Average	Average	Above Average	Outstanding
I. The Throughput Processes, *cont.* Area 5—Facilitating Cultural Change, cont.										
22. Shaping and developing collective management skills in support of the desired culture.	1	2	3	4	5	1	2	3	4	5
23. Aligning all HR processes, programs, and systems with the core values and strategic direction.	1	2	3	4	5	1	2	3	4	5
24. Designing structures and management roles needed to facilitate desired change to the culture.	1	2	3	4	5	1	2	3	4	5
25. Developing change experts and the capabilities of all employees to support and implement the desired organizational changes.	1	2	3	4	5	1	2	3	4	5
	Area 5 Average (total score/5) =					Area 5 Average (total score/5) =				
	COMMENTS:					COMMENTS:				
Area 6—Collaborating with Stakeholders										
26. Developing the knowledge, awareness, and skills of employees to operate in a global environment.	1	2	3	4	5	1	2	3	4	5
27. Developing and maintaining strategic alliances and networks.	1	2	3	4	5	1	2	3	4	5
28. Maintaining a positive people environment and competitive advantage in the marketplace.	1	2	3	4	5	1	2	3	4	5
29. Creating an intense customer focus and commitment by all employees.	1	2	3	4	5	1	2	3	4	5

Best People Practices	1. Business Importance					2. Current Performance				
	Not Relevant	Not Important	Some Importance	Very Important	Critical	Poor	Below Average	Average	Above Average	Outstanding
I. The Throughput Processes, *cont.* **Area 6—Collaborating with Stakeholders,** *cont.*										
30. Contributing to society, including customers, shareholders, community, cultures, and countries.	1	2	3	4	5	1	2	3	4	5
	Area 6 Average (total score/5) =					Area 6 Average (total score/5) =				
	COMMENTS:					COMMENTS:				
II. More Inputs										
31. Defining roles in leveraging people as a competitive advantage.	1	2	3	4	5	1	2	3	4	5
32. Installing a strategic leadership development system with an executive or employee development board.	1	2	3	4	5	1	2	3	4	5
33. Developing leadership competencies/skills.	1	2	3	4	5	1	2	3	4	5
34. Partnering among staff, management, customers, and HR.	1	2	3	4	5	1	2	3	4	5
35. Integrating HR processes with the strategic plan.	1	2	3	4	5	1	2	3	4	5
36. Repeatedly articulating the strategic direction and core values to everyone.	1	2	3	4	5	1	2	3	4	5
	Section II Average (total score/6) =					Section II Average (total score/6) =				
	COMMENTS:					COMMENTS:				

Best People Practices	1. Business Importance					2. Current Performance				
	Not Relevant	Not Important	Some Importance	Very Important	Critical	Poor	Below Average	Average	Above Average	Outstanding
III. The Fundamental Core Input										
37. Developing a strategic people/HR plan to position the organization's people practices to add value to employees, customers, shareholders, and the community.	1	2	3	4	5	1	2	3	4	5
	Section III Score =					Section III Score =				
	COMMENTS:					COMMENTS:				
IV. The Outer Circle										
38. Alignment with the corporate strategic plan/need for the entire organization to have people-related values and vision.	1	2	3	4	5	1	2	3	4	5
39. Attunement with people's hearts and minds so fully invested/motivated in the work.	1	2	3	4	5	1	2	3	4	5
40. Number one core competency—how close are we to creating people as a competitive advantage through increasing the range and depth of our leadership competencies (and associated skills) by each of our collective first-line, middle, and senior management members.	1	2	3	4	5	1	2	3	4	5
	Section IV Average (total score/3) =					Section IV Average (total score/3) =				
	COMMENTS:					COMMENTS:				

Best People Practices Scoring Sheet

Best Practice Areas	1. Business Importance	
	Average Score	Relative Ranking (1 = high, 6 = low)
1: Acquiring the Desired Workforce		
2: Engaging the Workforce		
3: Organizing High-Performance Teams		
4: Creating a Learning Organization		
5: Facilitating Cultural Change		
6: Collaborating with Stakeholders		
	Total Score		Average
I. People Management Best Practices (Q's 1–30)		/30 =	
II. Leadership Roles and Competencies (Q's 31–36)		/6 =	
III. Strategic Human Resource Planning (Q 37)		/1 =	
IV. Outcomes and Results (Q's 38–40)		/3 =	
V. Best HR Practices (Q's 1–40)		/40 =	

Best Practice Areas	2. Current Performance	
	Average Score	Relative Ranking (1 = high, 6 = low)
1: Acquiring the Desired Workforce		
2: Engaging the Workforce		
3: Organizing High-Performance Teams		
4: Creating a Learning Organization		
5: Facilitating Cultural Change		
6: Collaborating with Stakeholders		
	Total Score		Average
I. People Management Best Practices (Q's 1–30)		/30 =	
II. Leadership Roles and Competencies (Q's 31–36)		/6 =	
III. Strategic Human Resource Planning (Q 37)		/1 =	
IV. Outcomes and Results (Q's 38–40)		/3 =	
V. Best HR Practices (Q's 1–40)		/40 =	

The 2005 Pfeiffer Annual: Training.
Copyright © 2005 by John Wiley & Sons, Inc. Reproduced by permission of Pfeiffer, an Imprint of Wiley. www.pfeiffer.com

Based on your total score, circle how important your organization regards creating a People Edge (200 possible points).

A.	161–200	Critical to Success
B.	131–160	Very Important
C.	110–130	Some Importance
D.	80–109	Not Important
E.	40–79	Not Relevant

Based on your total score, circle your organization's *current performance* in creating a People Edge (200 possible points).

A.	161–200	Outstanding Performance and Culture
B.	131–160	Above Average Performance
C.	110–130	Average Performance
D.	80–109	Poor Performance
E.	40–79	Failing Performance

Best People Practices Action Planning Sheet

Which people management practices need the most improvement according to your answers on the Assessment? Write them in below and then order them by priority, filling out who will be in charge of the effort and by when action will be taken.

Item	Priority Order	Who's to Lead	Timeframe

Introduction
to the Articles and Discussion Resources Section

The Articles and Discussion Resources Section is a collection of materials useful to every facilitator. The theories, background information, models, and methods will challenge facilitators' thinking, enrich their professional development, and assist their internal and external clients with productive change. These articles may be used as a basis for lecturettes, as handouts in training sessions, or as background reading material. This section will provide you with a variety of useful ideas, theoretical opinions, teachable models, practical strategies, and proven intervention methods. The articles will add richness and depth to your training and consulting knowledge and skills. They will challenge you to think differently, explore new concepts, and experiment with new interventions. The articles will continue to add a fresh perspective to your work.

The 2005 Annual: Training includes twelve articles, in the following categories:

Individual Development: Developing Awareness and Understanding

Learning from Diversity Training: Outcome Assessment Strategies, by Anne M. McMahon and C. Louise Sellaro

Individual Development: Personal Growth

Let's Talk, by Carolyn Nilson

Communication: Technology

From Stand Up to Sit Down: Translating Classroom Presentations to Computer-Based Classes, by Niki Nichols

Growing Community Online, by Zane L. Berge

Problem Solving: Models, Methods, and Techniques

How You Know What You Know, by Herb Kindler

Groups and Teams: Techniques to Use with Groups

Semi-Structured Online Debate, by Chih-Hsiung Tu

**Consulting/Training: Organizations:
Their Characteristics and How They Function**

Creating the People Edge, by Stephen G. Haines

Consulting/Training: Strategies and Techniques

Does Executive Education Improve Business Performance?
by Adrian Furnham

Facilitating: Techniques and Strategies

Establishing a Stimulating Environment for Communication and Learning,
by Robert William Lucas

Leadership: Theories and Models

A Comprehensive, Effective, Proven Model to Develop Leaders,
by Lois B. Hart and Charlotte S. Waisman

Leadership: Strategies and Techniques

Management Rhythm, by Peter R. Garber

Leadership: Top-Management Issues and Concern

Performance-Management Techniques for Developing Self-Sufficient Workers, by Teri Lund and Susan Barksdale

As with previous *Annuals*, this volume covers a wide variety of topics. The range of articles presented encourages thought-provoking discussion about the present and future of HRD. We have done our best to categorize the articles for easy reference; however, many of the articles encompass a range of topics, disciplines, and applications. If you do not find what you are looking for under one category, check a related category. In some cases we may place an article in the "Training" *Annual* that also has implications for "Consulting," and vice versa. As the field of HRD continues to grow and develop, there is more and more crossover between training and consulting. Explore all the contents of both volumes of the *Annual* in order to realize the full potential for learning and development that each offers.

Learning from Diversity Training:
Outcome Assessment Strategies
Anne M. McMahon and C. Louise Sellaro

Summary

This paper focuses on assessing the outcomes of diversity education, particularly education that focuses on changing individuals' diversity orientations. An assessment study of such changes associated with a course on managing diversity in a college of business curriculum is described. The design is offered as a possible model for assessment of training effects in business and for the effects of employees' formal education on job performance.

The assessment was carried out using a pretest/post-test, nonequivalent control group design. The results indicate that students in the course do undergo specific changes in their diversity orientation and that the changes are related to the goals and content of the course. Ongoing, longitudinal uses of this design are claimed to produce state-of-the-art practices, reports, and diversity planning.

Businesses and business education programs in the United States are recognizing the significance of diversity factors to overall mission effectiveness (Cox, 1993; Muller & Parham, 1998; Ryan, 2001; Smith & Associates, 1997). Since the early 1990s, programs aimed at managing diversity more effectively have been increasing in number, and emphasis is being placed on demonstrating the impact of such programs for the organization's outcomes (Brown, 2001; also see the Society for Human Resource Management's diversity web page: www.shrm.org/diversity; the American Association of Colleges and Universities' *Diversity Digest* quarterly publication; and most business consultants' web pages). Further, publications such as *Fortune, USA Today,* and *Newsweek* regularly carry diversity in the workplace articles and special issues on diversity initiatives.

Among the typical initiatives are training sessions addressing various diversity topics. Some training is directly behavioral in that employees are tutored in specific practices, techniques, and activities that improve the organization's responses to defined diversity issues. In that case, the connection of the behaviors to the outcomes may be manifestly obvious, requiring little documentation for validity. The issue primarily becomes one of compliance to the training behaviors.

However, often training does not appear straightforwardly connected to a business's outcomes. The assumption is that the information and experiences provided during training will raise the employee's awareness and understanding of diversity issues and that those internal changes will be reflected in a desirable way through self-chosen performance changes (Grunig & Grunig, 2001).

Assessing outcomes of this typical type of diversity training is a challenge. The specific attitudes, awareness, information, and internal changes are rarely specified, and their connections to performance are left up to the individual and vaguely identified. In addition, robust effects are expected from training programs that typically last less than one day (Brown, 2001).

These same assumptions often apply to diversity courses in educational institutions as well. It is assumed that intensive emphasis on diversity will, in fact, change students' beliefs and attitudes. Further, it is assumed that changes in the manner in which students are aware of and think about diversity will reflect themselves in later conduct that enhances an organization's diversity status. Employers may depend on gaining skills, diversity and otherwise, based on the prior education of the people they hire, and such claims are rarely assessed (Beale, 1993; Juffer, 2001; Orlitzky & Benjamin, 2003).

The Management Department in the Williamson College of Business Administration has offered a Managing Diversity course that was designed with those assumptions. Some specific behavior competencies were addressed and evaluated, but for the most part, the effect of the diversity orientation of students is presumed. Further, it is presumed on face value that such changes will reflect themselves in later job performances that enhance an organization's ability to leverage diversity for effective overall outcomes.

In this paper we summarize an initial assessment process undertaken to identify attitude changes related to the Managing Diversity course. We identify the steps taken, the challenge of designing appropriate comparisons for measures of beliefs and attitudes, and the main outcomes of that evaluation process. We also identify some recommendations for efforts to address similar outcomes in other educational and training settings. The objective is to use this example to learn about how diversity training might have effects, not only in the classroom setting, but also in actual work settings and between educational and work settings (Benson & Dresdow, 1998).

The Assessment Process: Attitude Change

We followed ordinary design principles for our assessment (Babbie, 2003). They included the following:

- Identify relevant outcome goals;
- Identify a tool to measure those changes;
- Define a group to receive training and a comparable comparison group(s);
- Administer the tool before and after training;
- Administer the tool, at comparable intervals, to the comparison group(s);
- Conduct an analysis identifying changes in both groups;
- Compare the before and after results of both groups; and
- Compare the changes to the outcome goals.

These steps are more challenging for short-term training experiences than for long-term ones. Changes might be more substantial in long-term training and therefore more easily identified than changes generated by a short-term workshop. It might also be easier in an educational situation to gain access to an appropriate comparison group at comparable time intervals than in a work setting.

Identifying Goals

The course goals focused on a progression from a focus on micro issues to understanding organizational issues and then to institutional issues. The goals also assumed that students would move from increased passive awareness to an active orientation to diversity issues. They also assumed that students would progress from recognizing injustice and problems related to diversity to a proactive orientation involving constructive activities that foster good diversity management. We chose a tool that would capture changes in diversity orientation and that could be interpreted for these goals (Stinson, 1991).

Although identifying which goals are to be assessed and linking them to particular changes in a person's orientation to diversity is not a clearly defined process, it is often possible to target at least some outcomes that seem strongly related to goals and to find ways to determine whether or not those outcomes occur. However, this latter is difficult when the outcomes are changes in an individual's internal orientation to diversity topics.

Measuring the Change

We chose the *Diversity Awareness Profile* (Stinson, 1991), which invites respondents to identify actions they might take in a given diversity situation. Some actions described are more proactive than others, and some are more grounded in organizations than others.

Unable to find validity or reliability data associated with this questionnaire, we decided to conduct the study over several semesters to ensure that our findings were not a single event happenstance. This required us to use our own analysis of the data, not the interpretation scheme provided by the original author. We assessed just a couple of the goals for the course.

The research used a pretest/post-test, nonequivalent control group design. In the social sciences, evaluative research measuring training outcomes is often conducted using this approach (Babbie, 2003). While process indicators are used in developing measurements, there must be preliminary evaluation of both the training and the comparison groups to determine their equivalency on the selected measurement prior to administration of the treatment. In this case, the training group was the class given diversity training and the comparison group was made up of individuals taking an unrelated course within the same time frame.

We also administered the questionnaire to later classes in order to learn about changes over time as well as changes between groups. This practice creates a continuous database that helps the evaluator determine whether the groups, over time, start out in different places, as well as whether the changes are related to training in a stable way.

Comparing Groups

We compared responses to the items in the questionnaire for each group for degree of attitude comparability at the beginning of the training sessions. We also compared them at the end of the course for change by each group and between groups. This enhances confidence in the interpretation that the change is related to the training (Grunig & Grunig, 2001). It also allows one to judge how the population of incoming trainees changes over time and whether changes in incoming groups require changes in the training.

Results

The chi-square analysis to determine whether the training group and comparison group were different in their diversity orientations at the outset showed that they did not differ statistically in their responses to thirty-four of the forty items. These results were taken to indicate that the two groups were largely homogeneous (although not strictly comparable in the narrow laboratory sense) at the outset on diversity orientation issues addressed by the questionnaire.

The results of a one-tailed sign test for significant changes in item responses in the training group showed that, for twelve of the forty items, the students in the Managing Diversity class experienced significant change in diversity orientation. All changes were in the direction of increased diversity competence. An inspection of the frequencies for the responses to the items by the training group revealed that, for five items, there was no change, but for the other thirty-five, there was some change, although not necessarily significant, and all were in the desired direction. Simple chi-square values between the training group and the other groups support the same interpretation.

The post-test scores for the group not receiving training cannot, strictly speaking, be interpreted since that group received no intervention. However, an inspection of the frequencies for that group showed that there was no change on four items, negative change on six items, and some positive change on the remaining thirty items, seven of which were statistically significant at the .05 level or greater. Only two items were significant for both the training and comparison groups. We take these results to indicate that the course does lead to changes in diversity orientation different from any unspecified changes that might occur over time.

Comparing responses to course goals, we concluded that students in both groups appear to be equally oriented toward organization-level issues, as distinct from a more micro focus on diversity themes. This may be an artifact of the questionnaire or it may be due to the fact that all respondents were students in management classes. Future investigation will further assess that issue. Continued investigation of patterns of responses to the items and of the open-ended comments on the questionnaire showed that a progression from passive awareness to action was more likely on the part of students who had the diversity class.

To investigate the reliability of the questionnaire, we conducted chi-square analyses for possible differences between groups over two semesters. These groups were homogeneous; differences were very few. We also conducted a reliability analysis for the instrument on ten samples of students over three semesters, using Cronbach's Alpha. Reliability ranged from .88 to .94, and all were significant at $p = .0000$. Results support our decision to stay with this measurement tool in future designs (Ward, 2000).

These results are summarized in Table 1.

Table 1. Research Results

Assessed Outcome	Results Summary
Comparability of comparison groups	Significant differences between the training and control groups existed for six of the forty items prior to training ($p = <.05$).
Changes in diversity orientation	The training group revealed significant differences on twelve items ($p = <.05$).
	The control group expressed significant differences at the same level on seven items.
	Only two items showed significant changes for both groups.
	Changes in the training group were consistent with course goals; changes in the comparison group were not.

Reliability of the questionnaire items was evaluated for ten samples of students over three semesters. Chronbach's Alpha ranged between .88 and .94 ($p = .000$).

Lessons Learned for Future Assessment Design

Our experience with this study leads us to a number of recommendations for useful assessment activities. These recommendations are extendable to assessment designs in work settings.

Before and After Comparisons Are Not Sufficient

Even when changes appear robust as a result of comparing post-training outcomes with pretest outcomes, it is not possible to conclude that the training induced the change. It is necessary to document that some other untrained group did not demonstrate equivalent change. Some change always occurs. Indeed, it is this fact that underlies the basic scientific research design calling for comparison groups.

Even with a suitable comparison group, over time it becomes necessary to distinguish between training-induced changes and others that can be expected to occur in any case. Hence, it is important to compare information across time on the starting states of new trainees with employees not yet trained. When these comparisons are repeated over time, they may reveal changes in the outcomes that occur over time independent of training. Information such as this is useful in identifying training needs.

Assessment Is an Ongoing Process

The goal of a strong assessment process, then, is to maintain a longitudinal database that includes the types of comparisons just described. In addition, records need to be kept as to other diversity-related initiatives. Such initiatives will affect both trainees and those who are not trained. Further, over time the number of persons trained increases, creating a culture base that may have direct effects on diversity orientations. Training results are never static. Some changes occur after initial assessment. Alternatively, change sometimes erodes, and sometimes it leads to further changes that alter outcomes again. Thus, it becomes important to reassess samples of those who have received training and those who have not.

Assessment Does Not Occur in a Vacuum

All effective educational programs reach beyond the boundaries of their enrollments. When they do, learning is not only improved for those in the program, but extends beyond the boundaries of the training population. Training occurs in a specific social context. If it has effects, it also changes the context. In the case of our class, students discussed topics with their families and with students outside the class over an entire semester. They engaged not only these individuals but all those involved in their projects, which included their employers, retailers who supported the projects, and others. Change is systemic. The outcomes of training are not fixed at the end of the session. Connections between the training and events in the larger community and in the media can also have synergistic effects on change. Any conduct resulting from an orientation change will also change the context. These consequences may affect those within the system who have not had training.

Assessment Enhances Learning and Change

Ongoing assessment activities are likely to force a number of state-of-the-art practices: the development of a longitudinal database on system- and individual-level diversity progress; reports that improve understanding of what diversity is about and how it affects the organization; the use of firm-specific information in the design and assessment of diversity initiatives; and a recognition of the ways in which diversity competence is an imperative component of performance.

Complex ongoing assessment activities can open the door to learning about effectiveness issues (Banta, 1993). It may become possible to assess effects of background education on later job performance. Efforts to provide "pure" comparisons under "comparable" conditions (mimicking laboratory experiments) may encourage designs that limit such learning opportunities. What is required is a longitudinal database that permits interpretations by comparing results in complex ways.

Measuring Conduct Outcomes

Connecting changes in individual diversity orientation to specific conduct is also a murky undertaking. However, at least some connections of that sort must be demonstrated if a strong case for training is to be made. Again, while not all conduct linkages can be assessed, some can. Changes in number of lawsuits, grievances, and the like can be recorded over time. Further, the training history of those involved can be compared to the training status of those with different rates of problems. Changes over time on other performance issues can also be compared to training histories (Grunig & Grunig, 2001).

Keeping a record of cultural changes over time can also be very informative. Recording symbols used, as well as language chosen in letters, documents, and everyday speech, begin to reflect the kinds of systemic change good training sets out to enact. Whenever possible, such measures can be compared to the training history of the groups or parties involved. In addition, details of the cultural change and related discourse and symbols can be compared to training terms and symbols.

In the same vein, it is useful to keep a record of new initiatives, messages, and programs, as well as reductions in problems. Students in the Managing Diversity course offered dramatically more suggestions in the post-test responses than did individuals in the comparison group, and the suggestions were likely to indicate actions they might take when facing diversity situations. It is possible that as training increases over time or as the number who come to be trained increases, this effect is multiplied.

References

Babbie, E.R. (2003). *The practice of social research* (10th ed.). Florence, KY: Wadsworth.

Banta, T.W. (1993). Summary and conclusions: Are we making a difference? In T.W. Banta and Associates (Eds.), *Making a difference: Outcomes of a decade of assessment in higher education.* San Francisco, CA: Jossey-Bass.

Beale, A.V. (1993, January/February). Are your students learning what you think you're teaching? *Adult Learning*, pp. 18–26.

Benson, J., & Dresdow, S. (1998). Systemic decision application: Linking learning outcome assessment to organizational learning. *Journal of Workplace and Learning, 10*(6/7), 301–307.

Brown, B.L. (2001). *Diversity training myths and realities no. 13*. Education Resource Information Center [Online]. Available: http://ericacve.org/docgen.asp?tbl=mr&ID=103

Cox, T.H., Jr. (1993). *Cultural diversity in organizations: Theory, research and practice.* San Francisco, CA: Berrett-Koehler.

Grunig, J.E., & Grunig, L.A. (2001, March). *Guidelines for formative and evaluative research in public affairs* [Online]. Available: www.instituteforpr.com/pdf/2001_guide_formative_research.pdf

Juffer, J. (2001). The limits of culture, Latino studies, diversity management, and the corporate university. *Nepantla: Views from the South, 2.2*, 265–293.

Muller, H.J., & Parham, P.A. (1998). Integrating workforce diversity into the business school curriculum: An experiment. *Journal of Management Education, 22*(2), 122–148.

Orlitzky, M., & Benjamin, J.D. (2003). The effects of sex composition on small-group performance in a business school case competition. *Learning and Education, 2*(2), 128–138.

Ryan, C. (2001). The challenge of inclusion: Reconsidering alternative approaches to teaching and research. *Journal of Business Communication, 38*(3), 256–260.

Smith, D.G., & Associates (1997). *Diversity works: The emerging picture of how students benefit.* Washington, DC: Association of American Colleges and Universities.

Stinson, K. (1991). *Diversity awareness profile.* San Francisco, CA: Pfeiffer.

Ward, J.A. (2000, April). Clinical investigator's corner [Online]. Available: www.bamc.amedd.army.mil/DCI/articles/dci0400.htm

Anne McMahon, *Ph.D., is a professor of management in the Williamson College of Business Administration, Youngstown State University, Youngstown, Ohio. She received her Ph.D. from Michigan State University and has published articles on diversity topics. She serves on the Society for Human Resource Management's National Workplace Diversity Committee and organizes the Partners for Workplace Diversity, an alliance of employers that provide diversity initiatives for themselves and for the larger Youngstown community.*

C. Louise Sellaro, *DBA, is a professor of management in the Williamson College of Business Administration, Youngstown State University, Youngstown, Ohio. She received her doctorate in business administration from Kent State University and has published articles and cases in the areas of health care, strategic management, and diversity. She also does consulting related to program development focused on education of the disadvantaged.*

Let's Talk

Carolyn Nilson

Summary

Learning leaders and employees alike are searching for new ways of learning at work and from work. Time pressures, budget pressures, and the isolating and dehumanizing features of technology all work against positive learning experiences and suggest that a better way be found to reconnect people at work with one another. The difficult topics and complex relationship problems at work require new ways of thinking about them—ways that maximize the value of individual problem solvers at any organizational level.

Structured dialogue—in the form of a "LET'S TALK" session—is one way to reconfigure training so that learning happens when it needs to happen. A series of sessions spaced over weeks or months can have a positive cumulative payoff in building stronger collaborative and collegial relationships and in organizational problem solving.

Managers, supervisors, team leaders, and other persons who function as group facilitators are called on with increasing urgency in today's workplaces to design and deliver learning opportunities to employees quickly and effectively. Shorter, smaller, just-in-time learning sessions are preferred to manager-mandated offsite, hotel-based mega-training workshops and seminars. According to *Training* magazine's Annual Industry Report (Galvin, 2003), expenditures across the industry on seminars and conferences are down 9 percent, and they are down 21 percent on generic off-the-shelf materials from the previous year. Lean, customized, learner-selected learning opportunities are clearly the wave of the future. Budgets are shrinking, technology doesn't necessarily fulfill its promise, and employees want to learn from each other and from the work itself.

Learning facilitators and leaders, whatever their titles, must find ways in which to support workers in learning. Tough issues like preventing harassment, ensuring gender equity, managing conflict, maintaining workable teams, and a host of other complex workplace concerns are the responsibility of leaders and employees to address. Structured, informal learning sessions driven by employee interest and organizational need and based on dialogue are one way to do this.

This article presents ideas for developing dialogue sessions. Here, we give you the characteristics to include in a "LET'S TALK" session, provide you with an example of a workplace dialogue session, and suggest a list of possible dialogue starters for creating a series of learning sessions based on this approach.

Each LET'S TALK session suggested here is based on individual interest and present need, is structured using principles of creative problem solving and communication techniques, and is presented in a lean format taking one hour or less. A LET'S TALK session can be held anywhere and at any time there's a free hour—over lunch, over coffee, in someone's office, in a conference room, in a training room, on a commuter bus. Each session is designed to be led by a facilitator and features a handout known as a "Dialogue Starter."

The Structure of Dialogue

Dialogue is a way of talking that leads to understanding. It differs from "discussion" or "speaking up" at meetings in that dialogue intentionally is based on mutual awareness and definition of big ideas and key processes. Dialogue has a discipline about it, enabling individual expression of ideas, values, and beliefs through self-examination, suspension of judgment, and reflection. Dialogue has the added dimension of being situated in real work experiences and of encouraging cultivation of communities of practice. The dialogues of LET'S TALK encourage individual learning.

Dialogue, in the classical sense, depends on defining a large truth, testing assumptions about it, questioning, and exploring one's own relationship to that truth. The LET'S TALK dialogues are an update on this model. They are set within a broader context of creative thinking, problem solving, and action learning. Each dialogue session follows a five-point structure in open, informal learning sessions, self-selected based on interest:

1. Awareness of the topic.

2. Definition of the topic.

3. Examples of the topic in use.

4. Self-examination and reflection on the topic.

5. Action planning.

A Sample LET'S TALK Starter

Following is a sample LET'S TALK dialogue starter on the topic of the needs and contributions of individual team members. For an actual session, you'd make a copy of the Dialogue Starter handout (Exhibit 1) for each learner in the session and distribute it to the participants as they entered the room.

1. Awareness of the Topic

In this step, participants are first introduced to the topic. In the example, team members have been encouraged to write thank-you notes to persons anywhere in the company who have been helpful to them. The handout is made up of some that have been received. The handout is distributed to the session participants (who may not be the writers of the notes). The facilitator instructs the participants to read the handout to gain some understanding of the needs and contributions of team members.

2. Definition of the Topic

After the participants have read the handout, the facilitator might say something like the following:

> "From these thank-you notes, you can see several needs being expressed by the writers. Some needs are obvious; other needs are somewhat hidden. What needs for these team members can you identify? Note that there are six persons named in these thank-you notes—Carla, Manuel, John, Scott, Neshira, and Noel; each probably has some needs as a team member."

Probable responses to this query include the following:

- Carla would be a good mentor to Manuel in other situations and maybe to other persons too; maybe other team members need mentors also.

- The John/Scott note points up the need for a team talent bank that's updated regularly—people have hidden talents that we don't know about.

- Noel has uncovered a training problem; maybe Neshira could hold a workshop for him and others with the same need.

Exhibit 1. Dialogue Starter Thank You Notes

Dear Carla,

You have made such a difference in my life, and I wanted to thank you as we both go forward into the next adventure. You are more than a colleague to me—you are an inspiration and a source of the best information!

Sincerely,
Manuel

Dear Neshira,

I admire your way of keeping track of things. I need to learn a way to stay organized. I only know how to pile stuff up. Could you explain to me how you organize your files and papers and if your system would work for me?

You're the best!
Noel

Dear John,

I never write thank-you notes. But I think I could be persuaded. I'm not much of a writer, but just putting pen to paper makes me think of my plain good luck at being on your team. If you ever need somebody to be in charge of refreshments at your board meetings, let me know if I can help. I love to make fancy appetizers.

Sincerely,
Scott

3. Examples of the Topic in Use

Next, the facilitator asks the participants to identify several examples of ways their organization learns of the needs and contributions of individuals. Examples might include team member surveys every six months, a members' feedback form at the end of team projects, conversations with a manager, and exercises and games in team-training workshops.

4. Self-Examination and Reflection on the Topic

This next step is an opportunity for participants to consider what they've learned so far. The facilitator might explain the following:

> "The essence of dialogue is self-examination and assertion of self into the way you talk with colleagues at work. Dialogue is nonjudgmental; it is based first on a look inward and then on the addition of self to the existing context. Engaging in dialogue means knowing oneself and suspending judgment of others in that self-discovery. 'I think,' 'I believe,' 'I understand,' and 'I value' are all ways *in* to self-discovery and *out* to dialogue.
>
> "Take some time in this group to state your ideas, your self-revelations, about the examples in use and the needs identified in the thank-you notes.
>
> "Take some time before the end of this session to think in a synthesizing way about the dialogue that has happened thus far. Consider points of view, learning styles, personality differences, and, above all, your own perspectives and contributions. Reflect on your particular and unique self-expression. Ask other team members whether they understand your point of view. Give them feedback on their contributions and points of view. Think of a 'sharing' model—you give something of yourself, and you receive something of others. Be open, welcoming of others' ideas, and build bridges of understanding."

5. Action Planning

Finally, participants should be given an opportunity to plan what they will do as a result of this session. The facilitator might instruct them as follows:

> "From what you learned in this LET'S TALK session, you could very well see more clearly some specific action you can personally take to improve your working environment, the way you communicate, or the other work processes you engage in daily that might need a fresh examination. If you intend to take some action,

whether in the way you think, feel, or behave, take some time to record these actions. [The participants might be provided a handout or blank paper for this purpose at the session.] Focus on the topic of this dialogue, needs and contributions of individual team members. Use today's date as a reminder to start right away."

Ideas for Dialogue Starters

The sample session in the exhibit uses a dialogue starter of three thank-you notes to begin a discussion on the needs and contributions of individual team members. Following is a list of five major categories of ideas with several dozen suggestions for dialogue starters that can introduce important issues that need to be talked about at work:

- Graphics (photographs, art pictures, symbols, cartoons);
- Text (stories, case studies, parables, news headlines, poetry, recipes, quotations, rules of thumb);
- Cognitive exercises (true-false statements, examples of learning styles, math formulas, force-field analysis, crossword puzzles, games, music);
- Operational structures (rules, systems, standards, leverage points, diagrams, timelines, tipping points, flowcharts, checklists); and
- Personal assertions (journal entries, worries, ratings, assumptions, incentives, celebrations, rewards).

Reference

Galvin, T. (2003, October). Annual industry report. *Training*.

Dr. Carolyn Nilson *is the author of twenty-seven books on training and learning, including the best-selling training games books published by McGraw-Hill. Four of her books have been listed on amazon.com's list of "50 Best-Selling Training Books." She is an experienced training developer, instructional designer, training manager and executive, consultant, and mentor. She has served Fortune 500 companies, non-profits, and government agencies.*

From Stand Up to Sit Down:
Translating Classroom Presentations to Computer-Based Classes
Niki Nichols

Summary

Many of us in the training field have spent our careers developing courses and the associated materials for classroom presentation. As our talents matured, we learned to decorate our flip charts, turn text into workbooks, play games, operate a plethora of multi-media, and tame unwilling participants. Now we are being asked to leave the classroom and convert these same courses into a computer-based format.

New Employee Orientation and Equal Employment Opportunity Compliance are mandatory classes for many organizations. This article outlines the process for translating a full day of this type of classroom instruction into two-hour computer-based classes.

Employee time and travel are big expenses for organizations in today's business climate. They are also among the expenses that can be directly controlled by efforts from within. So word comes from on high (executive level) that more training must be done online, that participant travel must be reduced, and that classroom time (for non-job-essential instruction) must be limited.

As professionals we have read articles and books on computer-based training. We have attended conferences and talks on the subject. We may have tried a demonstration or taken a class on our computer. The two initial questions for meeting the mandate are "Which classes involve participant travel and non-job-essential topics?" and "Where does the process begin?"

In the Beginning

The answer to the first question was easy for our training group. The classes that involved the most participant travel and that covered non-job essential topics were New Employee Orientation (NEO) and Equal Employment Opportunity Compliance (EEO). The organization in question had three thousand employees with two-thirds of them scattered among more than two hundred small field offices around the state of Texas. Each month approximately fifteen new employees came to headquarters for two days of training. This was reduced to one day when the EEO training was put on video and distributed to each site.

Thus, we could focus on the New Employee Orientation. Once we committed to an electronic NEO (e-NEO), we investigated the capabilities of the organization. To begin the process, we asked, "Exactly what technology is available?" and "Who has the skills and resources to move the program to the new medium?" The answers came during a scoping meeting.

Scoping Meeting

The scoping meeting included the training manager and the NEO trainer, the web master, and a web developer. We each arrived with some basic information and some fundamental needs and primary concerns. On the training side, we had a general idea of what e-NEO should look like and what the content areas were, but almost no idea of what the web staff could accomplish. The web folks understood the capabilities of the system and had been looking at various courseware packages since the mandate for computer-based training was issued.

The training manager wanted an interactive program that would engage the new employees. We also needed a tracking system so there would be a record of who had completed the class.

The web experts confirmed that not everyone in our organization was connected to the network and that there was a wide range of operating systems as well. They determined that they could develop the e-NEO as they learned the course-building software. They also brought up the issue of accessibility.

The scoping meeting resulted in several agreements. One, this would be a team effort—a collaborative effort that included ongoing, open communication. The primary players were the NEO trainer and the web developer, with a back-up designated for each. Two, a timeline was set. We gave ourselves a year for this first project—for learning, for quality, for working around other obligations. And three, the final product would be available on both the intranet and on CD for maximum accessibility and should take no more than two hours to complete. The hope was that it would also provide a template for future projects, and thus reduce future development time.

Planning

The next meeting—this one between the trainers and the web developers—dealt with details. We discussed the mood and "feel" of the program. The trainers were adamant that this should not appear as miles and miles of text. We wanted video, lots of pictures, and lots of color. We brought the handouts, activities, videos, and PowerPoint® presentations that we currently used.

The web developers had some questions (and suggestions) about basic navigation, such as, "Will the participant need to leave and reenter the program?" "Do the modules/sections have to be completed in a specific order?" and "Where should the *back* and *forward* buttons/arrows be placed?" The developers persisted in their concerns about accessibility for our physically challenged employees.

We also discussed whether or not we should use links to connect the participants to existing organization web pages. The advantages would be that this material was already available and that it would reduce development effort. The primary disadvantage was that participants could follow a series of links and have difficulty getting back to the program. They could also use a lot of time exploring our internal website. The decision was to provide relevant web addresses that could be copied and accessed at a later date.

The Middle

At this point the primary web developer and the lead trainer went to work. The developer reviewed the training materials and built a foundation for this program. The trainer worked on the script, and a human resources manager made the call to address accessibility issues on a case-by-case basis through reasonable accommodation.

The Script

The developer attended a regularly scheduled NEO to become reacquainted with the program and, while learning the development software, began applying the information to our course. E-mails flew back and forth to members of a development software users' group when various aspects of the tutorial or instructions were unclear.

Over on the training side, the script took shape. Since we really didn't know what we were doing, we fell back on the familiar—the facilitator's guide. The left-hand column, which is usually for the trainer, was now dedicated to notes, instructions, and requests for the developer. The larger right-hand column was devoted to text. Figure 1 shows the first page of the e-NEO script as an example.

Throughout course use photos/video of people, places plants, critters, fish, TPW buildings	The mood of this course should illustrate the passion, commitment, and diversity of Texas Parks & Wildlife (TPW). It should be bright, active, and touch the senses. It should have a balance of media and not be overwhelming.
Opening screen	Logo, Welcome to Texas Parks & Wildlife New Employee Orientation
Insert voice & pic	Bob Cook welcomes new employees to TPW
Screen Insert photo of HQ	Title: Purpose of New Employee Orientation This program has several objectives. First, it is a way to welcome you to the Department. We also want you to: • Become familiar with the Texas Parks & Wildlife Mission and Philosophy and • See how that translates into an enthusiasm and even passion for what we do. We would like you to: • Know the organizational structure and the areas of responsibilities for each of the Divisions, • Clearly understand the expectations that Texas Parks & Wildlife has for each of its employees, and • Finish with a sense of connection and commitment to the TPW culture.
Screen	How to make this program work: Instructions *(next & back buttons (right & left arrow keys?), quizzes, leaps of faith)*
Log in Screen Is it possible for more than one participant to log in at one time? Print screen	Please introduce yourself to us. • Name • Social Security number • Division • Location • Supervisor • Classification Date (that's state lingo for hire date) And please tell us, "What excites you about working at TPW?"
Screen Insert voice & pic	Texas Parks & Wildlife Mission To manage and conserve natural and cultural resources for the use and enjoyment of present and future generations. *(Lupita Barrera – picture and quote)*

Figure 1. First Page of e-NEO Script

Articles and Discussion Resources

Quiz Should be able to go back to text to find correct answers		What do we do? For what kind of resources? Why? For whom? (fill in the blank? multiple choice? or some other kind of game?) For example: The Texas Parks & Wildlife Mission is to _____ and _____ our _____ and _____ resources for the _____ and _____ of _____ and _____ generations.
Screen		Texas Parks & Wildlife Philosophy We seek to balance outdoor recreation with conservation as we achieve greater self-sufficiency. On one hand, we must manage and protect our natural and cultural resources. At the same time, we must generate increased revenue by adding value through more and better public services. We affirm that a culturally diverse well-trained staff will best achieve this balance.
Insert voice & pic		*(Darlene Lewis — picture and quote)* And we must never forget, not in the haste of business, nor in the pride of science, that the outdoors should above all be a source of joy! Providing outdoor experiences, whereby young minds form values, will be our greatest contribution to the future.
Quiz Insert photos Should be able to go back to text to find correct answers		*(Insert pictures of kids swimming and prairie dog)* What do we seek to balance? _____ with _____ *(Insert pictures of scientist, Buffalo Soldier, and big horn sheep capture)* What do we affirm will best achieve this purpose? A _____ and _____ staff *(Insert pictures of Palo Duro, rock climbers, and a butterfly)* And what should we never forget that the outdoors should be? A source of _____.
Screen		Overview of the Organization We work for the people of Texas, who elect the Governor, who appoints the Commission that oversees the Department. *(Insert organizational chart)*
Insert photos of Commissioners		The Parks and Wildlife Commission has 9 members appointed by the Governor and confirmed by the senate. Members of the Commission hold office for staggered terms of six years. They are appointed in February of odd number years to coincide with the legislative session.
Insert photos of Commission in session		The current Commissioners are:

Figure 1. First Page of e-NEO Script, *continued*

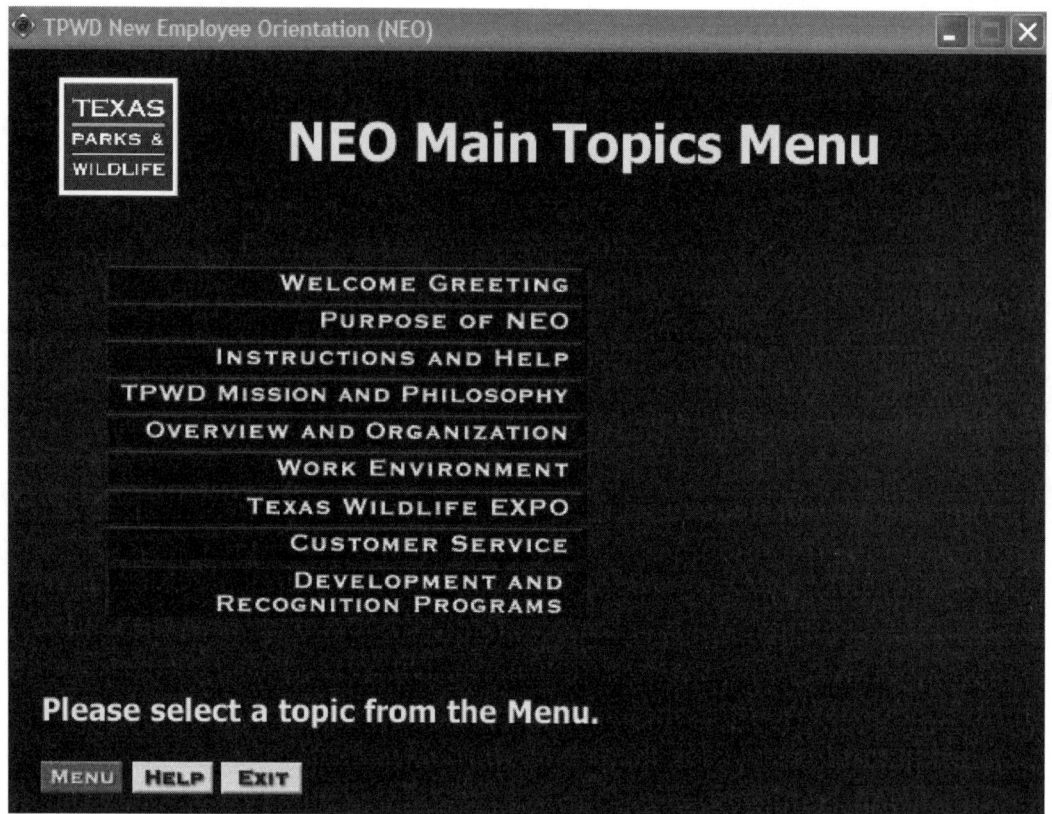

Figure 2. Main Topic Areas

Our organization is diverse and has sites and activities in some of the most beautiful areas of the state. We also have an extensive collection of film and photos taken in these locations. This archive was available to us and proved to be a great resource for conveying our mission and our passion to our new employees.

Our goal was to capture their enthusiasm and help it to become their commitment to fulfilling our responsibilities to our state, our constituents, and our environment. And we needed to present an overview of the organization, work rules, and customer service. We decided to use a welcome from the executive director and film clips of employees in a variety of jobs and locations. Figure 2 shows the main topic areas of the program.

Some information we expected the new employees to retain and some we just wanted to introduce. In order to indicate the completion of each section, we added some quizzes—mix-and-match, drop-and-drag, fill-in-the-blank. Figures 3 and 4 provide an example of a drag-and-drop quiz.

Articles and Discussion Resources

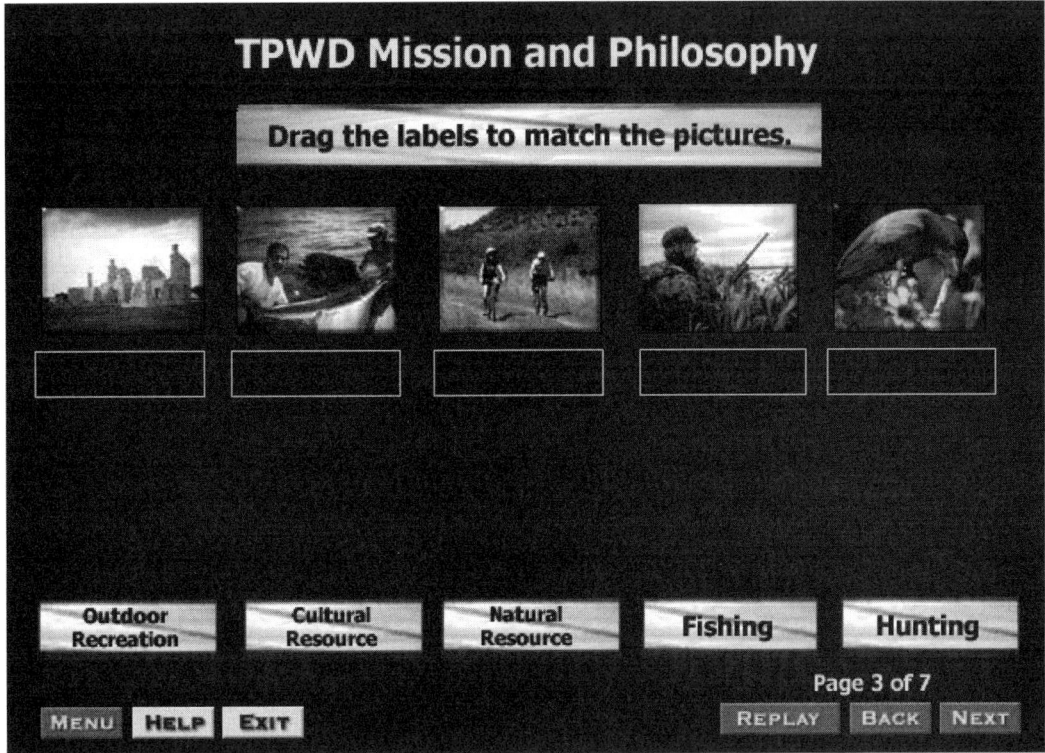

Figure 3. Example of Quiz

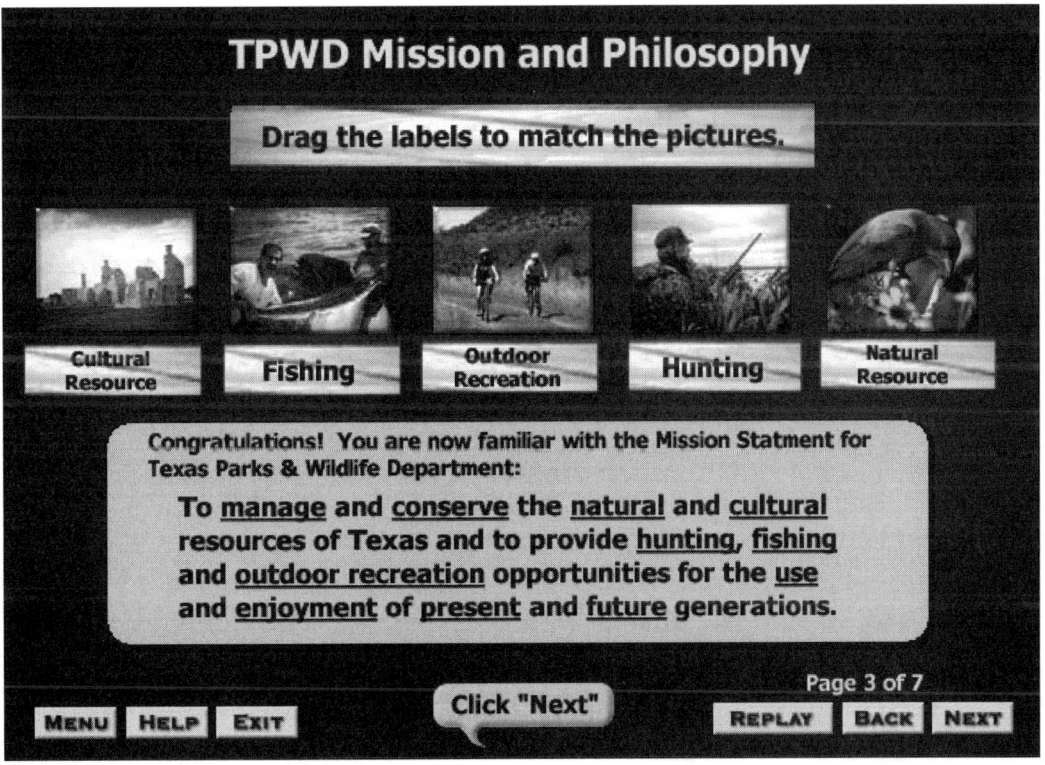

Figure 4. Example of Quiz

The 2005 Pfeiffer Annual: Training.
Copyright © 2005 by John Wiley & Sons, Inc. Reproduced by permission of Pfeiffer, an Imprint of Wiley. www.pfeiffer.com

Snags

As with any project, there were snags along the way. One of the most important was addressing the accessibility issues. The developer was able to build in various keystroke/arrow/mouse options to the navigation. Synchronized text was added to each audio segment. The introduction and instructions also directed employees to contact us if they needed other accommodation.

A technical snag resulted in our not being able to use video. Video demands so much band-width that the program would be slow to load and might tie up some computers for an unacceptably long time. After some research, the developer suggested we use scrolling photos coordinated with sound bites and text, since audio uses less band-width.

Because the project took a year to complete, we encountered an ongoing issue of keeping the material current. Not only did the organization hire a new executive director, but that generated a restructuring of the executive level. For us that meant a new welcoming script, new pictures and job descriptions of deputy executive directors, and, of course, a new organizational chart. There were also changes to address within various divisions. Sometimes it seemed that for every step we took forward, there was a correction, deletion, or change in a part we thought was complete. All we could do was keep our sense of humor, collaborate, communicate, and handle each change as it came about.

The End

This was truly a collaborative effort. As one part of the script was being developed into a computer-based class, the next module was being written into a script format. At each juncture, we met to discuss the progress on our individual parts. We shared our frustrations, our brilliant ideas (some of which turned out not to be so bright), and our successes. We often stopped by each other's offices just to touch base.

Throughout the development phase, colleagues played each module as if they were new employees. They provided valuable feedback on what worked and what did not. They asked questions and made comments that spurred us on. There were times when the frustration level was daunting and we pulled each other along. And at the end of a year, we had an e-NEO ready for a trial/beta run.

Two remote sites volunteered employees to take the class online. We sent CDs as back-up and we waited. The student tracking system that the developer built into the program included a certificate that students could print for their records and an automatic email to the training group with information for posting to the employee record. (This organization does not have an electronic HR information system for automatic tracking.) Cheers went up when the first email notifications arrived. IT WORKED! And employees liked it.

And then Information Security came knocking on our door saying that it was illegal to send unencrypted Social Security numbers by non-network email—oops! We then reverted to an old, tried-and-true method of notification that was being used to track EEO compliance training. We asked the students to print their certificates and fax them to our secure HR fax machine.

The beta testing continued, with a few other problems coming to the surface. There were some compatibility issues with individual computer systems. There were some kinks worked out on who would handle ongoing content updates and how often these should be tackled.

E-NEO was launched and is now the only orientation available to new employees. People who have been with the organization for years are also sneaking a peek and sending compliments to us. As a trainer, I really miss the opportunity to meet and greet each new employee—to share their enthusiasm and positive energy. There are now individuals here whom I have never met. On the other hand, all of us in the training department have more chances to stand up and present other programs. And we now have a template for converting other courses to computer-based classes.

This e-learning project was a wonderful opportunity for each of us who was involved. The Association for Conservation Information, Inc. (ACI) awarded our New Employee Orientation E-Learning second place in the Internal Communication category of its 61st Annual Conference Award Program. This was indeed affirmation that our efforts had paid off.

Niki Nichols *is a training specialist for Texas Parks & Wildlife Department, where she develops training materials, coordinates and conducts training sessions, and promotes training services. She has written articles on a variety of subjects, including change management and assessing training needs. Ms. Nichols takes this opportunity to thank her Texas Parks & Wildlife colleague Holly Hollan, who was the developer on the e-NEO project.*

Growing Community Online
Zane L. Berge

Summary

Although the advent of electronic communication allows for more flexibility and greater geographic reach in training and learning, this increased ease does not necessarily translate into improved learning. The physical separation of the members of the learning group can cause challenges. One way to overcome some of these challenges and to take better advantage of the online environment is to grow community. Growing community is the responsibility of both instructor and students; however, this article is largely directed at the instructor, providing suggestions for encouraging participation and social interaction among students and between students and the instructor.

It is common for online instruction to be conducted with several students at a time. Call it what you wish—groups, classes, teams—but the idea is that there are multiple people learning together with an instructor guiding the learning activities and providing feedback.

For our purposes here, an online community is a group of students using social interaction and collaboration for learning purposes. Membership in a learning community requires interdependence and reciprocity. Online community is a general sense of connection and belonging that can develop over time among members of an online group of learners who share a common purpose or commitment to a common goal (Conrad, 2002a).

The transition from classroom learning to online learning requires a cultural change as much as a technology change. It is perceived by students as a different kind of learning experience than in-person training and education, and there are often different barriers to be overcome than in the traditional classroom. Clark (1998) suggests that online learning communities should be grown rather than built. Growing a community takes time, especially since not all members within a course will have the same sense of community at the same time (Lock, 2003).

For students to grow and succeed, it is important to consider social aspects of the group of learners. Much like scaffolding at a worksite is a temporary support from which workers can perform tasks at heights above the ground, "social scaffolding" (Kim, 1998) refers to aspects of the learning environment, such as roles, rituals, features, activities, and leadership, that support the growth of community development.

"Social presence" is an important concept for online learning. Garrison and Archer (2000) developed a research-based model and identified aspects contributing to social presence—emotional expression, open communication, and group cohesion. Within these categories they list many other behaviors that reflect group community: humor; self-disclosure; expressions of emotion; reciprocal and respectful exchanges; mutual awareness in attending to the contributions of others; levels and type of contact; recognition of others' ideas; agreement, acceptance, and complimenting others on their ideas; and establishing and contributing to a sense of group cohesion (Conrad, 2002b; Garrison, Anderson, & Archer, 2000; Garrison & Archer, 2000). Student satisfaction is directly related to the amount of social presence of the instructor and other students in the class.

Researchers have discussed online community in terms of motivating performance, promoting greater self and collective growth, fostering harmony and inclusiveness among learners, overcoming feelings of remoteness, and students' feelings of greater satisfaction with the learning experience (Rovai, 2002; Ubon & Kimble 2003; Woods, 2001). Greater satisfaction usually means higher retention rates as well.

The Instructor's Role in the Online Environment

When I describe the roles and responsibilities of online instructors, I often categorize them into four areas: pedagogical, managerial, technical, and social (Berge, 1995). Certainly, some of the most important roles of online instructors revolve around their duties as educational facilitators. The instructor uses questions and probes for student responses that focus discussions on critical concepts, principles, and skills.

Creating a friendly, social environment in which learning is promoted is also essential for successful online instruction. This suggests that promoting human relationships, developing group cohesiveness, maintaining the group as a unit, and in other ways helping members to work together in a mutual cause are all critical to success of any online learning activities.

The managerial, organizational, procedural, or administrative role involves setting the agenda for the learning activities, the objectives of the discussion, the timetable, procedural rules, and decision-making norms. Managing the interactions with strong leadership and direction is considered a sine qua non of successful online instruction that is based on discussion.

The instructor must make participants comfortable with the system and the software that the online course is using. The ultimate technical goal for the instructor is to make the technology transparent. When this is done, the learner may concentrate on the academic task at hand.

The concept of community, or community of practice, falls squarely into the social category (Wenger, 1998). The more students can connect with the instructor and with other students in meaningful ways, the better the chances that the learning experience will be successful.

How to Grow Community Online

Some suggestions for ways the instructor can help to grow community online follow (Blunt, 2001; Kim, 1998; McLoughlin & Luca, 2002; Misanchuk & Anderson, 2001; Salmons, 2001; Smith & Stein, 2003).

Create Distinct Types of Gathering Places

Learning communities need both public and private places for members to meet. For example, if activities call for teams or study groups, the instructor can facilitate "neighborhood" forums where each group can meet that are separate from the entire class forums. Additionally, learning communities often find off-topic meeting places helpful as well. For instance, in a learning environment, many participants occasionally want to announce something or ask a question of the community that does not have anything to do with the content of the course. I provide a forum for that discussion called the "water cooler." On the other hand, what if students have questions about an assignment or some other aspect of the class? I also provide a forum called "Ask Zane," where students can direct questions to the instructor. The answers, which may be beneficial for the entire class, can be posted for all to see. No matter the type of forums that you create, the following suggestions apply:

- *Encourage students to share.* Reciprocity and help are two important hallmarks of community. Students who take an interest in each other's well-being, both academically and socially, will have more of a support system than if these elements are missing.

- *Use role differentiation.* Online learning environments provide students a place to assume multiple participatory roles. This enables varying levels and forms of responsibility for contributing, questioning, mentoring, and demonstrating expertise. Differentiation places learners in alternating roles of novice, researcher, and expert. Reciprocal teaching enables learners to develop process skills, self-regulation, and confidence (Bonk & Cunningham, 1998).

- *Use synchronous chat.* Using synchronous or real-time chat is a tool for developing social relationships among students. This allows for spontaneous comments and student expression (Murphy & Collins, 1997).

Create Member Profiles

Obviously, participants may not wish to divulge a lot of personal information, especially to people they do not know. If participants are new to one another, however, there is a need for introductions. Keeping them general and simple at the beginning starts to build *spirit* and *trust* in the community. More detailed profiles by participants can be added later, if useful, as the community develops. The following tips will help to make the most of your member profiles:

- *Highlight individuality.* Model the biographical information you wish students to give, which may include more than what might be found on your resume. Talk about your interests and what you enjoy.

- *Use names.* People like to be recognized; using their names helps create a warmer, trusting environment.

- *Encourage posting photos.* Connecting people's names and faces is a first step to forming bonds.

- *Personalize email.* Sending a few individual, private emails to students is another way to build connections. These can be a few lines of words of encouragement or support. This is especially true in the case of students who are not actively participating; you'll want to find out why and try to address their concerns.

Promote Effective Facilitating, Leadership, and Hosting

As with any formal training or education, the instructor is expected to lead the facilitation of the learning environment and experience. There are several websites that make recommendations regarding effective online hosting and facilitation (see, for example, Berge, 1995); therefore, I will include only the barest essentials here.

- *Answer promptly.* Time may cause a thought to die. Plus, students need to feel that the instructor is interested in their well-being, academic or otherwise.

- *Provide feedback.* Instructor-student interaction is improved by prompt feedback to the student. Well-timed, constructive feedback increases students' perception of positive social presence (Gunawardena, 1995).

- *Ask a question.* When leading a discussion, it is often better to pose a question than to give an answer (Berge & Muilenburg, 2000).

- *Encourage and model verbal immediacy.* Immediacy is the extent to which selected verbal and nonverbal communication enhances intimacy in interpersonal communication and reduces the perceived distance among people. Behaviors such as initiating discussion, addressing individuals by name, asking questions, or using examples about experiences may increase psychological closeness among learners (Woods & Ebersole, 2003).

Encourage Collaboration

Social constructivist theory may be driving the design of many online environments, but that does not mean students come prepared with skills to maximize learning in these environments. The following suggestions will help learners take fuller advantage of the collaborative possibilities of online learning:

- *Design collaborative learning activities.* In addition to individual activities, team or group learning is important. The value of peer or social interaction goes beyond teamwork and relationship building and goal achievement. Social constructivists, drawing on the work of Vygotsky (1978, 1986), theorize that a great deal of learning takes place in a social context and is spurred by interactions with other people (Berge, 2002).

- *Use peer review.* It is important to develop a positive, critical review of other community members' work. In order for a newly formed group of students to move to community, they must change the quality of their interactions. The community should move toward successful use of collaboration, in addition to the continued use of group discussions and cooperative tasks (Misanchuk & Anderson, 2001).

Define a Code of Conduct and Accommodate a Range of Styles

In general, workplace or organizational learning events are not marked by a high degree of conflict or personal attacks. If such behavior does occur, it must be stopped quickly and privately. However, learning in a community of practice can and often should be characterized by debate about differences of opinion regarding the content and ideas. Also, the community needs to accommodate the different interpersonal communication styles of the individuals in the group. The following guidelines will help ensure clear communication:

- *Avoid humor and sarcasm.* These are often misunderstood online.

- *Reread what you write.* Before you send a message, it is good to reread it because often what you say in the forums can be easily misinterpreted.

Organize and Promote Cyclic Events

If the online learning program lasts for several weeks or months, develop patterns in the activities. Doing so lets students know what to expect and allows them to plan better for learning activities and online participation.

Conclusions

Socio-cognitive theories of learning state that all knowledge and learning is socially constructed through social interactions (Vygotsky, 1978, 1986). Online education is particularly well-suited for promoting and supporting social learning because of the nature of asynchronous communication and discussion—many more people from a variety of backgrounds and geographic locations can be included. Still, online learning environments are not inherently interactive. The interactivity depends on the instructional design, including frequency, timeliness, and the nature of the asynchronous messages posted or the real-time chat used (Eastmond, 1995). The good news is that computers and communication systems allow interaction. The bad news is, well, that computers and communication systems allow interaction. How the instructor and students grow community can go a long way toward helping learning in the online training and education classroom.

References

Berge, Z.L. (1995). Facilitating computer conferencing: Recommendations from the field. *Educational Technology, 35*(1), 22–30.

Berge, Z.L. (2002). Active, interactive, and reflective elearning. *The Quarterly Review of Distance Education, 3*(2), 181–190.

Berge, Z.L., & Muilenburg, L.Y. (2000). Designing discussion questions for online, adult learning. *Educational Technology, 40*(5), 53–56.

Blunt, R. (2001, November). How to build an e-learning community. *e-learning, 2*(11), 18–22.

Bonk, C.J., & Cunningham, D.J. (1998). Searching for learner-centered, constructivist and socio-cultural components of collaborative educational learning tools. In C.J. Bonk & K.S. King (Eds.), *Electronic collaborators* (pp. 25–50). Mawah, NJ: Lawrence Erlbaum.

Clark, C.J. (1998). *Let your online learning community grow: Three design principles for growing successful email listservs and online forums in educational settings.* (Online). Available: www.plocktau.com/portfolio/online_community/3Principles_Online_Comm.pdf

Conrad, D. (2002a). A brief learners' guide to online community. (Online). Available: www.unbf.ca/education/conrad.pdf [last accessed March 1, 2004]

Conrad, D. (2002b). *Community, social presence, and engagement in online learning.* Unpublished doctoral dissertation. Edmonton, Ontario: University of Alberta, Edmonton.

Eastmond, D.V. (1995). *Alone but together: Adult distance study through computer conferencing.* Cresskill, NJ: Hampton Press.

Garrison, D.R., Anderson, T., & Archer, W. (2000). Critical inquiry in a text-based environment: Computer conferencing in higher education. *The Internet and Higher Education, 2*(2–3), 87–105.

Garrison, D.R., & Archer, W. (2000). *A transactional perspective on teaching and learning: A framework for adult and higher education.* Amsterdam: Pergamon.

Gunawardena, C.N. (1995). Social presence theory and implications for interaction and collaborative learning and intellectual amplification. *International Journal of Educational Telecommunications, 1*(2/3), 147–166.

Kim, A.J. (1998, January). Nine timeless principles for building community: Erecting the social scaffolding. *New Architect Magazine.* (Online). Available: www.webtechniques.com/archives/1998/01/kim/ [last accessed February 13, 2004]

Lock, J.V. (2003, June 7–11). Designing online courses that foster the development of learning communities. *Proceedings of the 20th CADE-ACED Conference.* St. John's, Newfoundland, Canada. (Online). Available: www.cade-aced2003.ca/conference_proceedings/Lock.pdf

McLoughlin, C., & Luca, J. (2002). Enhancing the quality of the student experience online: Revisiting the imperative of learning as socially based. (Online). *HERDSA.* Available: www.ecu.edu.au/conferences/herdsa/main/papers/ref/pdf/McLoughlin.pdf [last accessed February 16, 2004]

Misanchuk, M., & Anderson, T. (2001, April 8–10). Building community in an online learning environment: Communication, cooperation and collaboration. *Proceedings of the Sixth Annual Mid-South Instructional Technology Conference.* (Online). Available: www.mtsu.edu/~itconf/proceed01/19.html [last accessed February 13, 2004]

Murphy, K.L., & Collins, M.P. (1997). Communication conventions in instructional electronic chats. *First Monday, 2*(11). Available: www.firstmonday.dk/issues/issue2_11/murphy/index.html [last accessed March 1, 2004]

Rovai, A.P. (2002). Building sense of community at a distance. *International Review of Research in Open and Distance Learning, 3*(1), 1–16. Available: www.irrodl.org/content/v3.1/rovai.html [last accessed February 16, 2004]

Salmons, J. (2001, June 19). Virtual community-building for nonprofit organizations. *TechSoup.org.* (Online). Available: www.techsoup.org/howto/articlepage.cfm?ArticleId=301&topicid=5 [last accessed February 13, 2004]

Smith, S.J., & Stein, D. (2003, September 9). Never say never: Musings of online learning facilitation. *Master Facilitator Journal* (Issue #0117). Available: www.masterfacilitatorjournal.com/archives/skill117.html

Ubon, A.N., & Kimble, C. (2003, July). Supporting the creation of social presence in online learning communities using asynchronous text-based CMC. *Proceedings of the 3rd International Conference on Technology in Teaching and Learning in Higher Education* (pp. 295–300), Heidelberg, Germany. Available: www-users.cs.york.ac.uk/~adisornn/Research/TTLHE.pdf.

Vygotsky, L. (1978). *Mind in society.* (M. Cole, V. John-Steiner, S. Scribner, & E. Souberman, trans./eds.). Cambridge, MA: Harvard University Press.

Vygotsky, L. (1986). *Thought and language* (A. Kozulin, trans./ed.). Cambridge, MA: The MIT Press. (Originally published in Russian in 1934.)

Wenger, E. (1998). *Communities of practice: Learning, meaning and identity.* Cambridge, UK: Cambridge University Press.

Woods, R. (2001). Connecting for success: Effective strategies for building online community in the cyber-classroom. (Online). Available: www.ipfw.edu/as/tohe/2001/Papers/ebersole/ [last accessed February 13, 2004]

Woods, R., & Ebersole, S. (2003, March). Social networking in the online classroom: Foundations of effective online learning. *Ejournal,* 12/13(1). Available: www.ucalgary.ca/ejournal/archive/v12-13/v12-13n1Woods-browse.html.

Zane L. Berge *is an associate professor in the Instructional Systems Development Graduate Program at the University of Maryland, Baltimore campus. His scholarship is in the field of computer-mediated communication and distance education. He consults internationally in distance education and can be contacted at berge@umbc.edu.*

How You Know What You Know
Herb Kindler

Summary

This article describes two basic ways by which we understand: (1) *reasoned knowing*—logic, analysis, and inference—and (2) *direct knowing*—intuitive, instinctual, and holistic insight. The *Thinking Preference Profile* is introduced to guide trainers and trainees in identifying their current preferred mode of learning. Their understanding is enhanced by balancing these complementary modalities.

Basic to management training is the capacity to see possibilities, feel into the "rightness" of each alternative, make appropriate judgments, and take sound action. This article suggests how managers and trainers can integrate the two building blocks for effective action—*reasoned knowing* (inferring thoughts from prior thoughts) and *direct knowing* (attuning to gut reactions, emotional responses, and intuitive insights). Balancing these human capacities requires inquiry and empathy, analysis and synthesis, abstract conceptualization and inner sensitivity.

Reasoned Knowing

Reasoning is helpful in almost every facet of our complex, technological lives. Reasoning enables us to get where we want to go, record a TV program, compare and contrast costs and benefits, take the right vitamins, and understand why there are funny noises under the hoods of our cars.

Because reasoning is used to test the validity of a hypothesis or theory, it speaks in the language of numbers. It divides complex problems systematically into manageable components. Analytical reasoning is central to how organizations function by making explicit the division of labor among individuals and groups. Analysis reveals power structures and communication links. It helps managers understand subsystems to make them mesh productively. It helps accounting managers predict quarterly outcomes and engineers to refine product designs. The quantitative orientation of reasoning (when used alone as the basis for action) may cause the user to miss such qualitative influences as commitment, trust, morale, and ethical behavior.

Reasoned knowing takes root in early childhood in Western cultures, where it is reinforced with social approval (high grades, acceptance into good schools, and career progression).

Direct Knowing

Your "inner voice" connects you to hunches about opportunities that cannot be reached by linear reasoning. Intuition is central to nonlinear thinking. In bypassing inference, analysis, and logic, intuitive stimuli light up the brain's sensory switchboard (the thalamus), which directs incoming information to the emotional control center (the amygdala) before the thinking cortex can intervene. Bypassing the cognitive part of the brain was probably a protective mechanism for primitive man. On hearing a twig snap, he needed to act instantly and reflexively against what might be a dangerous intruder.

Intuition suggests we know more than we can say because it is rooted in body sensations, emotions, and symbolic images. It is implicit knowledge hidden from our everyday awareness. Most routine skills are executed with implicit, or tacit, knowing that relegates routine tasks—such as driving a car, singing from memory, digesting a meal, or serving a tennis ball, to the unconscious. Imagine how cluttered your mind would be if you had to think about every detail of every repetitive procedure. The capacity to go on "automatic pilot" frees our minds of clutter and makes room for creative and aesthetic expression. When a music student failed to shift from rote execution to "heart-felt" expression, master cellist Pablo Casals urged the student to use both modes of thinking, saying, "You played the notes; now play the music."

Even though both processes—direct and reasoned knowing—are complementary, practitioners with a strong preference for one mode often demean people who prefer the other. For example, persons who rely largely on logic, numbers, and objective evidence are sometimes labeled *impersonal nerds* or *bean counters*; while those who lean on their intuition and instincts for insight are sometimes called *impractical dreamers* or *touchy-feely* types.

Teaching and learning are enhanced when participants appreciate:

1. Whether they have a preference for direct or derivative knowing and, if so, how strong a preference or bias.

2. Means by which they can strike a better balance between both orientations to improve their decision-making effectiveness.

Thinking Preference Profile*

To help you assess your preference, following is an abbreviated version of the *Thinking Preference Profile*.

For each pair of statements, allocate exactly 3 points (no fractions please) between the two statements. There are no right or wrong answers. Use this scoring key to indicate your behavior:

3 = very often   2 = moderately often   1 = occasionally   0 = rarely or never

_____ 1A. I approach relationships after considering whether or not likely rewards are worth the effort.

_____ 1B. I approach relationships prompted by the desire to connect with another person.

_____ 2A. I am attracted to people who are intellectually stimulating.

_____ 2B. I am attracted to people who are emotionally expressive.

_____ 3A. The most important factor in making a life-altering change (such as a primary relationship, career change, or major relocation) is basing the change on verifiable facts.

_____ 3B. The most important factor in making a life-altering change (such as a primary relationship, career change, or major relocation) is feeling it is right for me.

_____ 4A. I am cautious about accepting advice when it is not supported by sound logic.

_____ 4B. I am cautious about accepting advice when it is not supported by empathic understanding.

_____ 5A. I decide whether or not to take an expensive vacation after asking myself if I can afford it.

_____ 5B. I decide whether or not to take an expensive vacation after asking myself if it will add joy to my life.

---

*Copyright © 2003 by Herb Kindler. All rights reserved. Requests for permission to reproduce this material should be directed to Herb Kindler at herbkindler@aol.com.

Allocate exactly 3 points (no fractions) between each pair of words or phrases in the following section to reflect the degree of influence on your *behavior*. There are no right or wrong answers. Use this scoring key to indicate:

   3 = very strong influence   2 = strong influence
   1 = moderate influence   0 = little or no influence

_____ 6A. Facts

_____ 6B. Feelings

_____ 7A. Information

_____ 7B. Instinct

_____ 8A. Systematic

_____ 8B. Spontaneous

_____ 9A. Logical deduction

_____ 9B. Inner knowing

_____ 10A. Figure out

_____ 10B. Tune in

"A" scores add up to: _____

"B" scores add up to: _____

Interpretation

Higher "A" scores (5 or more points higher than the "B" score) suggest that you prefer to seek truth and base decisions on reasoned-cognitive-analytical knowing.

Higher "B" scores (5 or more points higher than the "A" score) suggest that you prefer to seek truth and base decisions on intuitive-emotional-instinctual knowing.

A–B scores fewer than 5 points apart suggest a balanced approach (no strong preference) in how you know what you know. You have the flexibility to choose an appropriate mode of thinking based on each specific situation.*

---

*Note: The full *Thinking Preference Profile* appears in the book, *Clear and Creative Thinking* by Herb Kindler, available from Crisp in Menlo Park, California.

If your scores reflect an imbalance toward reasoned knowing (common in such professions as engineering, accounting, and information technology), practice getting in touch with your feelings and acting from both head and heart.

If your scores are skewed toward direct inner knowing (common in such professions as psychology, fine and performing arts, sales and marketing), practice giving more weight to your pragmatic judgment and common-sense thinking.

Herb Kindler, *Ph.D., is a former CEO, professor of organization behavior, and author of the best-selling* Managing Disagreement Constructively. *He is an M.I.T. engineering graduate with a doctorate in organization development from UCLA. He currently trains managers in building leadership skills at UCLA and UC Berkeley and in corporate settings.*

Semi-Structured Online Debate

Chih-Hsiung Tu

Summary

Online discussion methods are not limited to learners reading assigned materials and responding to questions posted by the instructor. Online debate is an effective discussion method for engaging online learners in a more interactive method of constructing meaningful knowledge. This paper discusses the use of a semi-structured online asynchronous debate to improve the analytic and communication skills of online learners through formulating ideas, defending positions, and critiquing counter-positions. The author describes the design of a semi-structured online debate that can enhance online learning and online training.

Online discussion is used extensively because it promotes several types of thinking—critical thinking, higher-order thinking, distributed thinking, and constructive thinking (Berge & Muilenburg, 2000). The type of thinking to be stimulated determines the discussion method used. Online discussion is not limited to learners reading assigned materials and responding to questions posted by the instructor. Online debate presents an alternative discussion strategy in computer-mediated communication (CMC). The purpose of this paper is to describe the design of a semi-structured online debate to enhance online learning and online training by asynchronous CMC technology.

Debate is a technique whereby learners are divided onto opposing sides, generally as teams, to dispute a contentious issue. Learners are afforded the opportunity to improve their analytic and communication skills by formulating ideas, defending positions, and critiquing counter-positions. Historically, a debate is a structured activity; however, online media permit a wider range of designs for online debates, from an inflexibly structured exercise to a process with minimal structure. When an online debate is more rigid, step-by-step instructions are provided for debate and defense, as in a formal face-to-face debate. When online debate is designed with less structure, it operates as an online discussion concerning a controversial issue. In this article, a semi-structured online debate is proposed. In this format, online learners (debaters) are assigned a particular issue and either a pro or con position and are expected to defend and justify that position. The design is meant to encourage online learners to exercise critical thinking, consider both sides of an issue, and appeal to the sensitivities of others. It is not intended to replace traditional online discussion. In fact, the intention is to identify potential and alternative effective online instructional design strategies.

Goals of Online Debate

Online debates have four goals: (1) construct meaningful knowledge, (2) engage in comprehensive speculation, (3) enhance learner-learner interaction, and (4) develop skills in persuasive argument.

Construct Meaningful Knowledge

The primary goal of an online debate is to focus the attention of learners on the interactive construction of meaningful knowledge and apply it to novel situations rather than acquiring and memorizing information (Shaeffer, McGrady, Bhargava, & Engel, 2002). The debating process requires participants to obtain and construct meaningful arguments to justify/defend their positions. Fragmented information or knowledge will place debaters in a vulnerable position.

Engage in Comprehensive Speculation

Training learners in the skills necessary to view an issue from multiple aspects is critical. One purpose of online debates, distinguishing them from online discussions, is to engage learners in observing an issue from multiple points of view (as opposed to online discussions, which permit learners to discuss issues from the aspect of their own preferred thinking). Since learners may be assigned to either side of an issue in an online debate, they must research and speculate about the strengths and weaknesses of both stands in order to strengthen their positions, defend the weaknesses of the opinion they are defending, and expose the weaknesses of the opposing position. This engagement obliges learners to establish a broader understanding of the issue being debated.

Enhance Learner-Learner Interaction

The structured, threaded, online debate forum is designed to enhance learner-learner interaction and encourages learners to make reasoned, persuasive, and concise arguments in areas where precise answers do not exist. As in the real world, debaters will be reflecting on issues that may be ill-structured and complicated. Learners are strongly engaged in learner-learner interaction because they must cogitate every posting and provide an opposing point of view.

Develop Skills in Persuasive Argument

An important goal of online debates is to improve the ability of learners to argue persuasively. Unlike most online discussion formats, an online debate appoints learners to actively engage in discussions of certain controversial issues and, through contention, attempt to persuade their peers to embrace their viewpoints (Engel & Schaeffer, 2001). The more effective learning outcome is that learners are able to solidify their opinion of the issue, or adopt a new opinion, while persuading others to adopt their assigned side of the issue.

Design

Important and practical guidelines for designing effective and successful online debates are listed below. The guidelines are organized into three stages, preparation, debate, and finalizing. Most tasks should be completed in the preparation stage. In other words, good preparation will assure the success of the online debate.

Preparation

The preparation occurs well before the actual debate begins. Instructors and instructional designers devise detailed formats, rules, and procedures. Comprehensive preparations will help eliminate confusion for the learners and help ensure a successful online debate.

Setting Debate Objectives. The instructors or the instructional designers should start by determining the objectives to be achieved through the online debate. This is when one reviews the four goals of online debates, discussed earlier. All four goals should be integrated into the design; however, depending on the context, the instructors or the instructional designers may want to emphasize one or more of these goals.

Selecting Debate Topics. The debate topic should be clear, authentic, and accompanied by appropriate statements and examples relevant to the debaters. The topic and its wording are instrumental in encouraging or discouraging active debate. Debaters are apt to be more engaged with authentic issues to which they can personally relate and can see addressed in the larger social context. A good topic would be controversial; allow debaters to take multiple positions, without one obvious best; contain enough complexity to allow it to be interpreted from multiple perspectives (e.g., stakeholders) and from multiple disciplines; and be relevant to learners. After a topic is determined, it should be stated as both pro and con positions.

For example: Should the curriculum be standardized for all students? The pro position: The curriculum SHOULD be standardized for all students. The con position: The curriculum SHOULD NOT be standardized for all students.

Determining Debate Format. Debate formats are determined depending on the degree of structure that one wishes to impose. The format can range from formal (more structured) to informal (less structured) and may be a mixture of formal and informal formats. The formal debate refers to a more structured design, such as Parliamentary Debate, while an informal debate will appear more like an online discussion or conversation on a controversial topic. This format described here is a semi-structured one that applies elements of both formal and informal debate.

A semi-structured online debate allows one to regulate the opening and closing statements for the debate. Both sides are required to post their opening and closing statements on a designated date. Between opening and closing statements, the floor will be open for free debates. During the open debates, there is no limit on the numbers of messages and no prescribed sequence for posting debate messages.

Devising a Timeline. The timeline applied depends on the form of CMC used, synchronous or asynchronous. Clearly, synchronous debate is analogous to regular face-to-face debate. The difference is that debaters are required to type rather than speak. Asynchronous debate is a new arena for debating. The characteristics of asynchronous communication allow debaters more time to prepare their responses. A period of at least one week of debate should be allowed, and when time permits, a period of two weeks is appropriate. Debates may become less focused if more than three weeks are allotted because it is more challenging for the debaters to concentrate their logistical reasoning over an extended period of time. It generally takes longer for asynchronous debaters to prepare their messages, but they tend to be more thoughtful, more logical, and have more evidence to support the arguments.

Supplying Supporting Materials. Providing resources for both positions is vital. The instructors or the debate moderators should direct the debaters to relevant resources before and during the debate so that debaters are equipped with facts and knowledge to justify their deliberations. In fact, a debate resource database can be established for the debate. Debaters, moderators, and instructors can contribute additional resources to the resource database throughout the entire debate process.

Establishing Rules. Guidelines are important to debaters because they state the instructor's expectations. Debate can be an intimidating process for those without experience in debating; therefore, the rules and guidelines must be detailed and descriptive. There are at least three types of guidelines to be prepared and provided: the debate guidelines, the conduct of online debates, and the debate moderation guidelines when learner moderation is applied. The debate guidelines should state clearly the duties, procedures, expectations, strategies, and tips. The conduct of an online debate regulates acceptable debating behaviors. Misconduct during the debate is most likely to occur because text-based CMC lacks nonverbal cues. Misunderstanding the plain texts with lean channels of communications could trigger flaming behavior. The moderation guidelines should communicate the roles and tasks of the moderator. See Exhibits 1 and 2 for examples of the three types of guidelines.

Exhibit 1. Example of Online Debate Instruction

Asynchronous Online Debate

Form: Team Activity
Time: Two weeks

Objectives:

- To obtain comprehensive understandings on multiple views on an issue.
- To critically assess and present the evidence and resources of the debate topic.
- To convince the audience that your position is the most reasonable.

Debate Topic:

Is an online collaborative learning environment able to foster sociability?
PRO: Online collaborative learning environments CAN foster sociability.
CON: Online collaborative learning CANNOT foster sociability.

Teams will be assigned a pro or con position by the instructor.

Rules:

Deadline	Tasks
10/06/03	Moderators cast their vote on either pro or con
	Moderators post the introductory statement of the debate topic (500 words)
10/08/03	Both pro and con sides post one opening statement (500 words)
10/09/03–10/16/03	Open debate. The numbers of postings and the lengths of postings are not limited.
10/17/03	Both pro and con make rebuttals (500 words)
10/19/03	Moderators post closing statement (500 words)
	Moderators cast their final vote to either pro or con

Debate Strategies

- Comprehensive research of relevant issues
- To develop persuasive arguments, debaters need to research and consider the relevant issues involved in both positions rather than just their position
- Identify strengths and weaknesses of both positions

continued

Exhibit 1. Example of Online Debate Instruction, *continued*

- Perform critical and logical processes
- Critically analyze the relevant information and issues obtained on both positions
- Synthesize the information
- Present it with more persuasive form
- Look for weaknesses in the opposing group's arguments.
- Prepare strategies to refute your opponent's arguments.
- Are the arguments relevant to the debate topics? Does the opposing group lack information to support their claims? Are the there any reasoning flaws?
- Know the common errors in thinking, such as logical reasoning fallacies, and use them effectively in the refutation.
- Predict counter-arguments and demonstrate that your position is the most reasonable. In other words, turn opposing position's weakness into your position's strengths.

Presentation

- Any argument, refutation, and defense should be concise and clear.
- Be mindful of your wording because all messages are permanent (in that they're written), unlike in an oral face-to-face debate.

Supporting Evidence

- Present the content accurately with support from authoritative and valid sources.
- Challenge the validity of evidence presented by the opponents.

Coordinate Team Tasks

- Coordinate debate partners and amalgamate the arguments to strengthen the position.
- Support and emphasize teammates' arguments.

Evaluation Criteria

- Afford strong and clear opening and closing statements.
- Justify the position effectively.
- Identify and reveal opponents' weaknesses and reasoning flaws.
- Present strong evidence to support the defending position and reveal opponents' flaws.
- Post messages in a timely and accurate fashion.
- Demonstrate the cohesion of team debating position.

Conduct of Debates

- Any misconduct may result in the postings being removed from the debate message board or disqualified for the debate.
- Questions or challenges should be professional and relevant to the debate topic.
- Insulting and offensive language is unacceptable. Any description or comment involving personal language or attacks will be considered offensive.
- Debaters should avoid impugning the motives of opponents and the moderators.
- Any debate message that is not relevant to the topic will be removed from the discussion board.

Debate Resources

- "Schools have made little progress towards being learning networks at the heart of the community" (www.cybertext.net.au/tct2002/debate/debate_main.htm)
- Introduction to the way of reason (http://debate.uvm.edu/code/001.html)
- Debate (www.42explore.com/debate.htm)
- Debate Central (http://debate.uvm.edu/)

Exhibit 2. Tasks and Guidelines for the Online Debate Moderator

Tasks

1. Facilitate online debate.
2. Post an opening statement that addresses the importance of the debate topic and raises the controversial issues.
3. Post a closing statement that summarizes the debate messages and close the debate.
4. Support and assist both sides to develop and organize their debating strategies.
5. Limit yourself to answering administrative questions.
6. Provide advice about where to find resources and how to search for them, but do not do the work for the teams.
7. Maintain and update the debate resource database.

Guidelines

1. It is inappropriate for moderators to participate in the creation of any work product for the teams. It may skew the debate positions.
2. The moderators may not participate in the actual debate; however, it is important to keep the debate on the tasks and relevant.
3. Frequently, a private message to the debaters may be more appropriate than a public one.
4. Remind the debaters that they are expected to participate during the debate.

Establishing Evaluation. The debate evaluation criteria should be stated clearly before the debate. Good evaluation criteria will inform the debaters of the expected focus and conduct of the debate. The evaluation criteria should be based on the goals of the debate; however, caution must be exercised to prevent determining the actual debate results because the purpose of a debate is to establish thoughtful processes, not to establish a solution for the topic under discussion. In fact, the preferred debate topic is a conundrum; debate is redundant if an answer is apparent. The evaluation of debates should lie on the processes of the debate rather than in the results of the debate. Good evaluation criteria should focus on the intended goals and allow debaters to demonstrate the following abilities:

- To clarify and understand positions;
- To identify, defend, and justify the strengths and weaknesses of a position;
- To provide appropriate supporting resources to sustain the argument;
- To post timely messages; and
- To demonstrate team cohesion on the position being supported in the debate.

Debating

A debate includes several vital processes: announcing the debate rules, grouping/assigning tasks, presenting opening statements, facilitating, and providing timely feedback.

Announcing the Debate Rules and Assigning Tasks. The debate should be initiated by announcing the debate rules that permit debaters to assume a proper stance during the debate process. At this time, the learners are divided into teams and assigned a pro or con position. If there are more than two teams, more than one team can be assigned to debate each side of the issue. Or one team can be assigned to be debate moderators. Alternatively, instructors can invite guest moderators who are experts on the particular debate topic.

Moderators answer administrative questions and give suggestions about how debaters might organize themselves, develop debate strategies, and prepare for the debate. It is appropriate to provide some advice about where to find resources but not to actually provide the resources.

Before the debate begins, the moderators are polled regarding their opinions on the issue. This initial vote regarding the debate topic serves to commit them to the debate. The instructor will collect the votes from the moderators and announce the results. This is repeated after the debate is closed to determine whether the debaters have been able to sway the opinions of the moderators.

Presenting Opening Statements. An introductory statement by the moderators is critical to prepare both positions to recognize weaknesses in the opposing argument. Any prejudice conveyed in these statements may potentially skew the results of the debate. The moderator's opening statement is followed by opening statements from both sides to support their positions. These statements should be posted by a specific time with a defined word limitation.

Facilitating. After the opening statements are posted, the floor is opened for debate by both positions and is impartially facilitated by the moderators. The open debate allows both positions to demonstrate weaknesses in the arguments of the opposition and justify their own arguments. Open debate should occur without limitations on the frequency of postings and the length of postings. The debaters should be allowed to debate and justify freely within the period of time given.

Moderators, while following the debate guidelines, should apply authoritative sources to assist the debaters in presenting their positions concisely and professionally. Debaters are led toward in-depth exploration through the assistance of appropriate facilitation. The lectures and assigned reading materials should provide relevant background information that can be drawn into the debate and should demonstrate the type of reasoning required to tackle the flow of the opponents' reasoning.

The role of instructors during the debate is to guide the debaters in attaining the objectives of the debate. The instructor remains on the sideline and does not participate in the debate. Less structured online discussions may not require the presence of an instructor, whereas the presence of an instructor is necessary during a debate to maintain the direction of the discourse and to intervene when the debate moves in the wrong direction.

Providing Timely Feedback. The instructors should observe the debate process closely and provide timely feedback. The debaters and the moderators may not be familiar with the debate process and the tactful use of effective debate strategies; therefore, the instructors are present to provide timely and constructive feedback to each team or each individual. A private communication may be necessary because the instructor's interference may alter the balance of the debate position and skew the results. The feedback should be constructive and suggestive, not judgmental.

Finalizing

In the final stage of the online debate, the moderators should post closing statements followed by rebuttals from both positions. The moderators' closing statement should illuminate the main points that each position presented. The moderators vote again on either the pro or con positions after the closing statements are posted. The instructors collect the votes and determine how many of the moderators were swayed to the opposite position and announce the results.

To wrap up the debate, the instructors should post overall comments and feedback for the entire debate. These should point out the critical issues that were not covered during the debate. It is important for the instructor to challenge the debaters to consider how the debate topic will evolve in the future. The instructor should also provide a summative assessment of the debate based on the evaluation criteria. This assessment should be a team evaluation. Individual assessments can be applied, if necessary.

Extended activities are valuable additions to the online debate if the time and circumstances permit, analyzing the pro and con arguments, and composing an improvement report. Each team should analyze the arguments and justifications presented by both teams to produce an after-action report addressing how future debates may be improved.

Final Words

Online debate is an alternative method utilized to enhance online learning, to encourage critical thinking, and to help learners appreciate opposing points of view. Online debates motivate learners to contribute and stimulate interest in what their opponents have to say. Learners actively build on each other's ideas and at the same time introduce new elements into the discourse. With appropriate online debate design, learners become more skilled at constructing persuasive arguments and knowledge.

References

Berge, Z.L., & Muilenburg, L. (2000). Designing discussion questions for online, adult learning. *Educational Technology, 40*(5), 53–56.

Engel, C., & Schaeffer, E. (2001). *Learning to persuade and persuading to learn: Design and evaluation of an online debate forum for large lecture classes.* Paper presented at the European CSCL Conference, Maastricht, Netherlands.

Schaeffer, E.L., McGrady, J.A., Bhargava, T., & Engel, C. (2002). *Online debate to encourage peer interactions in the large lecture setting: Coding and analysis of forum activity.* Paper presented at the Annual Meeting of the American Educational Research Association, New Orleans, Louisiana.

Chih-Hsiung Tu, *Ph.D., is an assistant professor at George Washington University, in Washington, D.C., and an educational/instructional technology consultant with extensive experience in distance education, eLearning, technology training in teacher education, online learning community, learning organization, and knowledge management. His research interests are distance education, socio-cognitive learning, socio-cultural learning, online learning community, learning organization, and knowledge management. He has edited or authored books, articles, and book chapters, and has presented conference proceedings.*

Creating the People Edge

Stephen G. Haines

Summary

This article's purpose is to present a way to create a strategic people/HR plan and to explain how to tie this plan closely to an overall organization-wide strategic plan. It will also present the six People Edge best practice areas for every organization.

The Challenge

How often do we utter the phrase, "People are our greatest asset"? Yet, at the same time, we fail to develop an overall systematic approach that strategically aligns and attunes human resource practices with organizational objectives.

For most organizations, the costs dedicated to staff salaries and benefits account for the single largest budget expenditure (varying from a low of about 60 percent in a manufacturing setting to a high of about 85 percent in a service organization). Thus, it makes both good common sense and good business sense to focus time and attention on the development of a strategic people management system that creates "the people edge" in the marketplace. But what's the best way of doing this?

Through our in-depth research, we have created a strategic people management plan as well as a companion model for examining the six People Edge best practice areas.

Strategic People Management Model

Our work with our Systems Thinking approach, applied to strategic planning and human resource management, has led us to look for practical, yet systematic, ways of positioning the people management function of an organization. People are the stewardship responsibility of senior and line management, not the HR function. This is

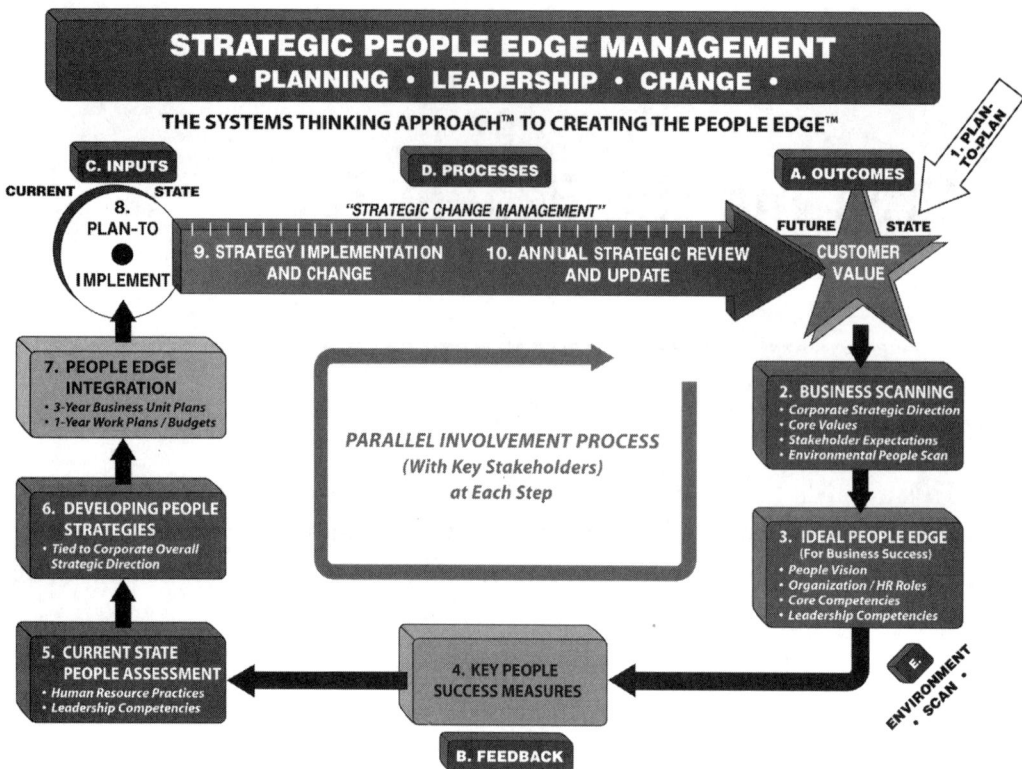

Figure 1. The Strategic People Management Model

why we use the phrase "people management" rather than HR management, which connotes the HR function having sole responsibility.

As a result, we have researched, developed, and refined our Strategic People Management model over the years to show organizations a straightforward Systems Thinking approach to create the People Edge necessary to develop and sustain a competitive business advantage.

Our Strategic People Management model is made up of five phases (A-E) and ten steps (see Figure 1).

Step 1: Plan to Plan

This is the prework stage of the process. It is required to determine organizational readiness and is an overall *educating, organizing, and tailoring step*. It answers questions such as, "Who needs to be involved in the planning to ensure ownership?" It also identifies strategic information that must be gathered for the planning process.

Usually, the final task in this step is to form an Executive Development Board to provide overall stewardship for the people in the organization to actually create the People Edge. This board also creates the opportunities for involvement of all key stakeholders in the people planning process.

Step 2: Business Scanning

There are three key elements in this step: (1) review the corporation's key business strategies, future direction, and core values with their people-related implications; (2) identify key stakeholder expectations; and (3) analyze key future environmental issues.

This step reinforces the importance of adopting a strategic approach to people management and linking people practices with the overall business direction. In particular, if there is a core strategy in the strategic plan regarding people, then all else that follows here in this article can be seen as implementing that strategy.

Step 3: The People Edge Vision

Based on our Systems Thinking approach of starting with the outcome first, developing a People Edge vision is the first planning task. It results in an inspirational statement describing where the organization wishes to be positioned to maximize its people as a competitive advantage. This also includes the articulation of the respective roles of senior management, line management, employees, and the human resources function in contributing to organizational success with people.

This step reinforces the essential principle of linking people practices to the strategic direction of the organization and the people strategy in the strategic plan.

Step 4: Key People Success Measures

Here we establish the high-level quantifiable outcome measures that will be used to measure employee success in adding value to customers, shareholders, and the community.

This enables senior management and the organization to measure progress and results toward achieving its People Edge vision. It often includes reducing turnover/absenteeism, increasing employee satisfaction (survey vs. your core values and do you "walk the talk"), and adding depth and quality to the talent pool (succession planning and development).

Step 5: Current State People Assessment

Next comes the assessment of the organization's current people practices against the six People Edge best practices (and forty specific practices) as the basis for strategy development.

These People Edge best practice areas were developed as a result of extensive literature review and research and are detailed later in the article. They are

- *Area 1:* Acquiring the Desired Work Force (the Individual Level of Living Systems).

- *Area 2:* Engaging the Work Force (the Interpersonal Level of Living Systems).

- *Area 3:* Organizing High Performance Teams (the Team Level of Living Systems).

- *Area 4:* Creating a Learning Organization (the Department-to-Department Level of Living Systems).

- *Area 5:* Facilitating Cultural Change (the Organization-Wide Level of Living Systems).

- *Area 6:* Collaborating with Key Stakeholders (the Organizational-Environmental Interface Level of Living Systems).

This is also where a 360-degree leadership competency assessment should be performed.

Step 6: People Strategy Development

Here we develop core people management strategies that are aligned to the direct business needs of the organization's delivery system and attuned to developing people's hearts and minds in support of serving the customer. Both the alignment and attunement strategies should relate closely and support the core strategies of the organization's overall strategic plan.

These core strategies will enable those who share responsibility for people management in the organization to realize their unique People Edge vision.

Step 7: People Edge Integration

This step involves the development of actions that outline the key activities for the next three years in support of the core strategies. A three-year layout of all needed actions and programs is created. Then these activities are reduced down to the top three to four priority "must do" actions for the next year.

This leads to the development of a one-year operational plan and budget for each major department in support of the people plan.

Step 8: Plan to Implement

One of the key reasons strategic people planning fails is due to a lack of implementation or a fatal reliance on the HR function to do it all. Management cannot abdicate its responsibilities for people stewardship. A one-year implementation plan is developed here, with the steps, processes, and structures required for successful implementation.

This includes how the plan will be communicated and how the change process will be managed and coordinated. The key element is regular follow-up by the executive development board mentioned in Step 1. They maintain and continually refine the plan as a living, breathing document.

Step 9: Strategy Implementation and Change

This is the point of actual implementation, change management, completion of tasks and priorities, and a period of adjusting actions as needed during the year.

It also involves managing the change process, measuring progress against the key people success measures, and celebrating achievements along the way.

Step 10: Annual People Review and Update

The people plan must be formally reviewed and updated on an annual basis. The key is to review the entire plan and update the annual priorities, taking into account ongoing changes in the business direction, the environment, and stakeholder expectations.

Achievements are recognized and celebrated. Strategies are reviewed and the three-year People Edge plan is updated.

Now the yearly cycle begins again, ensuring sustained high performance over the long term.

The People Edge Model

The People Edge model (see Figure 2) outlines the importance of developing people practices and processes to guarantee value to employees, customers, shareholders, and the community.

The model has at its foundation senior managers' leadership, commitment, and competence in people management, along with strong partnering arrangements with employees, management, customers, and the HR function. This is the center core of the model. Without it, the process already described is useless and the six People Edge best practices will never be achieved.

The core of the model is the organization's strategic people plan, which identifies the existing gaps between current practices and the desire to install best practices.

The second ring is the role distinction that helps to confirm "who does what" when it comes to people management. This second ring also signifies the need to do

Figure 2. The People Edge

an assessment of the six natural levels of leadership competencies for all members of management, starting with senior management. Based on this assessment, a strategic leadership development system is installed.

The third ring outlines the six best practice areas related to strategic people management.

The outer ring indicates that when these six best practices are imbedded within an organization, the result produced is the "alignment with the organization's strategic plan" and the "attunement of people's hearts and minds" as well. These are the two key results of successful implementation.

The Six People Edge Best Practices

The areas described below are the stewardship responsibility of senior management, with the expertise and staff support of HR professionals.

Area 1: Acquiring the Desired Work Force (the Individual Level of Living Systems)

One of the key challenges is the ability to attract and retain quality people. The key elements to address this problem include:

- Core organizational competencies and individual capabilities;
- Diverse, flexible, and alternative work arrangements;
- Work force succession and retention planning;
- Career development practices; and
- Comprehensive recruitment, selection, and orientation methods.

Area 2: Engaging the Work Force (the Interpersonal Level of Living Systems)

Winning the hearts and minds of employees continues to be a challenge for organizations, especially in times of "delayering," "rightsizing," and "downsizing."

Best practice organizations adopt multiple practices to re-engage their employees, including:

- Performance management systems that attune individual and team behavior with strategic direction and core values (i.e., goal setting, coaching, appraisal, development);
- Compensation linked to capability and contributions;
- Recognition systems that reinforce strategic direction;
- Flexible benefit programs to meet employee needs; and
- An accountability program designed to deal with poor performance in an effective, yet humane, manner.

Area 3: Organizing High Performance Teams (the Team Level of Living Systems)

The impact of empowered high performance teams on business success continues to be substantial. The key areas for organizing high performance teams include:

- Team design and development;
- Small unit team leadership;
- Empowered work teams;
- Participative management approaches; and
- Programs that reward and reinforce teamwork.

Area 4: Creating a Learning Organization (the Department-to-Department Level of Living Systems)

Building and sustaining intellectual capital as a core corporate asset across departments remains a key leverage area for competitive advantage. This also requires systems, processes, and information to support continuous learning and improvement throughout an organization, including:

- Development, growth, and sharing of intellectual capital;
- Systems Thinking institutionalized as an improved approach to better thinking and acting;
- Strategic human resource information systems (HRIS) in place;
- A cultural norm to debrief and learn from mistakes; and
- Encouragement of and support for creative thinking and innovation.

Area 5: Facilitating Cultural Change (the Organization-Wide Level of Living Systems)

Shaping the overall organizational culture to sustain a competitive advantage is a key best practice leverage point. This means:

- The collective management of the organization is developed as managers and leaders;

- A shared understanding of the desired culture and values is developed and implemented throughout the organization;

- Core human resource processes are aligned and streamlined with the values and strategic direction;

- Structures and infrastructures at the individual, team, and organization-wide levels reinforce the desired culture; and

- Strategic change agents and experts are identified to support and facilitate organizational change.

Area 6: Collaborating with Key Stakeholders (the Organizational–Environmental Interface Level of Living Systems)

Collaboration with multiple stakeholders, both within and external to the organization, is a means of meeting organizational needs. This is one of the emerging areas of leading-edge HR practices. It includes:

- Developing skills and knowledge to support global organizational initiatives;

- Ensuring strategic alliances are developed, including outsourcing HR administration and self-service systems;

- Developing a positive people environment and maintaining this as a competitive advantage;

- Creating an intense organization-wide customer focus; and

- Ensuring that collaboration and value-added contributions occur across organizations, customers, shareholders, communities, cultures, and countries.

Getting Started

To begin your own organization's work in people management, you can use the resources listed in the bibliography at the end of this article. You can begin anywhere in the Strategic People Management model and just continue from that point as you go through your yearly management cycle.

Bibliography

Bandt, A., & Haines, S. (2002). *Successful strategic human resource planning.* Menlo Park, CA: Crisp.

Brinkerhoff, R.O., & Gill, S.J. (1994). *The learning alliance: Systems thinking in human resource development.* San Francisco, CA: Jossey-Bass.

Buckner, M. (1993). *Succession planning.* New York: AMACOM.

Burack, E.H. (1988). *Creative human resource planning and application: A strategic approach.* Englewood Cliffs, NJ: Prentice Hall.

Dauten, D. (1999). *The gifted boss: How to find, create, and keep great employees.* New York: William Morrow.

Eastman, L. (1995). *Succession planning.* Greensboro, NC: Center for Creative Leadership.

Fitz-enz, J. (1995). *How to measure human resources management.* New York: McGraw-Hill.

Fitz-enz, J. (1997). *The eight practices of exceptional companies.* New York: American Management Association.

Gubman, E.L. (1998). *The talent solution: Aligning strategy and people to achieve extraordinary results.* New York: McGraw-Hill.

Haines, S.G. (2000). *Successful career and life planning.* Menlo Park, CA: Crisp.

Kravetz, D.J. (1986). *The human resources revolution.* San Francisco, CA: Jossey-Bass.

Lawler, E.E., III. (1990). *Strategic pay: Aligning organizational strategies and pay systems.* San Francisco, CA: Jossey-Bass.

Lawler, E.E., III. (1992). *The ultimate advantage: Creating the high-involvement organization.* San Francisco, CA: Jossey-Bass.

McAdams, J.L. (1996). *The reward plan advantage.* San Francisco, CA: Jossey-Bass.

Myers, M.S. (1991). *Every employee a manager.* San Francisco, CA: Pfeiffer.

Nelson, B. (1997). *1001 ways to energize employees.* New York: Workman.

Phillips, J. (1996). *Accountability in human resource management.* Houston, TX: Gulf.

Rothwell, S. (1990). *Strategic planning for human resources.* Oxford, England: Elsevier Science.

Rothwell, W.J. (1994). *Effective succession planning: Ensuring leadership continuity and building talent from within.* New York: AMACOM.

Ulrich, D. (1997). *Delivering results: A new mandate for human resource professionals.* Boston, MA: Harvard Business School Press.

Ulrich, D. (1998). *Human resource champions: The next agenda for adding value and delivering results.* Boston, MA: Harvard Business School Press.

Ulrich, D., Losey, M.R., & Lake, G. (Eds.). (1997). *Tomorrow's HR management.* New York: John Wiley & Sons.

Stephen G. Haines *is a CEO, entrepreneur, and strategist. He has over twenty-five years of working closely with over two hundred CEOs on strategy and positioning of different companies and organizations. He is a U.S. Naval Academy graduate, has a master's in OD from George Washington University, and has completed doctoral work in educational psychology at Temple University in Philadelphia. He is president and founder of both the Centre for Strategic Management and its sister company, Systems Thinking Press.*

Does Executive Education Improve Business Performance?
Adrian Furnham

Summary

The executive education industry likes us to believe that learning pays. But this is just like marketers assuming advertising works in that it ultimately increases sales above the cost of the advertising itself. The problem is that there is precious little evidence to substantiate the belief that sponsoring an employee on an MBA or similar program will even recoup costs, let alone significantly or even noticeably improve the bottom line. This article explores the potential worth of executive education for employers and ways that the impact of this education can be evaluated.

There is evidence that employees who obtain an MBA can expect a salary increase (*Financial Times*, 2004). This can therefore be seen as a good investment for self-financing, middle-aged, middle managers who want to break through to the next level of management. But what is the employer gaining in your average MBA graduate? Additional knowledge and skills, a guarantee of a particular personality profile, or merely a reputation for being "a mover and a shaker"?

Is It Worth It?

Knowledge and Skills

There is no doubt that executive education increases knowledge and, to some extent, skills. Whether they are relevant or quickly decline after the course has ended is uncertain. Graduates know a lot more about how business works and tend to have an impressively increased vocabulary—a sort of "business babble." They may also acquire or enhance particular analytic skills—some of which are more useful than others. Taking exams and writing reports may have limited usefulness back in the workplace, but the case-study method can teach people how to appraise complex scenarios analytically. It can, of course, also lead to analysis paralysis.

But an MBA does not affect ability or motivation. At some institutions, but possibly the minority these days, earning an MBA *is* an indicator of ability because acceptance to a program is conditional on scoring well on good, rigorous, well-normed ability tests. But the growth of business schools and the decline in applicants mean that many schools have relaxed their entrance requirements (*Financial Times,* 2004). An MBA is no guarantee either of ability or of *relevant* skills and knowledge to the business.

Personality Profile

Is an MBA an indicator of personality? Certainly, MBA students tend to be ambitious, need-for-achievement types. They have to be hard-working, well-organized, dedicated self-starters. Less charitable people would say they are characterized by avoriciousness, egocentrism, and short-termism.

Or does the MBA act as little more than a reputational placebo, the expensive sugar pill of management? Both the degree holder and those working with him/her believe in the ability, skills, and judgment and presume that the former has a resulting effect on the bottom line. However, it is more likely to be the beliefs and expectations of customers and shareholders that influence business performance than deluded, starstruck, or business-school-bamboozled certificate holders and their fellow travelers.

Based on my own experience teaching both MBA and non-MBA students, business school students are notoriously demanding. They are more characterized by pragmatic exam-orientation than by academic curiosity. They are hot on their rights and cool toward their responsibilities. They play to their strengths rather than attempt to compensate for their weaknesses. Their education/work/life (im)balance means they have little time for those most academic of activities like wide reading, reflection, recreational debate—the essence of an academic education.

Testing the Worth of an MBA

A Control Trial

Could you prove the proposition that education really improves performance? Could it be done through the use of techniques used to determine the efficacy of drugs, such as randomized, double-blind, control trials? Certainly that methodology does have a lot to say about how to demonstrate real results.

To do this, one would have to do the following. Managers of similar age, stage, ability, and experience from different parts of a large organization would have to be selected for the trial. They would have to be as "equivalent" as possible. Most importantly, they should be in departments where their ability, effort, and style can be directly related to both objective (revenue, costs, absenteeism, productivity) and subjective (ratings of satisfaction, management style, climate) measures. The more measures the better, as any one is possibly unreliable.

The managers should be randomly assigned to one of two or three groups: one group does business education, another moral philosophy, and a third yoga over the full duration. No one is to be informed to which group they were assigned and the secret is kept on their return. This is a randomized, single-blind, controlled study. Then, after six months and perhaps again twelve months later, you would measure the business performance of the managers' section, group, or department. If the business education group is significantly more successful in explicit, definable, and measurable terms, this is proof it works.

Parallels Between Therapy and Education

We know from psychotherapy research on efficiency that oddly *all therapies have roughly similar effects* (Smith, Glass, & Miller, 1980). It could be the same for education. Studying Aristotelian ethics may be no more or less beneficial than studying accounting because it is the educational *process* rather than the *content* that is important.

The various forms of psychotherapy do share some important features (Smith, Glass, & Miller, 1980), as do all types of education.

Psychotherapists all rely on the *therapeutic alliance*—a relationship between therapist and client that is characterized by acceptance, caring, respect, and attention. This relationship provides social support that helps clients deal with their problems and acquire social skills that they can apply to other relationships. Presumably, the longer and deeper the acquaintance, the more powerful the effect on the client. The same is true of the teacher/professor-pupil/MBA student relationship. Education of all sorts improves self-confidence.

In nearly all forms of therapy, clients talk about their beliefs and emotions, how they act, and why they act that way. They examine aspects of themselves that they ordinarily take for granted; in so doing, they gain self-understanding. Just explaining through talk—even to a tape recorder—may therefore have beneficial results. Again, the same is true in seminars, whatever the topic.

The mere fact of entering therapy (education), whatever the method, usually improves the clients' morale. The therapist conveys the message "You are going to get better"; the teacher "You are going to get more insightful." Clients begin to think of themselves as people who can cope with their problems and overcome them. Just expecting improvement can lead to improvement, although not of course if expectations are unrealistically high. The business school message is no different. You will become richer, more competent, more perspicacious.

Most important, perhaps, every form of therapy requires clients to *commit* themselves to making some sort of change in their lifestyle. Simply by coming to the therapy session, they are reaffirming their commitment to attempt to overcome their problems. They are also obliged to work on that change between sessions so that they can come to the next session and report progress. Improvement often depends as much on what clients do between sessions as on what happens in the sessions themselves. And this is the essence of adult education. Giving up free time to studying anything is a big commitment. It is a behavioral commitment to do things differently.

Evaluating Education

But at this point nervous business school deans and marketers start raising objections: we are all team workers and business performance is a team effort (not up to one manager); in some parts of the organization (i.e., HR), performance is not really measurable; and so on. That is flim-flam. Ask them about performance management or selection and promotion decisions and whether those are informed by data. Of course performance is difficult to measure, but it is not impossible. It takes time, care, and effort. What does exist exists in some quantity and can, in principle, be measured. The truth is, like the snake-oil salesman, they are fearful of the results of the trial.

Humble trainers, as opposed to sexy consultants, have long been asked to justify their budgets by proving that training works. People measure training by four methods (Kirkpatrick, 1998).

The first is *participant reaction to training*. Measures of trainee satisfaction through post-course "smile sheets" is cheap, easy, and relatively straightforward. But it is important to make sure the evaluators, and not the teachers, choose the questions you would like the course participants to answer. Trainers can easily bias the questions to their known strengths. Entertrainers get excellent feedback but teach little. Getting students to evaluate their MBA can lead to dissonance reduction or buyer's nostalgia. Most rationalize the idea that it was worth it, irrespective of what they really learned. This is therefore not a good measure.

Second, there is *learning*, which is the difference between pre- and post-course knowledge and skills. Again, this is not too difficult to measure, although there are two important caveats. It is easy to make the pretest very difficult and the post-test very easy so that it looks as if the trainee has learned a great deal. Also, learning, unless practiced and reinforced rather than punished, is all-too-soon forgotten. A 360-degree feedback assessment pre- and post- executive training can provide a good indicator of this.

Third, there is *behavioral change*, which is what the trainees do differently. This can take months to measure and, for most, involves considerable effort. It too may be best judged or rated by others—preferably by subordinates of the trainees/course attenders. It focuses on differences. This is an excellent way to measure performance, but behavioral change itself does not necessarily lead directly to improvement in section/department results.

Fourth, there are the elusive results from the bottom line. All sorts of things can be measured—sales or productivity up; rejects, absenteeism, or customer complaints down. Training and education are not only about this, of course. They could be seen as developmental opportunities that enhance employee satisfaction rather than company profit. That is a perfectly acceptable goal, but organizations must be honest about it.

If an individual's contribution to business performance cannot be measured, all human resource decisions must be based on guesswork. One only has to see small business—a pub, a bakery, a corner shop—change hands to know what a difference an individual manager can make.

Business schools need to invest in a study that proves business executive education really does improve performance if they want to make that claim.

References

The Financial Times. (2004, January 26).

Kirkpatrick, D.L. (1998). *Evaluating training programs: The four levels.* San Francisco, CA: Berrett-Koehler.

Smith, M., Glass, G., & Miller, T. (1980). *The benefits of psychotherapy.* Baltimore, MD: Johns Hopkins University Press.

Adrian Furnham *is currently a professor in psychology (ad hominem) at the University of London and is the founder/director of Applied Behavioural Research Associates. The organization specializes in research on corporate evaluation and design, performance appraisal, personnel and corporate assessment and selection, and state-of-the-art literature reviews. The author of thirty-six books, including* Culture Shock, *Professor Furnham has written for various management magazines and has authored over four hundred peer-reviewed scientific papers in international scientific journals.*

Establishing a Stimulating Environment for Communication and Learning*

Robert William Lucas

Summary

Communication is all around us. In no place is it more important than in the classroom when you are delivering important program content to a group of learners. For you to be successful as an instructor or educator, it is not enough to be comfortable with your subject matter. You must also understand various elements of human behavior, diversity, motivation, and a variety of other factors that influence how the brain attains, processes, and recalls information.

Recognizing and understanding the importance and role of interpersonal communication skills will aid you in sharing knowledge and skills with your participants while gaining information and ideas for yourself.

In this article, we will explore how to effectively apply strong interpersonal concepts, brain-based research, and the knowledge of human interaction to improve your training programs.

You, and most of the trainers that you probably know, spend hours developing lesson plans, setting a learning environment that incorporates active or brain-based learning concepts, and creating visual aids with pizzazz using such things as color, graphics, and artistic fonts. These things are often done because you read something in a book, saw someone else do so effectively, or were told to do so in a train-the-trainer program that you attended. Certainly, all of these elements add value; however, what many trainers

---

*Portions of this article/material originally appeared in *The Creative Training Idea Book* by Robert W. Lucas. Copyright © 2003 Robert W. Lucas. Used by the permission of the publisher, AMACOM Books, Division of American Management Association, New York, New York. All rights reserved. www.amacombooks.org

often fail to realize is that all the glitz and environmental preparation in the world cannot compensate for poor interpersonal communication skills and knowledge. Everything related to your training delivery should be designed to do one thing—aid your verbal and nonverbal messages. YOU have the knowledge and must deliver your program content in a captivating, intelligent, enthusiastic, and professional manner in order for learning to occur.

Setting the Stage for Communication

Creating an environment that facilitates eye contact, discussion, and clear communication is the first step toward making sure that information is exchanged effectively and efficiently. An easy way to set the tone for learning is to establish roles early in your program. This can be done by having learners create a list of "game rules" that

Exhibit 1. Sample Training Agreement

Please consider this program a "safe" environment. What we say here, stays here.

It's all right to...

- Express your ideas.
- Challenge the facilitator's ideas.
- Offer examples (please keep them generic with no names used).
- Question.
- Relax.

Your Role

- Be on time (from breaks and lunch).
- Participate.
- Learn in your own way.
- Provide honest, open feedback on evaluations.
- Enjoy yourself!

Facilitator's Role

- Start and end on time.
- Professionally facilitate the exchange of information and knowledge.
- Allow time for and encourage your input.
- Listen nondefensively.
- Help you grow personally and professionally

will be followed throughout the session or by preparing a "training agreement" like the one shown in Exhibit 1 to outline your roles and those of your learners.

Room Arrangement

Furniture arrangement is also an important part of setting the stage for communication. The importance of recognizing the best way to set up your room for maximum interaction based on the program content, room configuration, and desired level of participant contact cannot be overemphasized. Similarly, it is important to understand that the way in which you set up your furniture and equipment will have a definite impact on people psychologically. For instance, have you ever walked into a large room filled with chairs for a presentation and had only a small group of people actually attend? If you have, then you know that people often spread out and there is often a feeling of emptiness. In such situations, participants often have to be moved closer together before the session starts in order to encourage camaraderie and intimacy. Psychologically, these large open settings can send a message of "We were expecting more people, but they didn't show up." Attendees then start to wonder, "What do these absentee participants know about the session or instructor that I don't?" A similar problem arises from too many participants or chairs being stuffed into a smaller room. Such a space limits mobility, interaction, and the types of activities you can do. It also crowds people and can make them a bit claustrophobic. From a learning perspective, neither setting is good.

In an ideal communication environment, there are adequate tables, chairs, and space for planned activities and the number of people anticipated. Still, you should always have a few extra chairs and space for a few unscheduled attendees who show up.

From a communication perspective, it is best to seat people in a manner that they can see you and other participants and so that they can interact throughout the program. This helps build a sense of team, allows networking, facilitates two-way nonverbal communication, and provides ample opportunity for participants to ask questions or comment throughout the session. Round table configurations (see Figure 1) for small groups (5 to 8 learners) provide the best opportunity for interaction. It also allows you to see their nonverbal cues and monitor their unspoken messages so that you can react accordingly. The down side of such an arrangement is that it is difficult for you to get into the group and near each person throughout your program. It also limits interaction among all participants unless you have people move and regroup periodically throughout the program.

An alternative type setting is the crescent-shaped (see Figure 2) or U-shaped configuration (see Figure 3). Both allow you and participants to have ongoing eye contact and dialogue. They also allow your access into the group for better classroom management. The down side of these configurations is that people on either end of the tables sometimes have to lean forward or backward to look around others when

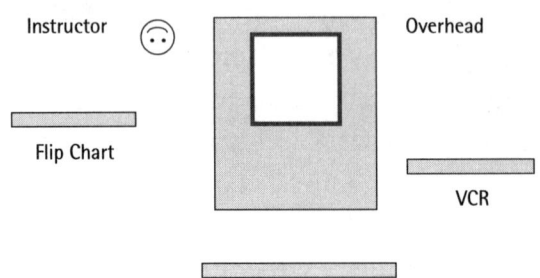

Figure 1. Round Table Configuration

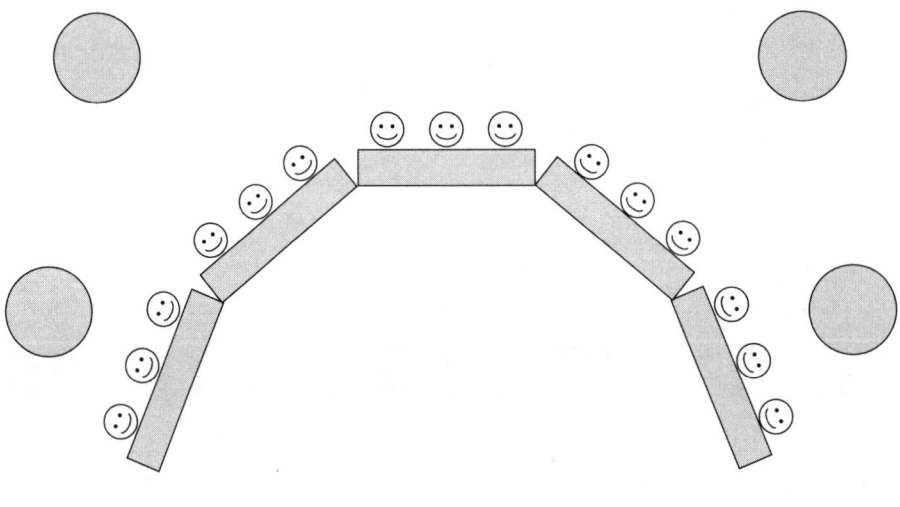
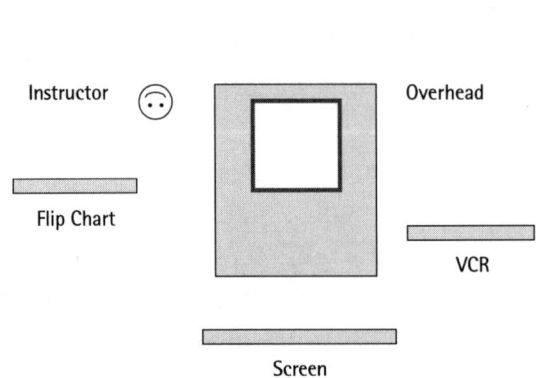

Figure 2. Crescent Configuration

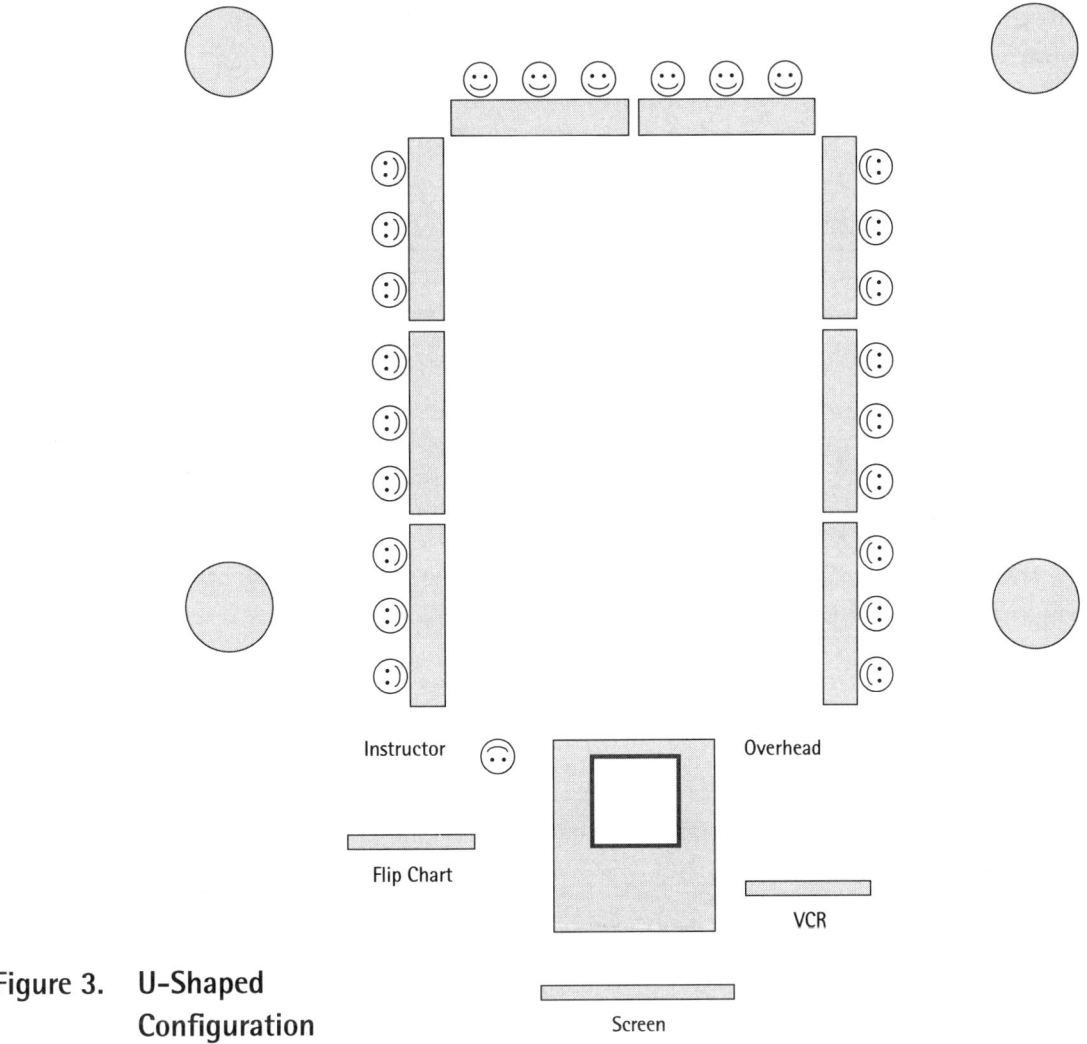

Figure 3. U-Shaped Configuration

participant discussion or comment takes place. If you decide to use such configurations, it is helpful to have extra chairs and/or tables in the room for small breakout group activities or discussions throughout the session.

Training Aid Design and Placement

Two additional elements related to environmental setup are the design and placement of your training aids. Since your visual aids are an important supplement to your message, consider their design and location carefully.

When creating visual aids, your goal should be simplicity and clear visibility in order to enhance their effectiveness. Also remember that you will have some learners with either sight impairments (diminished ability to see and light sensitivity) or color blindness. When creating your training aids, design them with those factors in mind. Additionally, when placing easels and screens in the room, make sure that they have appropriate amounts of lighting without glare or shadows. Failure to consider these elements could send a nonverbal message that you do not accommodate the needs of your learners. It could also result in reduced learning or transfer of knowledge.

The Role of Nonverbal Communication in Training Effectiveness

As an instructor, you should continually be alert to the nonverbal cues that you and your participants send. According to a classic research study on nonverbal message meaning (Mehrabian, 1968), 93 percent of the emotion from a message between two people comes from nonverbal cues. Fifty-five percent of that number comes from signals such as facial expressions, hand and body gestures, posture, physical appearance (e.g., dress, grooming, and jewelry). Another 38 percent comes from vocal cues (e.g., tone, inflection, rate of speech, volume, and pitch).

Depending on the cues you send, all of these signals can have a dramatic impact on message meaning and can lead to either positive understanding and rapport building or miscommunication and a breakdown in relationships. While this study was not focused on group dynamics, it has implications in the classroom. Skilled trainers and educators use nonverbal messaging to their advantage. They continually monitor their own nonverbal cues and rehearse their presentations before going in front of a group of learners to help ensure that they are aware of any distracting mannerisms or vocal patterns and eliminate them. They also practice accentuating key words and using a variety of voice qualities and gestures to strengthen or reduce emphasis throughout their presentation.

Many facilitators go so far as to videotape their practice sessions to detect any recurring gestures that they might use and that might detract from their spoken message. If you decide to try this approach, fast forward your tape and watch your gestures. Excessive, repeated gestures will be obvious and will almost look comical. This videotaping technique can help immeasurably because it can also help identify any common speech patterns or "pet phrases" that are used when presenting. Many people pick up colloquialisms (regional or ethnic terminology) and industry jargon or acronyms and use them frequently when talking without ever realizing it. Rehearsing and audio- or videotaping yourself can help identify and reduce such distracters.

Related to the impact of nonverbal communication, one Bulgarian researcher (Lozanov, 1991) stressed the power of the learner's unconscious brain in assimilating information. He parlayed his findings into language programs that allowed learners to gain and retain up to five hundred words per day with more than 90 percent recall weeks later. In part, Dr. Lozanov's programs were built around a principle that the human brain has a tremendous ability to capture messages in training on both a conscious and unconscious level. His contention is that every message (verbal and nonverbal) suggests a meaning and that all communication activity happens simultaneously. What this means in a training environment is that learners are very aware of the material and activities on which you are focusing. They are also aware of what you are NOT focused on. For example, when you display a visual aid and make a relevant comment, learners see the image and hear your message. They also take in any nonverbal gestures or nuances that you provide. This is why it is so important to rehearse program content and monitor your delivery. Presentation success depends on the congruence (agreement) of your verbal and nonverbal cues. You must send cues that match in their intent and portray a positive, non-distracting image. Nonverbal cues that conflict with your spoken messages can distract and cause an interruption in learning. For example, you announce during a program that you are running behind time (a negative message), yet you spend three or four minutes sharing a joke or story that does not enhance the program content. The messages that learners might get are that you are not really concerned with effective delivery of program material, that you are not organized and cannot prioritize, or that you lack professionalism.

The Role of Nonverbal Cues in Classroom Management

Nonverbal communication can also be an effective classroom management tool. For example, an easy way to build rapport and get to know learners is to have your room set up and all the preliminary activity completed before learners arrive. Once they arrive at the training location, you can greet them at the door with a smile and a firm handshake. The latter actually helps establish a nonverbal psychological bond with participants. By coming into physical contact and smiling (a relatively universal symbol of friendship), you create a relationship with learners. This bonding can be helpful later in a session since "friends" are less likely to challenge or heckle you.

Selecting and Setting the Right Environment

You can send many nonverbal messages about your ability, professionalism, and concern for the learner through the way that you set up and use your environment. Your training or education environment plays a huge role in the success or failure of a program or class. Unfortunately, many organizations and trainers fail to acknowledge or capitalize on this fact. Instead, they let expediency in delivering information or external factors (e.g., management/customer pressure, budget, business competition, or instructor availability) influence room and environment configuration. Certainly the external factors mentioned must be considered; however, their impact should be weighed against any potential impact on learners. If learners are not comfortable or able to maximize the learning situation, the training will be a potentially wasted effort. Keep in mind the findings of many theories of human motivation that abound (e.g., Maslow's [1970] Hierarchy of Needs and Herzberg's [1959] Motivation/Hygiene Theory) and how various factors influence human behavior and motivation. These research findings are certainly valid in a learning environment. As such, facilitators should continually think outside the box in preparing their learning environments.

Various research studies have shown that a variety of elements attract and hold attention while stimulating the brain (e.g., light, motion, color, sound, and novelty). These factors impact learning and can also affect learner mood and motivation. If your training room is dull and blank, add a splash of color or pizzazz. You can do this with the following:

- Quotes related to your topic on brightly colored poster board can provide additional program-related content and communicate messages or help motivate learners;
- Colorful balloons around the walls add a festive, upbeat feel;
- Colored paper for handouts adds pizzazz to the environment;
- Props such as hats, colorful scarves, foam animal masks, or rubber noses can add humor and novelty and can be used yourself or given to learners to use in a variety of ways;
- Party glitter and topic-related decorations on tables can reinforce the program theme and create connective memories that will help learners recall the session;
- Appropriate music as participants enter and during break can soothe, inspire, motivate, or just entertain and occupy the minds of learners during down times. (NOTE: If you use copyrighted music for public consumption you need to pay a license fee. Otherwise you are violating federal copyright law [see BMI and ASCAP in Trainer Resources].)

Configuring the Room for Maximum Communication and Learning

Researchers continually find that where participants are seated can impact the outcome of learning and their overall satisfaction with the learning experience and the facilitator. One study done with schoolchildren found that, when given flexibility in selecting a seat (or standing if they felt the need), it helped stimulate and improve learning (Dunn & Dunn, 1987). Requiring or assigning specific seating arrangements can actually inhibit a person's learning. This is an important consideration when deciding whether to have preassigned seats (e.g., with name tents) or allow a choice by participants. It is especially important that you accommodate the needs of all of your learners in today's diverse environment. Many people like to sit near the front of a room because of preference or due to a hearing or vision impairment. Some participants prefer the right or left side of the room. This could possibly be because of a hearing or sight impairment on one side or the other, because of their handedness (left or right), or just out of preference. Still other participants might prefer the rear of the room because of some type of mobility impairment or because they know they will need to exit early and do not wish to disturb others. These considerations should be remembered, and your personal preferences for seating participants should not be forced on the group. Another consideration is that, when moving people to small groups for activities, it is usually a good idea to allow participants the option of returning to their original seats when the activity ends.

Overall, the way in which you set up your tables, chairs, and equipment can impact effectiveness of the program and communication. For example, by setting up a classroom in one of the formats shown in Figures 1 through 3 or something similar, you are able to move closer to learners throughout a program. Closing the proximity with learners might be done to build rapport while you smile and make eye contact. It might also be done to nonverbally gain, regain, or retain learner attention while you speak. For example, when two participants are carrying on a side conversation and not focusing on you or session material, you might casually move toward the pair while continuing to deliver program content. Once directly in front of them (within three or four feet), you might pause the delivery to gain attention (silence and sound both attract attention), make direct eye contact, smile, and talk directly to one or both of the participants. In effect, the unspoken message is "Be quiet and pay attention." A question related to what you had just said in the program might even be asked of the two. This would cause them to realize they had not been paying attention. This latter technique is normally best used after other less subtle ones have failed. You have to be careful not to bring too much embarrassment on the pair, since this could turn them off to learning or cause resentment. If they do not know the answer, quickly ask the question again of the entire group. The point was made that the two were not focused and you can then move away and get on with the presentation.

Encouraging Effective Listening and Focusing Attention

Over the years, various researchers have determined that a "listening gap" often occurs when people are having a conversation. This is because the average person speaks at approximately 125 to 150 words per minute, while the human brain is capable of processing four to six times that amount of information. The result is that there is a gap and the mind sometimes becomes distracted. Many people call this "mind wandering" or "daydreaming." This phenomenon is absolutely normal and will likely regularly occur during your presentations. Your challenge is to recognize when it is occurring and do things to bring learner focus or attention back to you and your program content.

Many times you can detect participant distraction by watching mannerisms or eye contact or by asking a question of the group and seeing who seems to be confused or lost. Another easy way to gauge the attention level of participants is to put small, quiet (no noise-producing items), manipulative type toys on participant tables at the beginning of a session and tell learners that they can quietly "play" with them throughout the session. There are many types of items that can be used for this purpose. For example, Koosh® balls, spring toys, foam rubber squeeze toys in various shapes, wire puzzles, adjustable link type toys (e.g., Klixx® or Hoberman Spheres®), or bendable toys (e.g., little figures of animals or people). These can be found in many toy and hobby stores or at some of the resources listed in the Trainer Resources listing at the end of this article. When using such items while presenting session information, you can monitor participant behavior. If a lot of learners are fidgeting and playing with toys, this could be a nonverbal signal that you need to change your pace of delivery, that learners need a break, or that the material is not engaging or challenging participants and should be modified.

Communicating with Diverse Audiences

Another key factor in communication success as a trainer is having the ability to interact with and be able to effectively exchange information with all of your learners. The challenge in communicating in today's multicultural world is that there has been a constant blending of people and heritages. The result is that it is virtually impossible to find terms or names to accurately describe all people or to know how to deal with every type of person with whom you come into contact.

While it is dangerous to generalize and lump people and cultures together when interacting with someone, there are some general characteristics and common values shared by many people from various countries, geographical regions, and cultural backgrounds. By keeping these similarities in mind when interacting with your learners, you can enhance the opportunities for successful communication. Remember that such characteristics DO NOT apply to all members of a particular group. It is ALWAYS better to ask a person his or her preference and observe his or her reactions when you need to know something about the person. If you note annoyance or discomfort during a conversation, do a perception check to see whether you have said or done something to cause the reaction or whether there is another reason. Also, keep in mind that exposure to other cultures (acculturation) will impact what a person believes and how he or she acts. For example, a second or third generation Asian-American in the United States may relate more closely to Western values than to those of his or her native heritage.

Articles and Discussion Resources

To improve the chances of being understood by and understanding someone from a different culture, it is best to study and embrace diversity. Learn as much as you can about other countries, cultural sensitivities, heritage, people, and communication styles. It is not enough to speak a language; you must also understand the mind-set of the people who speak it. Exhibit 2 is a listing of various cultural groups and some general characteristics that many people from those cultures exhibit.

Exhibit 2. Cultural Awareness Tips*

When viewing these characteristics, keep in mind that these are general characteristics and not exhibited by all people from a given group. Other factors, such as age, gender, and mental and physical ability, could impact someone's behavior and communication style.

The following are definitions of the cultural groups described in this exhibit.

Hispanics, Latinos, or Chicanos include groups that trace their origins or background to Spain, Latin America, or Mexico. Note: The U.S. Census Bureau uses the term Hispanic for all these groups.

African-American or Black includes groups that trace their origins or background to Africa (sub-Saharan area). The descriptive term African-American is often used in the United States, while Black is often used by people in Latin America or the Caribbean.

Asians or Asian-Americans include groups that trace their origins or background to the Asian continent or to the Pacific Islands (e.g., China, Korea, Japan, or Samoa).

Native American includes groups that trace their origins or background to the continents of America.

European American, Anglo-American, or White includes groups that trace their origins or background to Europe, other than Spanish.

Hispanic/Latino/Chicano Cultures

Different terms are assigned to people of Hispanic background based on the region of the world from which they originate. Each country has its own unique culture; however, because of a common heritage, they share a number of general characteristics and values. The following are some things to keep in mind when serving people from this group:

- Family and group loyalty is an important concept in many Hispanic cultures. Long-term relationships are valued;
- Women are often admired and respected, especially mothers;
- Respect for elders and authority (for example, teachers) is often important. Direct eye contact is often avoided when talking with people who are older or of higher status as a show of respect. Additionally, many people often look away rather than making direct eye contact while listening;
- Time is viewed as flexible and the concept of hurrying to meet a deadline at the expense of disregarding others and what someone values can cause problems;
- Living "in the moment" and wanting to see what happens next is a common approach to life. Also, many people from this group take a more casual, spontaneous, and impulsive approach to life. This can influence relationships and communication style;

continued on the next page

*This material is adapted from *Customer Service Skills and Concepts for Success* by R.W. Lucas. Published by McGraw-Hill, New York, 2005. Reproduced with permission of McGraw-Hill.

Exhibit 2. Cultural Awareness Tips, *continued*

Hispanic/Latino/Chicano Cultures, *continued*

- Religious affiliations are often strong;
- Courtesy (use of diplomacy and tact), dignity, honor, and loyalty are valued in business as well as in family affairs;
- Many men tend to be more assertive than women in business, although women are often more assertive and men are often more aggressive in their communication approach;
- Direct argument or contradiction is typically viewed as rude and disrespectful;
- Emotions are readily displayed by many (crying, laughing, touching, and smiling);
- Material objects are often viewed as a necessity versus an end in themselves;
- Many Hispanics are in tune with their environment. They tend to touch, smell, feel, taste, and come in close proximity with objects or people who have their attention.

African-American/Black Cultures

Depending on the country of origin and personal background, there will be differences among individuals; however, there are some general characteristics shared by many African-Americans or Black people.

- Emotion or expressiveness is often seen in communication. To this end, voice volume and inflection are often elevated;
- Focus on unity or group is strong;
- Close relationships with group and family are often valued by many in this group;
- Assertiveness and directness may be common and valued by many in this group;
- Religious affiliations are often strong for many in this group;
- Direct eye contact when speaking, rather than when listening, is common. This is often as a show of respect and learned at a young age. Contrarily, a prolonged glance may be viewed as sexual interest or disrespect, depending on the parties involved;
- More spatial distance is often preferred when talking to others, especially strangers;
- Touching or patting of a child's head, especially by a white person, is often viewed as condescending;
- Use of nonverbal cues is often limited (for example, head nodding while listening);
- Use of direct questions is sometimes considered harassment. For example, asking an African-American participant who is trying to decide between two items or choices, "Can I clarify what I said?" might appear as if you are rushing him or her;
- Conversations between two people who know one another are typically viewed as private. Therefore, anyone who interrupts without permission is viewed as eavesdropping and is often rebuked. For example, if two African-American learners were discussing their views on a topic raised and you interrupted to emphasize additional elements, you might offend them;
- When they are speaking to each other, conversations can become loud and animated;
- Time is viewed as flexible, not linear. Life issues may take priority over keeping appointments, and many people are "present-oriented." Older African-Americans tend to be more punctual and more willing to wait than their younger counterparts;

continued on the next page

Exhibit 2. Cultural Awareness Tips, *continued*

African-American/Black Cultures, *continued*

- Adoption and use of a "Black" dialect or terminology by people outside of the cultural group without authorization is often viewed as mocking and an insult;
- Interrupting during conversation is usually tolerated. Competition to speak is often granted to the person who is most assertive;
- Asking personal questions of a person met for the first time may be seen as improper and intrusive;
- Emotions are often not readily displayed by men (crying, for example), especially among strangers;
- The terms "you" or "your people" are typically seen as pejorative and racist;
- Men may wear sunglasses and hats indoors as adornments, much like jewelry might be worn by other groups.

Asian/Asian-American Cultures

Some shared values and characteristics by people with Asian heritage include the following:

- "Family" is important to many people in this group, since many Asians typically value collectivism;
- Maintaining a low personal profile and working for the betterment of family or the group is important. This can sometimes be tied to "face" or esteem;
- Face, harmony, and obligation are important elements in dealing with others. Doing things that cause someone else to be embarrassed, ridiculed, or put in a lower position can damage a relationship with an Asian person;
- In regard to group orientation, many Asians prefer terms like "we," "us," and "ours" to "I," "me," and "mine";
- Ranks and titles are important to many Asians and used frequently. This may even surface in an informal training environment where everyone has been told to use first names and people are acquainted. An Asian learner might refer to someone as Mr. Bob or Miss Betty;
- Time and the concept of hurrying to meet a deadline at the expense of disregarding others and what they value is a foreign concept;
- Religious affiliations are often strong;
- Physical contact and facial expressions are often minimal. Patting someone on the back or putting an arm around someone's shoulder in the workplace is not typically done;
- Touch between strangers, especially those of the opposite sex, is typically frowned on;
- The head is often considered the residence of the soul; therefore, touching a person's head potentially places him or her in jeopardy or invites evil in the mind of many Asians;
- Personal cleanliness is valued and expected;
- Sitting with legs crossed and the soles of feet facing someone is considered rude and insulting in a number of countries, since the foot is the lowest part of the body;
- Space between individuals is often at least six inches farther than what many Westerners consider comfortable;
- Some see animated expressions or gestures as a sign of a lack of control;
- Respect and humility are key cultural values. This is often demonstrated by avoiding direct eye contact or lowering eyes when talking, especially to someone older or who is an actual or perceived superior (socially or in the workplace);

continued on the next page

Exhibit 2. Cultural Awareness Tips, *continued*

Asian/Asian-American Cultures, *continued*

- Privacy is valued, especially among strangers. Discussions or inquiries regarding a person's occupation, income, politics, current events, controversial topics, family life, or spouse should be avoided. Any of these could potentially lead to disharmony or a loss of face;
- Trust is a crucial element in business. Before getting down to business, you will need to spend time (possibly months and numerous meetings) to establish trust before broaching negotiations or business topics;
- An indirect style of communication is often used, along with silence. For example, instead of saying "no" (which could cause someone to lose face) to an assertive facilitator, an Asian learner might agree to lead a small group discussion. She or he may later regret or resent being forced into the role and stop participating in the session or fail to return for future training;
- Facial expressions are often suppressed;
- Belching after a meal is often considered a show of satisfaction;
- Some people of this group use laughter or giggling to hide embarrassment, anger, sorrow, discomfort with a situation, nervousness, or displeasure. A hand is often used to cover the mouth when laughing or giggling.

European American/Anglo-American/White Cultures

Since the continent of Europe extends so far and encompasses many ethnic groups and cultures, this list applies primarily to European, Anglo-American, and White Westernized countries and people. Some shared values and characteristics by people with European American/Anglo-American White/Westernized heritages include the following:

- Direct nonverbal communication is prominent among many Westernized people (eye contact, nodding while listening, or facing a speaker when seated);
- Use of direct questions for personal information is permissible and often appreciated;
- Emotions are often not publicly expressed, especially among strangers or men;
- Hand gestures are often prominent during communication (for example, an "A-OK" symbol);
- Touching in public between opposite sexes is viewed as rude in many countries (England, Germany, and Scandinavia). In the workplace, inter-sex touching is typically not condoned (United States) because of legal restrictions and the fear of harassment charges;
- Spatial distance preferences tend to be wider (in Northern Europe), especially among strangers;
- Sunglasses and hats are considered functional items to be worn only outside and removed when coming indoors;
- "Taking turns" in conversation dictates that one person has the floor until all of his or her points are made;
- Showing emotions during disagreements is perceived as the beginning of conflict, which can escalate if left unchecked;
- Inquiring about the jobs, family, and so forth of a newcomer or participant from this group is often viewed as being friendly;
- Many cultures are past-oriented and change-resistant;
- Individualism is common in relationships or when handling problems, rather than relying on others;
- Long-term business relationships are often preferred over "quick sales."

Exhibit 2. Cultural Awareness Tips, *continued*

Middle Eastern Cultures

Some shared values and characteristics by people with Middle Eastern heritage include the following:

- Emotion is expressed easily by many people from this group (smiling, laughing, crying);
- Grief or sadness is often exaggerated (crying or wailing);
- Direct eye contact is often used to show interest and help someone understand truthfulness of another person. Failure to reciprocate is often seen as a lack of trustworthiness;
- Speaking loudly often indicates strength, while a soft voice sends a message of weakness;
- Touching or passing items, especially food, with the left hand is a social insult since that is the "bathroom" hand used for toilet functions;
- In many Islamic cultures, touching between genders (even hand shakes) is inappropriate; however, touching (hand holding and hugs) between members of the same sex is appropriate and acceptable as a show of friendship;
- Body odors are often considered normal and appropriate (for example, breath that smells heavily of garlic or perspiration/body odor);
- Standing in close proximity is common when talking;
- Time is viewed as fluid; therefore, taking time to get to know someone and building trust are important elements in business. People and relationships are more important than a company or job;
- Honor and dignity are important personal characteristics; therefore, you should avoid expressing doubts or criticism about a person or his or her possessions when others are present;
- A circuitous speech pattern is common and it may take a while to "get to the point." Be patient and professional while listening;
- Changes in plans, schedules, and meetings are common;
- Giving special treatment to friends and family members is considered an obligation;
- Religious festivals and events normally supersede other events and business;
- Eating pork is often forbidden by law in countries where Islam or Judaism is the primary religion;
- Islamic law frowns on profiteering; therefore product pricing should not be viewed as excessive;
- Women have a lesser role in many Islamic-based cultures and they normally do not participate in business dealings. Also, when traveling in Islamic countries women are often required to dress in such a way that their arms, legs, torso, and faces are concealed (This includes foreign visitors);
- Asking a host about the health of his spouse is insulting.

Conclusion

Many factors are related to the environment that must be considered when preparing to deliver a training or educational program. When developing materials and preparing to deliver information, effective trainers and educators strive to incorporate a variety of tools and strategies to better communicate and to occupy learners. As research continues to find, novelty, enthusiasm, sound communication skills, and concepts of brain-based learning are some of the most effective tools for helping ensure that learning is taking place and that information gained is actually transferred back to the real world.

Bibliography

Dunn, R., & Dunn, K. (1987). Dispelling outmoded beliefs about student learning. *Educational Leadership, 44*(6), pp. 55–61.

Herzberg, F., Mausner, B., & Snyderman, B.B. (1959). *The motivation to work* (2nd ed.). New York: John Wiley & Sons.

Lozanov, G. (1991). On the problems of the anatomy, physiology, and biochemistry of cerebral activities in the global-artistic approach in modern suggestopedagogic training. *The Journal of the Society for Accelerative Learning and Teaching, 16*(2), pp. 101–116.

Lucas, R.W. (1994). *Effective interpersonal relationships.* Burr Ridge, IL: Irwin.

Lucas, R.W. (1999). *The big book of flip charts.* New York: McGraw-Hill.

Lucas, R.W. (2003). *The creative training idea book: Inspired tips and techniques for engaging and effective learning.* New York: AMACOM.

Maslow, A.H. (1970). *Motivation and personality* (2nd ed.). New York: Harper & Row.

Mehrabian, A. (1968, September). Communication without words. *Psychology Today*, pp. 52–55.

Trainer Resources

American Society of Composers, Authors, and Publishers (ASCAP), (800) 952-7227, www.ascap.com—License agreements for use of copyrighted songs and music.

The BrainStore, (858) 546-7555/(800) 325-4769, www.thebrainstore.com—Books and reference materials, props related to brain-based learning and teaching.

Broadcast Music Inc (BMI), (800) 925-8451, www.bmi.com—License agreements for use of copyrighted songs and music.

Creative Learning Tools, www.creativelearningtools.com—Themed buttons, creative products, books.

Creative Presentation Resources, Inc., (800) 308-0399, www.presentationresources.net—Toys, games, Koosh® balls, incentives, presentation aids, training books, articles, videos.

MindWare, (800) 274-6123, www.mindwareonline.com—Creative games, books, and materials.

Successories, (630) 820-7200, www.successories.com—Motivational posters, plaques, books, and incentives.

Robert William Lucas *holds dual roles as president of Creative Presentation Resources—a creative training and products company—and as a founding managing partner for Global Performance Strategies, LLC—an organization specializing in performance-based training, consulting services, and life planning seminars. He has extensive experience in human resource development, management, and customer service. Published works include* The Creative Training Idea Book: Inspired Tips & Techniques for Engaging and Effective Learning *and* The BIG Book of Flip Charts.

A Comprehensive, Effective, Proven Model to Develop Leaders

Lois B. Hart and Charlotte S. Waisman

Summary

In 1998, the authors launched The Women's Leadership Institute (WLI) with the following goal: to prepare women for more effective corporate leadership within their companies. Because of the many accomplishments that have been achieved as part of the WLI program, we are ready to identify some of the markers of our success with the Institute, the six elements in the comprehensive program, and, additionally, comment on the results to date.

Although this article focuses on our creation of a gender-specific program, we strongly believe that this leadership model will work with more diverse groups of developing leaders.

> Excellence is an art won by training and habituation. We do not act rightly because we have virtue or excellence, but rather we have those because we have acted rightly. We are what we repeatedly do. Excellence then, is not an act but a habit.
> —Aristotle

> **Monica Hahn, Aramark**
>
> I looked around and there was no other program out there that offered the same combination of content, application, and coaching. WLI spread it over a year, giving me a chance to apply what I'd learned (with my coach's help) in between sessions. For me the professional development planning done with my coach was the most important and valuable part of the program! The coaching really enabled me to customize the program to my individual and corporate needs. On another front, it can be lonely at the top—the further you move up the corporate ladder, the fewer people you know who are at your own level. WLI and the Women's Vision Foundation offered me a network of professionals to learn, grow, and laugh with.

The Genesis of the Women's Leadership Institute

In our professional lives, we have often had the opportunity to utilize materials and curricula from other colleagues and thought leaders. Over the years, as we explored others' fragmented approaches to leadership development, we were dissatisfied with their approaches. For example, we saw instances of the following:

- Training without contact with a manager;
- Training with no connection to a development plan;
- Coaching only the individual leader;
- Organization development interventions with no connection to personal or company development initiatives
- In-house mentor programs with no connection to training or coaching; and
- Programs with no follow-up, so participants left "high" from good training yet received no support for putting new learning into action.

We closely examined earlier leadership development and training models like those offered by Leadership Texas and Leadership America, programs offered by local Chambers of Commerce, and examples found in books like Linkage Inc.'s, *Best Practices in Leadership Development Handbook*.

Every program had features and benefits that were valuable; yet we still were not ready to adopt anyone else's approach. We tried to identify our major concerns. They centered on the disjointed elements we noted earlier, as well as a few additional essentials:

- Was it possible to improve the ROI organizations were receiving on their HRD dollars?

- What would be the impact of working with individual leaders for at least one year?

- Could we combine all aspects of professional development, education, and experiences?

So in 1998, Lois B. Hart, who already had over thirty years of experience working with all kinds of companies and was the author of twenty books and tapes, decided to move her long-time vision into action. She began discussing her ideas with colleagues, Charlotte S. Waisman among them. They knew that a successful business depended on skillful navigation by leaders who could manage people and resources to accomplish the organization's vision. They were also aware that, to remain competitive and viable, a company must invest in its employees.

Yet the statistics for women in business showed that this substantial sector of the workforce continued to be an underdeveloped resource, a detriment not only to the women themselves, but also to companies that were missing critical opportunities for profitability and growth. Women comprise 52 percent of the nation's workforce; yet this sector is largely ignored. Women held fewer than 6 percent of top leadership positions in corporations, even though women comprised almost 42 percent of middle management (U.S. Census Bureau, 2002).

To further develop their vision, a research and action team was formed with members who included various corporate women executives, leadership development experts, organization development consultants, and curriculum developers. Many of the team had, for some time, been thinking about the issues Lois and Charlotte posed. The team spent two years researching the status of women in corporations, identifying the critical leadership skills and competencies, and developing the comprehensive program.

The results of the study, thoughts, and practices of this group culminated in an organization called The Women's Leadership Institute (WLI), an all-inclusive program that fast-tracks mid-level corporate women to positions of greater responsibility and achievement within their organizations.

We hope that, by our disseminating our thoroughly tested WLI methodology, others will take our plan, use our model, and deliver exceptional leadership materials. We truly invite each of you to try our ideas, and we stand ready to aid and assist in any ways we can so that you too can provide an outstanding, comprehensive leadership development experience that will enable each participant to grow mightily.

Searching for a Leadership Model

There are, certainly, more books on leadership than one has the time or energy to read. Our planning team read many books and reviews and reported to one another on the results and the creative theories each espoused. This article is not meant as a review of that prior work. Our goal is to present our model, referred to as "Leadership Through Action," as it underlies every activity and idea of the WLI program.

We felt that we needed to find at least one of the many books on leadership that would provide a basis for our work, to augment what we were teaching, training, and espousing. The authors whose body of work spoke to us most clearly are Jim Kouzes and Barry Posner (K-P), especially their highly successful book, now in a third edition, *The Leadership Challenge*. Unlike so many others with leadership models, these authors have conducted continuous research that is inclusive. Women and minorities are clearly part of their investigations. We also saw that we could use the theoretical basis of their five practices (see below) and create action-oriented learning activities to "cement" their points as well as our own.

1. Model the Way.
2. Inspire a Shared Vision.
3. Challenge the Process.
4. Enable Others to Act.
5. Encourage the Heart.

As we reviewed other ideas and models, we also found that those leadership skills, practices, and attitudes cited would often fit into the K-P model as well as our own beliefs regarding what should be taught.

As we developed WLI, we created it as an amalgam of best practices, wherever we found them. WLI is therefore a potpourri of the best practices we have found. We will provide an example of how we utilize K-P's five practices and their 360-degree feedback instrument, both of which will be discussed as we disseminate our full WLI model.

> **Deb Morton, McDATA**
>
> One of the greatest gifts I received from WLI was getting myself back. Maybe a better way to say it is, I can be myself and succeed. I'm aware of so many more options in terms of dealing with conflict, entering a conference room, facilitating agreement, understanding the importance of vision, and making connections. I feel like I have choices and options in charting my course.

The WLI Leadership Model

Often in training, we begin by teaching what we know. This creates a linear model: from the teacher/trainer to the audience.

As shown in Figure 1, a more successful strategy is to place the participant in the center. This verifies her importance, the singularity of effort made for each person, and the commitment to personalize what will help grow each person.

Figure 1. The Program Design

Around this person, there are six additional circles that clearly support each element of the leadership program. Since the model is circular, we can enter at any point, so our discussion can start with any of these essentials. Yet each element/feature must be present and supportive if leadership through action is to create this positive leadership experience.

The Women's Leadership Institute expands women's leadership abilities with a wide-ranging approach to learning that takes place over a one-year period. An Institute *coach* assigned to each *participant* serves as the main link between the participant and the other elements of the Institute, providing personal guidance throughout the program.

WLI believes that for a woman to truly succeed in applying leadership skills, her *manager* must also be a partner. The manager works closely with the Institute coach in developing the participant's program. WLI participants identify the learning style that works best for them. The participant and her coach develop an individualized *Professional Development Plan*, identifying her job objectives and the most effective method by which to learn those skills. This plan is the foundation for her personal journey.

Every four to five weeks, participants attend a *workshop* to newly learn or reconnect with skills based on core leadership competencies. They also network with other businesswomen. Between workshops, participants work on assignments (learning applications) that immediately apply to their current positions or their career development.

Each participant is shown how to find a *mentor* from within her company or from her professional field. While the mentor guides the participant, the mentor interacts with the Institute coach to help the participant achieve her goals. Additional, customized coaching occurs when a woman needs supplementary assistance in specific job skills. In these cases, expert *resource people* act as short-term advisors to the participant.

Also, executives from the participants' companies (including the participant's manager and mentor) attend the annual WLI Culture Shift—Building Cultures for Long-Term Success program to learn about the best corporate practices used to develop, promote, and retain women leaders.

Continuing education units from Colorado State University are granted at the end of the WLI year-long program. Through this multi-tiered educational approach, WLI provides businesswomen and their companies a full toolkit to meet the challenges of effective growth and change.

The Coach Is Key to the Leader's Growth

Our WLI coaches are experienced professionals who are skilled in coaching, listening, problem solving, networking, learning, and achievement motivation. They also have at least one strong professional area of competency. For example, they may excel at interpersonal communication, negotiation, or change management.

Each participant is assigned a personal coach who serves as the link between her and the rest of the Institute program. The coach works with the participant approximately one hour a week. After an initial face-to-face meeting, most coaching is done on the telephone. As the participant's "touchstone" throughout the WLI program, the coach helps the woman identify her career goals as well as her leadership skill growth areas and development needs.

The core 360-degree instrument used both at the beginning and the end of the WLI year is the *Leadership Practices Inventory*, created and tested by Jim Kouzes and Barry Posner. Participants use the feedback received from those who observe their leadership practices—including their own manager plus direct reports and colleagues—to identify specific competencies where the participant wishes to expand or refine her skills.

Together the coach and the participant develop an individualized Professional Development Plan that identifies the participant's unique job needs, goals, and skills. The participant identifies her learning preferences, and learning activities are selected based on them.

This development plan will form the foundation for the application of leadership skills throughout the WLI year. At the end of the year it can also form the foundation of "Life After WLI." (We have in fact started a highly successful alumnae organization because of intense interest on the part of our participant/graduates.)

The Manager Partners with the Coach

We believe that for a leader to truly succeed in applying leadership skills, her manager must also be a supportive partner. In WLI, the manager works closely with the Institute coach to review the participant's goals, identify possible barriers to her growth, and identify resources within the company that may help the participant. The coach and manager have an initial face-to-face meeting lasting one to two hours. They continue to talk throughout the year's program, often touching base with a telephone call once a month.

Just-in-Time Coaching with Resource People

We know that sometimes we need additional resources to meet our participant's goals. In these cases, the Institute grants five hours with expert resource people who offer special skills and knowledge and who act as just-in-time, short-term coaches for the participant. For example, she may need help with fiscal management, project management, or information technology issues.

Monthly Workshops on Leadership

Participants attend eleven, day-long workshops, starting with a three-day offsite retreat. The remaining workshops are held approximately every four to five weeks. During the 100 hours of training, accelerated learning techniques are used, so participants quickly learn the skills found in effective leaders. The wisdom of guest executive women from other companies also enriches many sessions.

> **Kris Britton, Xcel Energy**
>
> I did not realize the true value of inspiring vision until WLI. "Inspiring Vision" helped me to align activities with those I work with. I learned the importance of documenting and revisiting vision, but most importantly, sharing it constantly.
>
> Networking is a skill that was non-existent for me until WLI helped me demystify it. In less than one year, my professional and personal network has increased dramatically. Because of my newfound network, I get things accomplished more effectively by tapping into the network and plugging others into my network of resources to help them with their needs. Networking has also allowed me to give back to others.

WLI participants complete workplace assignments, applying what they are learning to their actual work lives. There are also brief assignments that prepare them for upcoming workshop sessions.

For instance, in the workshop they clarify their own values and leadership vision. Then we ask them to read about the Kouzes and Posner practice, Inspire a Vision, found in their book, *The Leadership Challenge.* With the step-by-step directions we provide, as well as the reading they have done, the participants' learning application is to next lead *their* work unit or team in identifying shared values, vision, and mission.

The time for participants to complete workplace assignments varies depending on individual needs, but past participants indicate they spend one to three hours a week applying what they learned.

Some of the recent topics that workshops have featured include:

- Applying cutting-edge leadership theory to succeed in business;

- Learning skills based on the Kouzes and Posner leadership model and their 360-degree assessment, the *Leadership Practices Inventory*;

- Clarifying values and beliefs;

- Leading with a shared vision;
- Staying abreast of change and technology with innovative practices;
- Enhancing risk taking;
- Taking decisive action and planning strategically;
- Solving ethical dilemmas;
- Gaining political savvy and contacts;
- Practicing proven networking skills;
- Negotiating with confidence;
- Communicating with effective conflict resolution and presentation skills;
- Identifying one's leadership styles and expanding flexibility;
- Coaching and empowering employees appropriately;
- Integrating best practices to lead diverse employees;
- Addressing gender-based issues and behaviors;
- Using emotional intelligence to increase overall effectiveness;
- Creating balance in one's life;
- Utilizing the diverse talents of four generations of employees in the workplace; and
- Recognizing and celebrating both individual and team achievements.

There is often a gap between good ideas and effective action. The skill building fostered in The Women's Leadership Institute helps women to grow their strategic thinking and couple it with positive risk taking. What are the traps that can "get" you? Where are the pitfalls? Who are your strategic partners?

Learning these competencies in the workshops is the first step. Having a great support system is the next. Women not only work with a coach and gain the benefit of her years of experience in corporate America, but their support system to take those ideas to fruition is enhanced as the coach works with the participant's manager and mentor.

In WLI the approach changes. You no longer have to "think about it." You internalize how to take effective action. It becomes second nature. Then you start helping others, such as your peers and direct reports.

Mentors Show the Way

Throughout history, mentors have served to assist the passage of the apprentice to the level of master. People who are successful in their careers have received guidance, encouragement, and advice from more experienced individuals, who are often called mentors.

In the Women's Leadership Institute program, we want every woman to have the benefits of a mentor relationship. The mentor adds the dimension of healthy political knowledge and internal company history to each woman's specific work environment. The mentor champions as well as coaches the participant and opens doors of opportunity for her through participation on special projects or work teams.

> **Barbara Beckner, Qwest Communications**
>
> Others observed changes in me, including how I drive the team to accountable results, set clear objectives that are tied to measurable results, and how I networked within the company to identify individuals or teams that can help us achieve our goals. From my mentor I gained a totally new perspective, new resource pool, and professional guidance that has proven to be invaluable.

Using a separate mentoring booklet we provide at the beginning of the year, each participant assesses what she needs and wants from a mentor, expands her list of potential mentors, and learns how to find and work effectively with a mentor. The mentor may be from within the woman's company or from her professional field. Once selected, the mentor regularly communicates with the participant's Institute coach. Together they help the participant identify developmental goals, locate resources and opportunities to expand her horizon, and collaborate on potential barriers to her advancement.

Building Cultures for Long-Term Success

Once we developed the first five elements of our model—manager, coach, resource people, mentor, and workshops—we quickly realized that a critical element was missing—the work culture. Large numbers of women were leaving the corporate world, and for sound reasons, many of which were embedded in the work culture. With our experience in organization development, we decided to add this sixth element, Culture Shift, to our model, as our way to shift the company cultures in what we anticipated would be an effective direction.

Challenger, Gray and Christmas, a well-known outplacement firm, made some interesting predictions for 2004. Among their ideas is that more women will move into the executive suite. If this is true, then there is more reason than ever to assure that these women are well supported in their workplace culture and that their employers value their contributions.

Culture shift is a profound feature of the Women's Leadership Institute program. It involves executives from each participant's company, including her manager and mentor. We also include other key top executives and those who manage human resources, training, and development.

We hold an annual Culture Shift program. Our primary goal is to facilitate changes in the ways that companies recruit, develop, advance, and retain women leaders by showcasing best practices. Our secondary interest is to provide a meaningful professional network for these executives from diverse companies in which to share their successes.

We provide an assessment called the *Stages of Company Development: Basic, Progressive, and Best Practices* that covers four organizational categories: Leadership, Environment, Acquisition and Development, and Delivery. The executives rank what initiatives they are currently doing in each category. One of the most intriguing parts of the day occurs when they share their rankings with one another. Of course they gain ideas from one another as well!

In our Culture Shift day-long forum we present the business case that supports best practices found in companies. We demonstrate how to change internal policies and procedures that are barriers blocking the full development of businesswomen. Representatives from area companies explain how they engage top leaders, set up a women's network, develop an in-house mentor program, and establish accountability for diversity goals.

Two of our presenting companies in 2004, Ernst and Young and Accenture, had recently won the prestigious 2003 Catalyst Award. Other companies who attended and engaged in lively dialogue after the presentations included Qwest, Xcel Energy, TIAA-CREF, and Coors Brewing Company.

Learning Models and Methodology

In each part of the WLI leadership model noted above, the trainers and guests utilize a number of learning models and methodologies that enhance the overall program significantly.

These include, but are not limited to the following:

- Accelerated and adult learning concepts, which help to define what is taught and how it is presented;

- Assessment of "how they learn best," which guides the choice of training methods;

- Instruments that capture the skill level of various competencies are presented and thoroughly discussed; and

- Books and audiotapes of newer leadership theories and practices are circulated for reading and listening between sessions.

As designers and facilitators of training, we are committed to the use of varied training methods to both present a stimulating workshop experience and to assure that we meet the variety of ways people learn. As presenters we come with our own unconscious bias toward doing things according to our own learning needs and style, so it takes a conscious effort, but we have been successful! Our trainers review the information participants provided in the "How You Learn Best" exercise so we can ensure the variety of methodologies needed to accelerate their learning. (See the *2001 Annual* for a description of this activity.)

Our pool of methods includes but is not limited to case studies, journaling, assessments, role plays, movement, and discussion, among others that are fully described in the Glossary at the end of this article.

We follow a well-defined sequence that ensures learning is retained:

- 10 to 12 minutes to rouse the participants' attention, raise their curiosity, and set objectives for the module;

- 10 to 13 minutes to present new learning material, but not only in lecture/presentation format. We have structured activities that encourage discovery, shared information in small groups, and problem-solving cases and clinics;

- 15 minutes to help participants integrate the new knowledge through discussion in dyads, activity where skills are practiced, as well as review games;

- 10 to 12 minutes to identify action steps through a written plan, peer support, or developing a list of possible steps and, additionally, follow-up work with their coaches; and

- 7 to 10 minutes to break for refreshments, socialize, do stretching exercises, and switch where they are sitting.

Here are some additional guidelines all of the trainers have committed to following:

- Start off the session or topic with a brief intrapersonal activity where the learner writes down three problems or questions she has about the topic under discussion. Pair them up for 2 or 3 minutes to compare notes. With the total group, poll for some examples. Provide a list of the biggest challenges of the topic and address those in the presentation.

- When writing points on a flip chart, poster, or overhead acetate, use a variety of colors. Also vary the color of the handouts. Appropriate pictures are also helpful!

- Draw volunteers from the audience who can illustrate your points.

- Increase their memory of the key points by connecting to their experiences and knowledge. Chunk learning into no more than five to nine ideas or points so that the information means something to them. Provide an example of what you are describing either visually or orally, to further lock in your point.

- As you facilitate, be positive with your words, facial expressions, and other body language. Refrain from negative words such as "difficult" or "confusing," which might set up a negative suggestion to learners.

- Gently correct the learner's mistakes within 60 seconds. When "experts" from the audience become overly involved making comments or asking questions, you can get off track and irritate the rest of the audience. Handle this with a limit of one question from each person and offer to handle more questions privately, after the session.

- End with a review exercise that further locks in the learning.

- Carefully plan a closure that is a strong conclusion. Quotes, humorous stories about things to avoid, or a comment about looking to the future always work well.

Recommended Books

Two training handbooks provide our trainers with the basis of activities for the leadership skills' modules: *50 Activities for Developing Leaders, Vol. I*, written by Lois Hart and *50 Activities for Developing Leaders, Vol. II*, co-authored by Lois Hart and Charlotte Waisman.

We also recommend Lois' book, *Training Methods That Work*, for a review of seventeen different methods you can incorporate in workshop designs.

We provide participants with a core set of books, along with an extensive bibliography. Additional books and audiotapes may be borrowed. These resources expand the participant's knowledge of the subject. The books and tapes are brought to each workshop session and are shared.

Our core books are four; we give them to each participant and refer to them often within the sessions. As noted earlier, our foundational book is *The Leadership Challenge* by Jim Kouzes and Barry Posner. It gives a clear explanation of the five leadership practices. We assign readings from the book that support the topics presented in our workshops.

We also give each participant a copy of the *Managers' Pocket Guide to Dealing with Conflict* by Lois Hart (distributed in the Conflict Module). In our module on celebrations at work, we distribute *Celebrate!* by Lois Hart, Mario Tamayo, and Ken Blanchard. Finally, *Great Connections* by Anne Babor and Lynne Waymon is used to teach networking skills throughout the year.

Instruments

There are three instruments to highlight here that we utilize in the WLI program. The first is the *Leadership Practices Inventory* created by Kouzes and Posner. This is completed in the first month and then redone in the final month of the program. At the onset, the participants and coaches use the feedback to set professional goals for the year and the trainers use the summary to identify which of the five practices on which to focus. This instrument is now available in both paper and online formats.

Early in our program, participants are given Ken Blanchard's, *LBA II*, an excellent instrument where the participants themselves are able to identify their perceptions of their dominant and secondary leadership styles.

In our Conflict Module, we administer the *Thomas-Kilmann Conflict Mode Instrument*. The five styles—competing, collaborating, compromising, avoiding, and accommodating—are thoroughly discussed. We solicit examples from the participants and ask them to describe constructive and destructive behaviors for each type. Flexibility issues that personal leadership and conflict styles raise are also strategized.

Research and Results

Our hypothesis was that a comprehensive leadership development program design, combining the elements of training, coaching, mentors, and organization consulting, would result in significant differences in the company and in the individual leaders.

When we started WLI, we hypothesized that our participants would receive promotions, stay loyal to their companies, and model appropriate, effective leadership behaviors, both within their organizations and in their larger communities.

We also questioned what would be the impact of a one-year program, rather than shorter leadership training. We wondered as well whether we had the ability to create this combined development, evaluation, and experiential experience.

We were not disappointed. While WLI has not (at this time) developed quantitative measures, it is evident through close, serious evaluation and anecdotal information that WLI has made a significant difference on many levels.

Cost Savings

Establishing a "return on investment" is always difficult to track with educational programs, but it is apparent that our participating companies benefited financially. It is clear from our discussions with managers and mentors at our participating companies that the program pays for itself through cost savings or incremental revenue increase because of increased productivity.

John V. Noonan, in his excellent book *Elevators,* shows a way that, in addition to determining the quality of training programs that Donald Kirkpatrick wrote about many years ago, it is possible to compute a *dollar value* for every course. Noonan recommends that a monthly report to management include a spreadsheet that shows the value added to the business by every course, and he carefully details the process by which one might perform this exercise.

The Noonan model is based on four factors: salary, time invested, pre-training productivity, and post-training productivity. We are currently looking for a Ph.D. student who would be willing to do a longitudinal study based on Noonan's work, so that our anecdotal knowledge can be confirmed.

Retention of Competent Women Leaders

Our commitment is to the employer. We have an excellent track record of women who stay loyal to the company who sponsored them in the Women's Leadership Institute. The only individuals who are no longer with the company that sponsored them in WLI were those who were laid off during recent difficult economic conditions. With large numbers of people changing jobs every two to three years, we are quite pleased with this metric.

By creating an environment in which women can advance, companies avoid the costs associated with replacing women managers who may otherwise leave in search of more amenable workplaces. Currently, HR specialists estimate that it costs a company at least one to one-and-a-half times a manager's salary for one year to replace that individual (Denby, 2004).

It can also be argued that the "soft" measures of retention still contribute to cost savings for the company. These include factors such as employee motivation, a variable not measured in dollar terms, but nonetheless capable of influencing costs.

Utilization of Talent

Seventy-five percent of our graduates have received promotions to higher-level leadership positions, bringing to their companies new insights and skills. It is here that the one-year influence of the WLI program can be most clearly felt. Because the women practice the skills they learn all year, and their coach discusses this impact with them, the participants' talents are recognized and utilized on many work projects. We know that the executives are watching the women they send to WLI; after all, they are selected for their high potential. It has been very gratifying to us that several of our participants were promoted even during the program.

Increased Productivity and Efficiency

Our leadership program helps unblock highly qualified women so that they can perform at their peak.

Women who have been through the WLI program have increased productivity. They know how to handle barriers, those issues and problems that may affect their being accepted as full partners in the workplace. They have learned positive strategies for effective work challenges! They work well either alone or in teams. WLI women have enhanced and expanded the skill set they need to do their jobs more efficiently. They want to give back to their companies. WLI helps companies shift their cultures so women feel included; this has contributed to comprehensive results.

Leading Change

We teach leaders how to be effective change agents, leading others during difficult times. We teach them how to plan for major change, how to tie an initiative to the company's values and vision, and how to involve the employees. Even during the year's program, we observed our leaders effectively and confidently guiding their staff and teams through some rocky changes in their companies.

> **Sandra Kong, TIAA-CREF**
>
> I have become more focused and determined. I no longer walk away from uncomfortable situations. I am bolder about addressing issues. What I attained from WLI is the confidence I needed to be a more effective leader.

Reaching New Markets

Leadership experts have recognized the value of having a diverse workforce. Diverse teams are better positioned to anticipate the needs of a wider range of consumers. When a company commits to promoting diversity among its decision makers, it has the ability to capture and profit from varied market segments. In WLI we have developed women, both white and of color, to visibly lead in their companies.

Another remarkable benefit is that companies with a reputation for offering development and promotion opportunities attract other professionals, both men and women, to the organization as well. It is this result that led our team to feel confident that we had demonstrated a combination of development, education, and experiences that was most meaningful to our participants.

Impact on the Participants

Throughout this article, we have included some testimonials from those who have experienced our unique leadership program. They document specific impacts on their professional careers and their lives. But in addition, we want to describe three other ways we currently measure our program's effectiveness.

First, we continuously solicit feedback from the participants. At the end of every workshop day, we provide evaluations. They vary in what we ask so they reflect different kinds of evaluation. Sometimes the evaluations are verbal; most are written. Our Leadership Team reviews the feedback and incorporates appropriate changes in the programs and events that follow. The changes can be substantive (for example, "When discussing power I would like to talk about effective ways to work with those whose power style differs significantly from mine") or minor (for example, "More Diet Coke, please"), but we take them all seriously and strive to exceed our customers' expectations.

We do level II (Kirkpatrick) evaluations as often as we can. We also solicit feedback mid-year about their coaching experience.

Second, at the end of the year we conduct a very extensive evaluation of the entire year's program with participants. This allows for time and reflection to color their thoughts about the experience. Their comments are often widespread, yet truly identify that they are very appreciative of their WLI experience.

Third, we chose to administer the K-P *Leadership Practices Inventory* at the beginning and end of the year-long program, expecting that their scores would improve. We ensure that the same observers participate in the post-LPI.

Approximately 80 percent of our participants' scores improved as perceived by themselves and their observers. But another pattern was puzzling to us. We found that about 20 percent of our participants' scores dropped in one or two of the five practices.

We wondered how that could happen since we intentionally "taught to the K-P model"! After much discussion, including talking directly with Jim Kouzes, the creator, about this issue he agreed with us that this phenomenon could be caused by the following:

1. The leader reassessing her skills. At the beginning she felt she was quite competent at "Modeling the Way" but when she learned what that really involved, she realized that she still had work to do to improve this practice.

2. The observers "raised the bar" or reset their expectations. Knowing this person was in a very special executive program, they now expected more of her, something like, "Well, now show me what you've learned!" The observers may expect more dramatic changes. They may also know more about leadership because they "read" the items in the LPI.

In spite of these anomalies, we still highly recommend the pre and post use of the Kouzes and Posner LPI instrument in any leadership program that lasts four to six months or more.

Christine White, Coors

Wow!! What a year! Beginning with a retreat to meet all of these wonderful, high-energy leaders in the Denver area, and then to get to work with them on a monthly basis throughout the year was an amazing gift!! The time has gone so fast, and I am certain that the learning and networking will continue long afterwards.

> **Jill, Director of Corporate Development, WLI**
>
> As I've observed the growth and confidence that's taken place in women as they participate in WLI, I've wondered at times if they know how amazing their transformations have been. Reading the evaluations from those just completing the program made me realize that they do "get" the changes that have occurred. The following two statements reflect some other things that happen with and to our participants:
>
> > "Now, I have set my sights on moving up the ladder [to top positions]. I have also considered other positions that I might not have considered before. Moving up the ladder doesn't seem nearly as daunting or mysterious a process."
> >
> > "It didn't hit me until about halfway through the program that I experienced a significant shift in my thinking. I was at an event and noticed two of my co-workers hanging back. The first thought that popped into my head was, 'Take your place at the table, you belong here.' Previously, I had felt like I needed permission or an invitation to take my place at the table. I know now that I belong and am comfortable in a leadership position wherever that takes me. Sort of like Dorothy in the *Wizard of Oz*; the only permission I ever needed was my own."

How You Can Start

Start by adding one or two new features to what you are doing now!

If the WLI model and its record of achievement also stimulate you to think about ways you can incorporate some of its characteristics, begin to add our elements to whatever you are currently doing with leadership training.

One colleague of ours said that, at her company, leadership training was a one-day workshop done at a sales meeting once a year. During 2003 she added a coaching component for their ten male and female sales managers. This created a small group of leaders who were more fully bonded to the company, committed to their personal growth and to growing their market share, and to reaching out to tell others within the company of the marvelous feelings they had when their coaches substantiated their thoughts, ideas, and plans. For 2004, our colleague will add another incremental step.

Learn the Kouzes and Posner leadership model thoroughly. We encourage you to read their excellent primer *The Leadership Challenge*. Test out the *Leadership Practices*

Inventory for yourself, with you as the Leader. Attend their workshop and certification program (www.theleadershipchallenge.biz).

Create a leadership team. Include people from the following departments or other departments where you know you have a champion: OD, HR, training, sales, instructional design, operations, plus some executives who have been mentors and/or attended substantial leadership training themselves. People who are thoughtful and care about employee development can be outstanding supporters of leadership initiatives.

Read the books and research that provides a benchmark for your leadership program. We have included some of our recent reading in the bibliography.

Identify companies or compatible organizations where you could jointly design and implement a leadership program. For example, several smaller high-tech firms might combine resources to develop a program for their leaders.

Contact us. Give us feedback. Let us help you.

Visit the website of our sponsoring organization, The WomensVision Foundation, at www.womensvision.org.

> Leadership is the art of accomplishing more than the science of management says is possible.
> —Colin Powell

Glossary of Training Methods*

Application. The trainer provides instructions or an assignment that will put the new learning into practice or use.

Assessment. The individual learner reflects or takes an instrument to evaluate her/his strengths, values, position on issues, or developmental needs.

Card Sort. Multiple items or ideas are listed on separated pieces of paper or cards, and participants sort, group, or rank them.

Case Study. A printed description of a realistic problem or scenario, which provides sufficient detail for participants to determine appropriate actions they might take.

Demonstration. The trainer (or a participant) shows how something works or is used by "walking" participants through each step.

Discussion. The trainer encourages dialogue among the participants (either in the total group or small groups) about an issue or content from the workshop, using both preplanned and spontaneous questions.

From *50 Activities to Develop Leaders*, Vol. II, by Hart and Waisman.

Feedback. Use of a process (either verbal or written) that provides information back to the individual.

Journaling. Written record of thoughts, reactions, or feeling.

Metaphor. A word or phrase ordinarily and primarily used for one thing or purpose is applied to an explanation of another.

Movement. Activity that involves walking, milling about, and/or stretching, sometimes to music.

Presentation. A planned talk, sometimes called a lecturette, to inform, report, instruct, motivate, or persuade.

Reflection. A quiet activity to write or think about an issue or content from the workshop.

Role Play. Enactment of a real-life incident or event or a created dramatized story that gives participants the opportunity to practice and experiment with new behaviors and then receive feedback.

Round Robin. When, in an orderly fashion, participants verbally complete sentence stems.

Simulation. An activity that gives the appearance of a real-life situation or experience.

Storytelling. Telling of a happening or connected series of happenings, whether true or fictional.

Video. Visual form of a scenario.

Visualization. Formation of a mental image not easily present to one's sight; once developed it is often shared either verbally or in writing.

Writing. Putting thoughts, reactions, and feelings to paper or on a keyboard.

Bibliography

Books

Ackerman Anderson, L., & Anderson, D. (2001). *The change leader's roadmap: How to navigate your organization's transformation.* San Francisco, CA: Pfeiffer.

Baber, A., & Waymon, L. (2002). *Make your contacts count.* New York: AMACOM.

Blanchard, K., & Peale, N.V. (1988). *The power of ethical management.* New York: William Morrow.

Blanchard, K., & O'Connor, M. (1995). *Managing by values*. Escondido, CA: Blanchard Family Partnership.

Bodenhamer, B., Min, D., & Hall, L.M. (2000). *The user's manual for the brain*. Trowbridge, Wiltshire, UK: Crown House Publishing Limited.

Bramson, R.M. (1981). *Coping with difficult people*. New York: Dell.

Bridges, W. (1991). *Managing transitions: Making the most of change*. Reading, MA: Addison-Wesley.

Catalyst. (1998). *Advancing women in business: The catalyst guide*. San Francisco, CA: Jossey-Bass.

Challenger, J.E. (2004, January 4). Revved workplace revives perks, multilingual and women. *The Denver Post*, Section G, p. 1.

Christensen, C. (2000). *The innovator's dilemma*. Cambridge, MA: Harvard Business School Press.

Cooper, R.K., & Sawaf, A. (1997). *Executive EQ*. New York: Penguin, Putnam Inc.

Covey, S.R. (1990). *The 7 habits of highly effective people*. New York: Simon & Schuster.

Davenport, T.H., et al. (2003). *What's the big idea: Creating and capitalizing on the best management thinking*. Cambridge, MA: Harvard Business School Press.

Deal, T.E., & Key, M.K. (1998). *Corporate celebration*. San Francisco, CA: Berrett-Koehler.

Denby, E.R. (2004, January). Do your family friendly programs make sense? *HR Magazine*, p. 78.

Downey, D., et al. (2001). *Assimilating new leaders: The key to executive retention*. New York: AMACOM.

Duff, C.S. (1999). *Learning from other women*. New York: AMACOM.

Gallagher, C. (2000). *Going to the top*. New York: Penguin Books.

George, B. (2003). *Authentic leadership*. San Francisco, CA: Jossey-Bass.

Germer, F. (2001). *Hard-won wisdom*. New York: The Berkley Publishing Group.

Gerstner, L.V., Jr. (2002). *Who says elephants can't dance*. New York: HarperCollins.

Goleman, D. (1997). *Emotional intelligence*. New York: Bantam Books.

Goleman, D. *(2000). Working with emotional intelligence*. New York: Bantam Books.

Goleman, D. (2002). *Primal leadership*. Cambridge, MA: Harvard Business School Press.

Halpern, B.L., et al. (2003). *Leadership presence*. New York: Gotham Books.

Hart, L.B. (1990). *Training methods that work*. Menlo Park, CA: Crisp.

Hart, L.B. (1994). *50 activities for developing leaders, Vol. I*. Amherst, MA: HRD Press.

Hart, L.B. (1996). *Faultless facilitation resource guide*. Amherst, MA: HRD Press.

Hart, L.B. (1999). *Manager's pocket guide to dealing with conflict*. Amherst, MA: HRD Press.

Hart, L.B., Tamayo, M., & Blanchard, K. (2004). *Celebrate!* Denver, CO: Author.

Hart, L.B., & Waisman, C. (2003). *50 activities for developing leaders, Vol. II*. Amherst, MA: HRD Press.

Heim, P., with Golant, S.K. (1993). *Hardball for women*. New York: Plume.

Heim, P., & Murphy, S. (2001). *In the company of women*. New York: Tarcher Putnam.

Hiam, A. (1998). *The manager's pocket guide to creativity.* Amherst, MA: HRD Press.
Kelley, T. (2001). *The art of innovation.* New York: Doubleday.
Kouzes, J.M., & Posner, B.Z. (1993). *Credibility.* San Francisco, CA: Jossey-Bass.
Kouzes, J.M., & Posner, B.Z. (1999). *Encouraging the heart.* San Francisco, CA: Jossey-Bass.
Kouzes, J.M., & Posner, B.Z. (2003). *The leadership challenge* (3rd ed.). San Francisco, CA: Jossey-Bass.
Kravitz, S.M., & Schubert, S.D. (2000). *Emotional intelligence works.* Menlo Park, CA: Crisp.
Lancaster, L.C., & Stillman, D. (2003). *When generations collide.* New York: Harper Business.
LeCompte, A. (2000). *Creating harmonious relationships.* New York: Atlantic Books.
LeDoux, J. (1996). *The emotional brain.* New York: Simon & Schuster.
Linkage Inc. (2000). *Best practices in leadership development handbook.* San Francisco, CA: Pfeiffer.
Lynn, A.B. (2002). *The emotional intelligence activity book.* Amherst, MA: HRD Press.
Maccoby, M. (2003). *The productive narcissist.* New York: Broadway Books.
Maxwell, J.C. (1993). *Developing the leader within you.* Nashville, TN: InJoy Company.
McCoy, C.W., Jr. (2002). *Why didn't I think of that?* Englewood Cliffs, NJ: Prentice Hall.
McGartland, G. (1994). *Thunder bolt thinking.* Austin, TX: Bernard-Davis Company.
Michalko, M. (2001). *Cracking creativity.* Berkeley, CA: Ten Speed Press.
Morrison, A.M. (1996). *The new leaders: Leadership diversity in America.* San Francisco, CA: Jossey-Bass.
Nelson, B. (1994). *1001 ways to reward employees.* New York: Workman.
Noonan, J.V. (1995). *Elevators: How to move training up from the basement.* Wheaton, IL: Twain Publishers.
Peoples, D. (1992). *Presentations plus.* New York: John Wiley & Sons.
RoAne, S. (1997). *What do I say next?* New York: Warner Books.
Ruderman, M.N., & Ohlott, P.J. (2002). *Standing at the crossroads: Next steps for high achieving women.* San Francisco, CA: Jossey-Bass.
Simmons, A. (2001). *The story factor: Secrets of influence from the art of storytelling.* New York: Perseus.
Simon, S., Howe, L.W., & Kirshenbaum, H. (1995). *Values clarification.* New York: Warner Books.
Smart, B.D. (1999). *Top grading: How leading companies win by hiring, coaching, and keeping the best people.* Englewood Cliffs, NJ: Prentice Hall.
Tichey, N.M. (1997). *The leadership engine.* New York: Harper Business.
U.S. Census Bureau. (2002). *A report on the glass ceiling initiative.* Washington, DC: Author.
U.S. Department of Labor. (2000). *Report on the American Workforce.* Washington, DC: Author.
Utterback, J.M. (1996). *Mastering the dynamics of innovation.* Cambridge, MA: Harvard Business School Press.
Wellington, S.W. (1998). *Advancing women in business: Best practices.* San Francisco, CA: Catalyst.

Wilder, L. (1999). *Seven steps to fearless speaking.* New York: John Wiley & Sons.

Zichy, S. (2001). *Women and the leadership Q.* New York: McGraw-Hill.

Instruments

Leadership Practices Inventory by Jim Kouzes and Barry Posner. Published by Pfeiffer. Available in paper and online formats. Visit www.pfeiffer.com or www.lpionline.com.

LBAII by Ken Blanchard. Published by Blanchard Training and Development, Inc. 800-728-6000.

Thomas-Kilmann Conflict Mode Instrument. Published by XICOM, 800-759-4266.

Lois B. Hart, Ed.D., *is the founder and executive director of the Women's Leadership Institute (WLI), a unique, year-long program of mentoring, coaching, and training executive women. Dr. Hart's background includes training, organization development, coaching, and public education experience; she has also written more than twenty-two books and tapes, including* Faultless Facilitation-A Resource Guide *and* Learning from Conflict. *Dr. Hart has an Ed.D. from the University of Massachusetts, where she studied organizational behavior and leadership development with Dr. Kenneth Blanchard.*

Charlotte S. Waisman, Ph.D., *is a hands-on trainer/coach/leader and team motivator. Her extensive work history includes human resources and training positions. For the last three years she has been the director of human resources at Ischemia Technologies. Earlier positions include one at Keane, Inc., where she was in charge of employee career development. Dr. Waisman has a Ph.D. from the School of Communications at Northwestern University in Evanston, Illinois. Her background also includes fourteen years as a tenured professor.*

Management Rhythm
Peter R. Garber

Summary

This brief article is perfect for a summary following a management-development session. It could also be sent as follow-up after a training or coaching session.

The Rhythm of Management

A one, and a two, and a three—now you're getting into the management rhythm. Just like when stepping out on the dance floor, you need to have a certain amount of rhythm to be successful as a manager. Life is all about rhythms. These rhythms are what make up our daily routines. Rhythms are really nothing more than patterns. Each day we repeat certain patterns as we go through the tasks and rituals that make up our lives, including our jobs. Patterns provide us with something familiar, something that we are comfortable with because we have repeated them in the past. We become able to go through these patterns in our lives almost without thinking.

We become uncomfortable when we don't know what to expect next in our lives. When no discernable pattern exists, we have nothing familiar to rely on as a reference point. This can make you feel detached or as if you are in uncharted territory. Everything is a pattern if you step back far enough. You need to find these patterns and get into the rhythm they provide. *Management rhythms* give you a comfortable, predictable pattern to follow. You can anticipate what move you should make next based on these repeated patterns. You need to find your groove. Feel the beat, get with the rhythm, feel the vibes, get on down.

One, two, three, four; one, two, three, four; cha, cha, cha.

People will see the difference with you once you get into the management rhythm. You will seem more comfortable, confident, and in control of your job. They may not be able to exactly put their finger on what is different about you. They might not say anything, but they will notice. Nothing will faze you because you are in the "zone." You will know what your next step should be and what steps will follow. It is like having dance steps painted on the floor for you to follow. Fred Astaire or Ginger Rogers couldn't be smoother or more rhythmic than you on top of your management form.

You answer the phone, type a report, dash off to a meeting—all with a sense of timing and coordination as if you have done these things a thousand times before. In reality, you have. Why shouldn't you get into a rhythm? You just have to find your groove and stay in it.

One, two, three, four; one, two, three, four; cha, cha, cha.

As you effortlessly glide from one crisis to another, you have a flow, a cadence, yes, even a rhythm that you follow. You have danced this dance before. You take the lead and set the example for confidence and self-assuredness in your workplace. Colleagues may even feel a little (or a lot) jealous of you and your new attitude and wonder how they might get into this mode.

One, two, three, four; one, two, three, four; cha, cha, cha.

Eight Steps to Take to Get into Your Management Rhythm

Step 1. Identify what frustrates you the most about your job. The first step in any problem resolution process is to identify the root cause of the problem. This can often be much more difficult than you might think to accomplish. The true cause of a problem is not always readily apparent. Problems often disguise themselves as something else. For example, other people may often appear to be the cause of a problem when it really isn't their fault. They may simply be innocent victims of the true source of the problem. Perhaps it is something in your management process or system that is the true cause of the problem and not those who have to work with these deficiencies.

Step 2. Look for patterns in these sources of frustration. Finding these patterns may take some time. You may have to gather a significant amount of data in order to identify these problem patterns. Once you have enough data, review it carefully for trends. You may be surprised how readily apparent these trends are once you have collected enough data to see their existence. Just identifying these patterns to problems may provide insight into solving them.

Step 3. Find those aspects of the patterns that cause you the most frustration. Graphing or charting these patterns can help you identify precisely where in these patterns your problems at work might exist. You could probably also graph your frustration levels along these same problem patterns. The more you understand what and where the causes of your work frustrations are, the better you will be able to develop effective solutions to them.

Step 4. List ways in which these constant frustration sources might be eliminated or reduced. Making a list of the possible ways in which these might be eliminated provides you with a number of different options. Don't worry about the practicality of these solutions, at least not at first. The most important thing is to think of any and every way that the problem could be addressed. Once you are satisfied that you have come up with as many ideas as you can think of, begin eliminating those that would not be practical or effective. However, be careful not to scratch something that might be a good idea but presented in an impractical manner. Once you have whittled your list down to a manageable number, rank the ideas from most to least useful. Look at the ideas you ranked highest and decide which one(s) you will pursue.

Step 5. List what steps you need to take each time these patterns emerge. Look for commonalities in the solutions you developed. You may be surprised how one solution may correct any number of problems. Often there can be one source to multiple problems. It is often the variation of the problems that is random, not the source. Taking the same corrective action or actions can often be effective to solve any number of problems that on their surface appear unrelated. You may also find a way to correct the problem once and for all.

Step 6. Think about how many times you go through these same patterns on a regular basis. Take a step back and think about just how much frustration these problems have caused you in the past. You may see that the same unproductive syndrome has occurred over and over again. Think about how discovering the true cause of the problem could reduce the frustration you have been experiencing at work.

Step 7. Look for ways to improve your skills in performing these patterns. As they say, practice makes perfect. The more you perform these problem-correction patterns, the more natural they will become. Before long you will find that you no longer have to think about them, as they become part of your natural rhythm at work. But one word of caution—make sure that you develop good rhythms. Don't just learn different unproductive patterns. Make sure that your replacement pattern is the best way to make these problems go away and not reoccur.

Step 8. Identify the rhythm to the patterns. Look for new patterns as they emerge. Identify what follows what in sequence. You may have to take a step back to see the whole picture emerge. Each action you take can set off a series of other actions. Look for the consequences of these actions and subsequent patterns that emerge. Make sure that you get "upstream" far enough to intervene early enough in the process to have a positive impact. Once you have found the best solutions to these problems, look for the natural rhythms that are occurring. These rhythms may be in the way that others react to a particular situation. People's behaviors provide much of the natural rhythm that will occur in your workplace. Pay attention and take note of how people react to things that happen at work. You will begin to see patterns that lead to identifying natural rhythms.

Case Study

Steve Green felt like he was in a rut at work that he just couldn't find his way out of no matter how hard he tried. It was as if everywhere he turned he ended up on a dead-end street. Nothing seemed to work out the way it was supposed to. He just couldn't seem to get into a rhythm. Every day seemed to bring a different problem that he had never encountered before. He felt that he was adrift on a raft at sea being beaten constantly by pounding waves.

Then one day when the problems at work seemed particularly bad, he was so frustrated that he just sat down and began to think about what he could do to end this nightmare. As chaos was ensuing around him, he took a moment to look at the bigger picture. As he thought about it, he began to see a pattern to his problems. Steve began to identify the real cause of his frustrations at work (Step 1). He soon discovered the true root cause. Problems often disguise themselves as symptoms of the true cause. Many of the problems and frustrations he was experiencing at work were due to his own lack of organization. He seemed to spend inordinate amounts of time trying to find information that he had previously used, often just days before. We often focus on the wrong things when responding reactively to problems. He realized that he was experiencing the *same problems but under different rocks* each day. He kept placing blame for his problems on others when his lack of organization was really the root cause all the time.

Steve began to look for patterns in these sources of frustration (Step 2). Each day he kept a log of the problems and frustrations he experienced at work. Quickly he realized that most of the problems centered on information storage and retrieval. As he analyzed this data, he also discovered that a big part of the problem was the way he reacted each time. He would spend hours trying to find data that, if he had only filed it properly on the computer system, could have been quickly retrieved. He also saw what he could now understand was a predictable pattern. The pattern went like this: Poor information storage led to "lost" data; he then panicked, had to make new inquiries and search for the information, and finally discovered it, although by this time he was very frustrated. This process would then repeat itself the next day. It was apparent that Steve's work habits were at the root cause of the problem.

Steve decided he needed to understand which of the sources of his problems caused the most frustration (Step 3). He charted all of the problems he identified and then prioritized them from the most to least frustrating to him. He looked at all the ways in which he stored or saved information throughout his work day. He then could decide which problems would be his first priorities, beginning with the most frustrating problems first.

He began to list how problems could be better addressed and ultimately eliminated (Step 4). At first, he didn't worry about the practicality of his resolutions. He just wanted to get as many ideas down on paper as possible. On his original list were solutions such as hiring a personal assistant, buying a new personal computer that had expanded storage capabilities, taking computer training, getting assistance from subject-matter experts on organization, setting up more filing cabinets, and so on.

The next step was to identify how these ideas could help him develop realistic solutions to his problems and frustrations at work. He looked for a commonality, a pattern or approach that he could become comfortable with and that would be effective each time problems occurred. Steve now realized that he really needed to find a consistent approach to dealing with the challenges that his work presented (Step 5). Steve tried something completely different when the problems arose. Instead of reacting instinctively to each situation, he began to force himself to be more disciplined. With the help of a systems person at work, he developed an electronic filing system that enabled him to not only more quickly store information but to retrieve it more easily as well. At first this required a certain amount of discipline every day. However, it became more and more natural to him as time went by. Problems were less stressful because Steve knew what he would do when a situation came up. When he could readily find information he needed, he didn't revert to his old ways of frantically searching everywhere, but now could quickly go to an indexed filing system that led him directly to the information he was seeking.

He now could clearly see the patterns that had caused problems to occur in the past and solutions thus became more and more apparent (Step 6). Perhaps not surprisingly, Steve's ability to efficiently and effectively resolve problems increased dramatically. He began to utilize consistent approaches to other aspects of his job responsibilities as well. He learned to be much more organized and disciplined in a number of other aspects of his job and continued to become more and more comfortable at work as he adapted a natural rhythm for getting things done.

He also focused on making sure that the new management rhythms that he was adapting were effective in preventing problems and frustrations from reoccurring in the future (Step 7). He looked for cause-and-effect relationships between his repeated behaviors and problem resolutions. If a relationship wasn't positive, he adjusted his behaviors. Sometimes just doing things right wasn't enough. He also had to do the right things. In Steve's case, this involved storing the information that would be important at a later date.

He realized that he had to be careful not to establish unproductive management rhythms. If he spent all of his time saving the wrong information, he would have accomplished nothing. He might even make matters worse. He paid close attention to the rhythms that were emerging from his problem-solving process and ensured that he was taking a step far enough back to see the rhythmic patterns that were emerging and that he indeed was doing the right things. He liked what he saw and the rhythms that he now found himself in at work (Step 8). He now truly found his management rhythm.

One, two, three, four; one, two, three, four; cha, cha, cha. Good luck getting into your own management rhythm!

Peter R. Garber *has been working as a human resource professional for the past twenty-five years. He is currently manager of Equal Employment Opportunity for PPG Industries, Inc., headquartered in Pittsburgh, Pennsylvania. Mr. Garber is the author of a number of business books and articles, including his most recent book,* Giving and Receiving Performance Feedback. *He has been a regular contributor to the Pfeiffer* Annuals *for the past ten years.*

Performance-Management Techniques for Developing Self-Sufficient Workers

Teri Lund and Susan Barksdale

Summary

Globalization has created an opportunity for businesses to decrease costs by placing jobs worldwide. Yet, whether managers find themselves in the United States, Europe, Japan, Asia, or Africa, the same need surfaces... the need to determine whether worker performance is meeting the business need.

Understanding how to create and maintain meaningful performance indicators not only improves employee performance but it creates an environment in which recruitment, development, and promotion are aligned with the overall improvement of performance and productivity.

Providing managers, team leads, and supervisors with tools that help them develop self-sufficient workers is paramount in today's resource-scarce world. Techniques for doing so are outlined in this article.

Gaps in worker performance occur for several reasons: (1) a lack of understanding of performance goals and how those goals relate to the business's bottom line; (2) a need for more emphasis on development and performance-improvement opportunities; (3) a lack of identification of performance standards that are directly linked to the duties and responsibilities of a specific job; and (4) the need to improve performance conversations that focus on what was expected and how to further develop skills and knowledge that apply to the job and the business need.

Helping managers, team leaders, and supervisors to identify the part of the performance that is important for the business, for meeting management goals, and for individual workers is key to enriching the overall performance-management cycle.

Performance appraisals and related systems often fail because they are time-consuming and tend not to be related to the organization's business. Pat Crull, vice president and CLO at Toys "R" Us, points out that "Every penny counts every day. Even as the economy loosens, the lessons of the hard years have reached so many people that there will be no more room for anything that isn't focused on making organizations better. Once you're lean and efficient, there's no turning back" (Galagan, 2003).

It is critical that management teams possess skills to identify and motivate workers to perform at their highest levels. This article focuses on effective performance-management techniques that help organizations meet their business needs.

Identifying the Fundamental Performance-Management Need

As stated previously, there are several reasons why worker performance gaps may or may not be met through an organization's performance-management approach. These reasons range from a lack of understanding of the relationship between worker goals and business outputs to the inability to identify opportunities to develop one's own skills for the future. Therefore, it is important for the management team to identify the aspects of performance management that must be developed or improved.

In some organizations, growing the workforce is the most important performance-management need. The business is rapidly changing and workers have to be prepared to fill future jobs. In other organizations, the need may be to set clearer performance standards directly related to the job to be done. For example, an organization tends to measure special projects rather than the skills and knowledge needed to fill a specific job function. Even though these projects have ended long ago, workers are still being rated on the performance needs generated by the projects and not on their knowledge or skills. In this case, metrics have to be altered so that workers are evaluated on the knowledge and skills related to their current jobs.

The need to have a performance conversation rather than fill out forms or enter data into a system is critical to bolstering worker morale and helping employees understand how to be more efficient and effective in the organization. For the management team, the ability to clearly identify developmental opportunities that link to job needs is as important as being able to spend a limited budget wisely.

One method that has been used successfully to identify where to focus performance-management efforts includes the following steps:

- Identify performance-management activities initiated over the past few years. Did they work? Why or why not?

- Determine whether something else is needed to enhance performance management. Are performance conversations held? Are they effective? Why or why not or how or how not?

- Assess whether workers really understand how their job outputs relate to performance outputs.

- Determine whether there are opportunities existing within the organization (or that can be funded outside the organization) that would develop the skills or knowledge needed by the business unit to survive and be successful in the future.

- Agree to the performance indicators that should and will be communicated and measured to evaluate performance.

- Document the performance discussion in writing and have both parties review them.

Establishing an Understanding of Goals and Business Output

It may be difficult for workers to understand what may seem like esoteric goals and the relationship of those goals to a business output such as *improving competitive advantage*. For example, decreasing call time for a call center does not necessarily seem to improve competitive advantage. However, if customers spend less time on the phone voicing concerns or questions and feel satisfied with the information supplied, they tend to select that company over the competition when the opportunity arises.

How then does a member of the management team link a worker's or job's goals to the outcomes and bottom line of an organization?

Listed below are some questions to help both the manager and worker analyze goals for business performance.

- What are the "business outputs" associated with this job?

- How do the worker's or job's goals relate to these outputs?

- What tasks that are performed routinely by the workers or in the job relate to both the goal and the desired business output?

- How will meeting this goal benefit the organization?

- How will not meeting this goal hurt the organization?

- If this goal did not exist, would the overall performance be impacted? In what way?
- What are examples of the outcomes that would result if this goal were met by performing well versus meeting this goal through mediocre performance?

The management team can use these questions to define goal expectations for workers or in one-on-one conversations with workers when setting performance expectations.

Identifying Performance Indicators

Performance indicators describe the expected or accomplished level of workplace performance by individual worker or job. Performance indicators support the collection of data that is relevant and reliable and provide valid measurement information. The data collected should tell managers how they are fulfilling the organization's direction and how the worker and the job provide value to the organization.

The elements that comprise a performance indicator most often include (1) the output of a job (the amount produced, the yield, the quality, the productivity result); (2) the outcomes for the organization (results if this job is done well), (3) the product produced or by-product that results through completing the job (the final product or only part of the product, but it is helpful to identify an *audit trail* linked to a specific product); (4) the worker's ability to be self-sufficient and self-reliant.

By measuring a worker's self-sufficiency you are measuring the cost of having that individual in the job (or his or her consumption) versus what is produced (consumption < production [C < P]). Self-reliance is important to performance because it indicates the extent to which an individual can work alone without supervision or controls and still produce a quality product or be a part of the production.

An example of how a performance indicator may be created by using these elements is illustrated in Table 1.

Developing Skills and Knowledge Today and for the Future

One of the problems many managers, supervisors, and team leaders have in defining skills and knowledge, whether for today's need or future needs, is the tendency to lump knowledge and skill into one category rather than looking at each separately and identifying whether a worker requires a greater understanding of a task or if what the worker is *doing* is incorrect or being performed at the wrong level.

Table 1. Creating a Performance Indicator

Job Output	Organization Outcomes	Product or By-Product	Self-Sufficiency	Self-Reliance
Creation of cylinder with less than 2 percent scrap	Printer pricing is competitive; parts are not defective so customer is satisfied	Laser printer	Cost of worker* is met if scrap is less than 5 percent and worker produces more than fifteen cylinders	Team lead supervises and checks for overrun and quality at intervals
Twenty-two cylinders created in 1 hour	Printer production meets demand	Same as above	Same as above	Supervisor reviews output on hourly basis

*Included in worker cost: salary, training, benefits, worker's compensation, and space on production line.

A method to support this task—Bloom's taxonomy—was created in the 1950s and remains sound today. The method is often used to create educational objectives. Bloom's taxonomy can be used to classify cognitive processes into six levels or types (Anderson, 2000). The levels are defined as follows:

- *Knowledge*—the ability to *recall* information or *remember* content, to *identify* facts or concepts.

- *Comprehension*—the ability to *translate* information or *recognize* that new concepts are being introduced; working with the facts or concepts and determining when *new* facts or concepts are introduced.

- *Application*—*demonstrating* or using what was previously learned or knowledge that was deployed; *using* facts or concepts in new or different situations effectively.

- *Analysis*—the ability to break the whole into parts. Information is compared to other information or questioned or differentiated appropriately. *Analyzing* and studying the individual facts rather than just looking at the intact problem or situation.

- *Synthesis*—the ability to use parts to assemble a whole. Given the facts or concepts, the individual is able to create a totally different work or ideas are merged into a new product. *Creating* something new using the previous facts or concepts.

Table 2. Levels of the Bloom Taxonomy

Bloom's Level	Terms Related to Level
Knowledge	Recall, list, define, tell, describe, recognize, repeat, memorize, match, list, state, write, cite, quote, tabulate, collect
Comprehension	Summarize, translate, segregate, select, sort, discuss, recognize, identify, review, restate, interpret, classify, describe, distinguish, express, indicate, estimate, locate
Application	Apply, use, solve, demonstrate, teach, illustrate, show, sketch, schedule, operate, prepare, determine, complete, calculate
Analysis	Analyze, discriminate, differentiate, inspect, probe, compare, diagram, test, question, perceive, connect, classify, divide, infer, arrange, compare, explain
Synthesis	Combine, integrate, modify, rearrange, substitute, create, invent, formulate, rewrite, merge, improve
Evaluation	Assess, decide, rank, grade, test, measure, recommend, convince, select, judge, conclude, compare, summarize, evaluate, value, predict, estimate

- *Evaluation*—the highest level of Bloom's taxonomy is the ability to assess or judge whether another individual can operate or demonstrate the ability to work at all other levels. *Appraising a judgment* or *a decision* that used the facts or concepts.

This method can be useful to the management team, as it enables them to identify at what level an individual has to be working versus at what level he or she is actually working. For example, if a worker is able to recall the steps for solving a problem when a customer calls the help desk, that person is most likely working at the *Knowledge* level.

Table 2 is provided to help managers recognize the levels at which employees are working. By reviewing the terms listed in the table, members of the management team can identify what they have seen a worker exhibit on the job. For example, "I have seen Pat *modify* the call protocols effectively to meet a customer's concern or anxiety" (*modify* = working at the *Synthesis* level). Or "Perhaps Lee *probes* the customer with sound questions but is unable to *formulate* or *rewrite* the customer problem when escalating the problem to an engineer" (*probes* = working at the *Analysis* level; *formulate* or *rewrite* = the *Synthesis* level). Consequently Lee is able to analyze what the problem is and, if it fits the mold, he can respond to the customer. However, if a new process or product has to be created, Lee cannot communicate this need.

Identifying Development and Improvement Opportunities

If a member of the management team can accurately identify at what level an individual is working versus the level at which that individual should be working, then a development and improvement opportunity can be devised—whether it is in the form of a training experience, an on-the-job experience, or some other form of education.

Employees working at lower than expected levels have performance deficiencies and are not self-sufficient. In certain cases, these workers are costing the organization more than they are producing. In today's cost-conscious environment, this is a serious business issue. This situation can be remedied by identifying specifically what these workers need to do versus what they are currently doing. Sometimes it is simply a communication problem. In other cases it is a performance issue and may or may not be resolved with the proper learning opportunity.

In other situations management may find that an employee is working at a higher than expected level. This usually equates to a higher than expected C < P ratio, indicating that the worker has more potential. Identifying opportunities to further that worker's development is a service to everyone. Again, identifying the next level to which a worker can progress and giving that person the appropriate learning opportunities can increase production and productivity. Table 3 uses Bloom's Taxonomy to demonstrate how managers can determine which type of development opportunities to provide for their employees.

Improving the Performance Conversation

Too often performance is considered only when it does not meet organizational needs, and not when things are going well. It is important in today's environment to continually identify ways to increase employee satisfaction and productivity. Using the *TRUE* method shown below, managers can do both.

- *Timely discussion.* Schedule a meeting to discuss the individual's performance and development needs and opportunities. Don't put off a needed discussion. Make sure workers have, at minimum, a twice-yearly opportunity to hear how they are performing and what performance is self-sufficient, what is below, and what is above.

- *Realistic goals and agreed-on next steps.* When discussing future performance, be realistic in setting goals. Einstein did not learn all there is to know about physics in a month, so managers should not set unrealistic goals for workers, and workers should not agree to something they cannot or will not do. Honesty is important on both sides.

Table 3. Deciding Which Opportunities Are Appropriate

Bloom's Level	Types of Development or Improvement Opportunities that Relate to the Level
Knowledge	Knowledge acquisition is usually done through reading manuals or books, class work, online classes, or manuals. Workers are provided with information and expected to recall and recite it after the review.
Comprehension	In this case, workers have acquired the basic knowledge but need an opportunity to dissect it or interpret it in different circumstances. This can also be accomplished through role plays, testing, or simulations.
Application	Application is just that—applying what has been learned to a job task or activity. Therefore, workers may simply need an opportunity to do this. Another method of successful application is for workers to teach someone else to do the task.
Analysis	To develop at an analysis level, workers must be able to apply what has been learned and then compare and analyze some aspect of their work. For example, comparing and analyzing two products to determine which one has a flaw or explain why a solution given would not work to fix a customer problem.
Synthesis	To function at the synthesis level, workers need an opportunity to identify how to improve on a process or product or to create a new process or product based on their existing knowledge. Obviously, without the ability to work efficiently at the previous four levels, this does not happen. A good way to develop synthesis is to make a working lab available or to encourage workers to experiment with current products or processes.
Evaluation	Individuals working at this level are often thought of as masters. For workers to function at this level, they must have a great deal of autonomy and the ability to fail without consequence.

- *Understanding of individual needs.* Different workers need different types of learning opportunities. It is important to ask questions and listen so that individual needs are recognized and are remedied as realistically as possible. Be flexible so that employees can be retained and meet their potential, but be careful not to promise an employee something that cannot be done.

- *Expectations.* Clearly state your expectations regarding performance, timelines, outcomes, organizational results, self-sufficiency, and self-reliance. Don't have the conversation three months after expectations are set only to discover that each party had different expectations. When the discussion is completed, document the agreed-on expectations and follow up to determine whether assistance is needed in meeting the expectations.

Employees are an important part of a successful company's value equation. Each worker is worth the time it takes to discuss performance and expectations.

Conclusion

In today's workplace environment, managers must focus on performance to increase each worker's self-sufficiency. Thoughtful performance management is a critical part of sustaining double-digit productivity markers. Helping the management team fulfill performance-management requirements in a positive and dynamic way will increase worker satisfaction and ultimately organizational results.

References

Anderson, L. (2000). *Strategy for learning, teaching and assessing.* Boston, MA: Pearson, Allyn & Bacon.

Galagan, P. (2003, June). The future of the profession. *Training & Development*, p. 31.

Teri Lund *has been a consultant for twelve years. Previously, she held management positions for Barclays Bank and Kaiser Permanente. She has a bachelor of science degree from Montana State University and a master's degree in international business and finance from New York University. Ms. Lund has in-depth experience in implementing alternative methods of learning through technology. She is a recognized leader in the area of technology and its impact on learning and performance improvement.*

Susan Barksdale *has been a performance-improvement consultant to numerous corporations for the last fifteen years and speaks frequently at industry conferences. Previously, she managed training and consulting departments for two financial consulting firms. She holds graduate and undergraduate degrees in the behavioral sciences from the University of Wisconsin and served as a psychotherapist at Mount Sinai Medical Center and in private practice. She and Teri Lund recently co-authored ASTD's* Learning and Performance Workbook Series.

Contributors

Jean Barbazette
The Training Clinic
645 Seabreeze Drive
Seal Beach, CA 90740-5746
  (562) 430-2484
  email: jean@thetrainingclinic.com

Susan Barksdale
Strategic Assessment and Evaluation
  Associates, LLC
4534 SW Tarlow Court
Portland, OR 97221
  (503) 223-7721
  email: sbarksdale@att.net

Teri-E Belf
2016 Lakebreeze Way
Reston, VA 20191-4021
  (703) 716-8374
  fax: (703) 264-7867
  email: belf@erols.com
  URL: www.erols.com/belf
  URL: www.successunlimitednet.com

Zane L. Berge, Ph.D.
University of Maryland, Baltimore
  Campus
1000 Hilltop Circle
Baltimore, MD 21250
  (410) 455-2306
  email: berge@umbc.edu

Lois Danis
Performance Manager
State of Florida Department of
  Transportation
3400 West Commercial Boulevard
Ft. Lauderdale, FL 33309-3421
  (954) 777-4420
  fax: (954) 777-2293

Adrian Furnham
Department of Psychology
University College London
26 Bedford Way
London WC1 0AP
England
  (0044) 207-679-5395
  email: ucjtsaf@ucl.ac.uk

Paul L. Garavaglia, Ed.D.
OpMot
1520 South Lapeer Road, Suite 207
Lake Orion, MI 48360
  (248) 814-7675
  fax: (248) 814-7685
  email: paul@opmot.com

Peter R. Garber
PPG Industries, Inc.
One PPG Place
Pittsburgh, PA 15272
　(412) 434-2009
　fax: (412) 434-3490
　email: garber@ppg.com

Donna L. Goldstein, Ed.D.
Managing Director
Development Associates
　International, Inc.
3389 Sheridan Street, #309
Hollywood, FL 33021
　(954) 893-0123
　fax: (954) 893-0170
　email: devasscint@aol.com
　URL: www.DAInt.org

Gail Hahn, MA, CSP, CPRP, CLL
Fun*cilitators
11407 Orchard Green Court
Reston, VA 20190
　(866) 386-2896 (866.fun.at.work)
　fax: (530) 326-2979
　email: gail@funcilitators.com
　URL: www.funcilators.com

Stephen G. Haines
Centre for Strategic Management
1420 Monitor Road
San Diego, CA 92110-1545
　(619) 275-6528
　fax: (619) 275-0324
　email: info@csmintl.com
　URL: www.csmintl.com
　URL: www.SystemsThinkingPress.com

Lois B. Hart, Ed.D.
Women's Leadership Institute
11256 WCR 23
Ft. Lupton, CO 80621
　(970) 785-2716
　email: lhart@seqnet.net

Herb Kindler, Ph.D.
Herb Kindler & Associates
427 Beirut Avenue
Pacific Palisades, CA 90272
　(310) 459-0585
　email: herbkindler@aol.com

George E. Krock
PPG Industries. Inc.
One PPG Place
Pittsburgh, PA 15272
　(412) 434-3413
　fax: (412) 434-3490
　email: krock@ppg.com

Deborah Spring Laurel
Laurel and Associates, Ltd.
917 Vilas Avenue
Madison, WI 53715
　(608) 255-2010
　fax: (608) 260-2616
　email: dlaurel@ameritech.net

Robert William Lucas
President
Creative Presentation Resources, Inc.
P.O. Box 180487
Casselberry, FL 32718-0487
　(800) 308-0399/(407) 695-5535
　fax: (407)695-7447
　URL: www.presentationresources.net

Teri Lund
Strategic Assessment and Evaluation
 Associates, LLC
4534 SW Tarlow Court
Portland, OR 97221
 (503) 245-9020
 email: tlund_bls@msn.com

Anne M. McMahon, Ph.D.
Department of Management
Youngstown State University
One University Plaza
Youngstown, OH 44555-3071
 (330) 941-3071
 URL: www.cc.ysu.edu/~ammcmahon/

Lenn Millbower
Offbeat Training®
329 Oakpoint Circle
Davenport, FL 33837
 (407) 256-0501
 email: lennmillbower@offbeattrain-
  ing.com
 URL: www.offbeattraining.com

Niki Nichols
P.O. Box 628
Burnet, TX 78611
 (512) 389-4467
 fax: (512) 756-7065

Carolyn Nilson, Ed.D.
38 Rood Hill Road
Sandisfield, MA 01255
 (413) 258-3369
 email: ttc12672@taconic.net

Edwina Pio, Ph.D.
Auckland University of Technology
Faculty of Business
Mer-Level 2, 46 Wakefield Street
Private Bag 92006
Auckland 1020
New Zealand
 +64.9.9179999, ext. 5130
 fax: +64.9.9179884
 email: epio@aut.ac.nz

Robert C. Preziosi
Professor of Management
H. Wayne Huizenga School of Business
 and Entrepreneurship
3301 College Avenue
Ft. Lauderdale, FL 33314
 (954) 262-5111
 fax: (954) 262-3965
 email: preziosi@huizenga.nova.edu

Frank A. Prince
Unleash Your Mind LLC
512 North McClurg Court, Suite #4807
Chicago, IL 60611
 (312) 828-9245
 URL: www.speedsleep.com
 URL: www.unleashyourmind.com

John Sample
2922 Shamrock South
Tallahassee, FL 32309
 (850) 644-8176
 fax (850) 644-6401
 email: sample@coe.fsu.edu

C. Louise Sellaro
Department of Management
Youngstown State University
One University Plaza
Youngstown, OH 44555-3071
   (330) 941-3071
   URL: www.Webed.org

Robert Shaver
Program Director
University of Wisconsin-Madison
School of Business
601 University Avenue
Madison, WI 53715-1035
   (608) 441-7334
   fax: (608) 441-7325
   email: bshaver@bus.wisc.edu

Steve Sphar
2870 Third Avenue
Sacramento, CA 95818
   (916) 731-4851
   fax: (916) 739-8057
   email: sphar1@earthlink.net

Linda Byars Swindling, JD, CSP
Passports to Success
3509 Cimarron Drive
Carrollton, TX 75007
   (972) 416-3652
   fax: (972) 416-0220
   email: Linda@PassportsToSuccess.com
   URL: www.PassportsToSuccess.com

Chih-Hsiung Tu, Ph.D.
Assistant Professor
Educational Technology Leadership
Department of Educational Leadership
Graduate School of Education &
   Human Development
The George Washington University
2134 G Street NW
Washington, DC 20052
   (202) 994-2676
   fax: (202) 994-2145
   email: ctu@gwu.edu

Charlotte S. Waisman
30334 Inverness Lane
Evergreen, CO 80439
   (303) 674-2345
   email: Jottin1303@aol.com

Ryan Watkins
The George Washington University
2134 G Street NW, #103
Washington, DC 20052
   (202) 994-2263
   email: rwatkins@gwu.edu

Contents of the Companion Volume, *The 2005 Pfeiffer Annual: Consulting*

Preface	xiii
The Difference Between Training and Consulting: Which Annual to Use?	xvii
Introduction to *The 2005 Pfeiffer Annual: Consulting*	xxi

Experiential Learning Activities

Introduction to the Experiential Learning Activities Section	1
Experiential Learning Activities Categories	5
Picture Yourself: Gaining Self-Awareness *Deborah Spring Laurel*	11
Take a Risk: Practicing Self-Disclosure *Ira J. Morrow*	17
At the Movies: Building Cross-Cultural Sensitivity *Teresa Torres-Coronas*	25
All Power Is Relative: Checking Ourselves Against Others *Robert Shaver*	35
The Association for Community Improvement: Dealing with Hidden Agendas *Donna L. Goldstein and Luis R. Morales*	43
Give Brands a Hand: Generating Ideas *Arthur B. VanGundy*	55
Pass It On: Using an Alternate Brainstorming Technique *Brenda Hubbard and Susan Crosson*	59
Altair the Ant: Influencing Performance *Lorraine L. Ukens*	63
The Hats We Wear: Understanding Team Roles *Kristin J. Arnold*	69

The Last Team Member: Building a Team *Connie Phillips*	73
Plunge In: Using Openers to Connect Groups and Their Work *M.K. Key*	77
Want/Give Walkabout: Sharing Expectations *Gail Hahn*	81
Three Roles of Leaders: Understanding Leadership *Parth Sarathi*	85
To Be the Best: Determining Aspirational Values *Cher Holton*	91

Editor's Choice

Introduction to the Editor's Choice Section	101
Corporate Meeting: Building Understanding of the Vision *Doug Campbell, John Howes, Carrie Reese, and Saundra Stroope*	103
Advice to a Protégé *Kristin J. Arnold*	109
26 Ways: Selecting Team Leaders *Robert Alan Black*	117

Inventories, Questionnaires, and Surveys

Introduction to the Inventories, Questionnaires, and Surveys Section	121
Evaluation of Performance in Team Presentations *Ira J. Morrow*	123
Organizational Citizenship Behavior Inventory: A Conceptual and Validation Analysis *Biswajeet Pattanayak, Rajnish Kumar Misra, and Phalgu Niranjana*	137

Articles and Discussion Resources

Introduction to the Articles and Discussion Resources Section	147
Consultants on the Cutting Edge *Barbara Pate Glacel*	149

Cultural Identity and Self-Concept: Implications for Influencing Others *Phyliss Cooke*	157
Mentoring: Empowering Human Capital *Mohandas K. Nair*	163
Managing Sideways *Peter R. Garber*	171
An Integrative Model for Leading Change in Organizations *Linda Russell and Jeffrey Russell*	177
What If We Took Teamwork Seriously? *W. Warner Burke*	189
A Structural and Behavioral Model of Human Resource Planning *A. Venkat Raman*	193
Evaluation, The Final Phase of Consulting *Charles L. Fields*	209
Value-Added Diversity Consulting *Tyrone A. Holmes*	219
The Write Stuff *Richard T. Whelan*	229
The Systemization of Facilitation *M.K. Key*	235
Leadership Coaching: Avoiding the Traps *Jan M. Schmuckler and Thomas J. Ucko*	243
Corporate Values and Bottom-Line Performance: The Value of Values *Steve Terrell*	251
Contributors	269
Contents of the Companion Volume, *The 2005 Pfeiffer Annual: Training*	274
How to Use the CD-ROM	277
Pfeiffer Publications Guide	279

How to Use the CD-ROM

System Requirements

PC with Microsoft Windows 98SE or later
Mac with Apple OS version 8.6 or later

Using the CD with Windows

To view the items located on the CD, follow these steps:

1. Insert the CD into your computer's CD-ROM drive.
2. A window appears with the following options:

   Contents: Allows you to view the files included on the CD-ROM.

   Software: Allows you to install useful software from the CD-ROM.

   Links: Displays a hyperlinked page of websites.

   Author: Displays a page with information about the author(s).

   Contact Us: Displays a page with information on contacting the publisher or author.

   Help: Displays a page with information on using the CD.

   Exit: Closes the interface window.

If you do not have autorun enabled, or if the autorun window does not appear, follow these steps to access the CD:

1. Click Start -> Run.

2. In the dialog box that appears, type d:<\\>start.exe, where d is the letter of your CD-ROM drive. This brings up the autorun window described in the preceding set of steps.

3. Choose the desired option from the menu. (See Step 2 in the preceding list for a description of these options.)

In Case of Trouble

If you experience difficulty using the CD-ROM, please follow these steps:

1. Make sure your hardware and systems configurations conform to the system requirements noted under "System Requirements" above.

2. Review the installation procedure for your type of hardware and operating system.

It is possible to reinstall the software if necessary.

To speak with someone in Product Technical Support, call 800-762-2974 or 317-572-3994 M–F 8:30 a.m.–5:00 p.m. EST. You can also get support and contact Product Technical Support through our website at www.wiley.com/techsupport.

Before calling or writing, please have the following information available:

- Type of computer and operating system
- Any error messages displayed
- Complete description of the problem.

It is best if you are sitting at your computer when making the call.

Pfeiffer Publications Guide

This guide is designed to familiarize you with the various types of Pfeiffer publications. The formats section describes the various types of products that we publish; the methodologies section describes the many different ways that content might be provided within a product. We also provide a list of the topic areas in which we publish.

FORMATS

In addition to its extensive book-publishing program, Pfeiffer offers content in an array of formats, from fieldbooks for the practitioner to complete, ready-to-use training packages that support group learning.

FIELDBOOK Designed to provide information and guidance to practitioners in the midst of action. Most fieldbooks are companions to another, sometimes earlier, work, from which its ideas are derived; the fieldbook makes practical what was theoretical in the original text. Fieldbooks can certainly be read from cover to cover. More likely, though, you'll find yourself bouncing around following a particular theme, or dipping in as the mood, and the situation, dictate.

HANDBOOK A contributed volume of work on a single topic, comprising an eclectic mix of ideas, case studies, and best practices sourced by practitioners and experts in the field.

An editor or team of editors usually is appointed to seek out contributors and to evaluate content for relevance to the topic. Think of a handbook not as a ready-to-eat meal, but as a cookbook of ingredients that enables you to create the most fitting experience for the occasion.

RESOURCE Materials designed to support group learning. They come in many forms: a complete, ready-to-use exercise (such as a game); a comprehensive resource on one topic (such as conflict management) containing a variety of methods and approaches; or a collection of like-minded activities (such as icebreakers) on multiple subjects and situations.

TRAINING PACKAGE An entire, ready-to-use learning program that focuses on a particular topic or skill. All packages comprise a guide for the facilitator/trainer and a workbook for the participants. Some packages are supported with additional media—such as video—or learning aids, instruments, or other devices to help participants understand concepts or practice and develop skills.

- *Facilitator/trainer's guide* Contains an introduction to the program, advice on how to organize and facilitate the learning event, and step-by-step instructor notes. The guide also contains copies of presentation materials—handouts, presentations, and overhead designs, for example—used in the program.

- *Participant's workbook* Contains exercises and reading materials that support the learning goal and serves as a valuable reference and support guide for participants in the weeks and months that follow the learning event. Typically, each participant will require his or her own workbook.

ELECTRONIC CD-ROMs and web-based products transform static Pfeiffer content into dynamic, interactive experiences. Designed to take advantage of the searchability, automation, and ease-of-use that technology provides, our e-products bring convenience and immediate accessibility to your workspace.

METHODOLOGIES

CASE STUDY A presentation, in narrative form, of an actual event that has occurred inside an organization. Case studies are not prescriptive, nor are they used to prove a point; they are designed to develop critical analysis and decision-making skills. A case study has a specific time frame, specifies a sequence of events, is narrative in structure, and contains a plot structure—an issue (what should be/have been done?). Use case studies when the goal is to enable participants to apply previously learned theories to the circumstances in the case, decide what is pertinent, identify the real issues, decide what should have been done, and develop a plan of action.

ENERGIZER A short activity that develops readiness for the next session or learning event. Energizers are most commonly used after a break or lunch to stimulate or refocus the group. Many involve some form of physical activity, so they are a useful way to counter post-lunch lethargy. Other uses include transitioning from one topic to another, where "mental" distancing is important.

EXPERIENTIAL LEARNING ACTIVITY (ELA) A facilitator-led intervention that moves participants through the learning cycle from experience to application (also known as a Structured Experience). ELAs are carefully thought-out designs in which there is a definite learning purpose and intended outcome. Each step—everything that participants do during the activity—facilitates the accomplishment of the stated goal. Each ELA includes complete instructions for facilitating the intervention and a clear statement of goals, suggested group size and timing, materials required, an explanation of the process, and, where appropriate, possible variations to the activity. (For more detail on Experiential Learning Activities, see the Introduction to the *Reference Guide to Handbooks and Annuals*, 1999 edition, Pfeiffer, San Francisco.)

GAME A group activity that has the purpose of fostering team spirit and togetherness in addition to the achievement of a pre-stated goal. Usually contrived—undertaking a desert expedition, for example—this type of learning method offers an engaging means for participants to demonstrate and practice business and interpersonal skills. Games are effective for team building and personal development mainly because the goal is subordinate to the process—the means through which participants reach decisions, collaborate, communicate, and generate trust and understanding. Games often engage teams in "friendly" competition.

ICEBREAKER A (usually) short activity designed to help participants overcome initial anxiety in a training session and/or to acquaint the participants with one another. An icebreaker can be a fun activity or can be tied to specific topics or training goals. While a useful tool in itself, the icebreaker comes into its own in situations where tension or resistance exists within a group.

INSTRUMENT A device used to assess, appraise, evaluate, describe, classify, and summarize various aspects of human behavior. The term used to describe an instrument depends primarily on its format and purpose. These terms include survey, questionnaire, inventory, diagnostic survey, and poll. Some uses of instruments include providing instrumental feedback to group members, studying here-and-now processes or functioning within a group, manipulating group composition, and evaluating outcomes of training and other interventions.

Instruments are popular in the training and HR field because, in general, more growth can occur if an individual is provided with a method for focusing specifically on his or her own behavior. Instruments also are used to obtain information that will serve as a basis for change and to assist in workforce planning efforts.

Paper-and-pencil tests still dominate the instrument landscape with a typical package comprising a facilitator's guide, which offers advice on administering the instrument and interpreting the collected data, and an initial set of instruments. Additional instruments are available separately. Pfeiffer, though, is investing heavily in e-instruments. Electronic instrumentation provides effortless distribution and, for larger groups particularly, offers advantages over paper-and-pencil tests in the time it takes to analyze data and provide feedback.

LECTURETTE A short talk that provides an explanation of a principle, model, or process that is pertinent to the participants' current learning needs. A lecturette is intended to establish a common language bond between the trainer and the participants by providing a mutual frame of reference. Use a lecturette as an introduction to a group activity or event, as an interjection during an event, or as a handout.

MODEL A graphic depiction of a system or process and the relationship among its elements. Models provide a frame of reference and something more tangible, and more easily remembered, than a verbal explanation. They also give participants something to "go on," enabling them to track their own progress as they experience the dynamics, processes, and relationships being depicted in the model.

ROLE PLAY A technique in which people assume a role in a situation/scenario: a customer service rep in an angry-customer exchange, for example. The way in which the role is approached is then discussed and feedback is offered. The role play is often repeated using a different approach and/or incorporating changes made based on feedback received. In other words, role playing is a spontaneous interaction involving realistic behavior under artificial (and safe) conditions.

SIMULATION A methodology for understanding the interrelationships among components of a system or process. Simulations differ from games in that they test or use a model that depicts or mirrors some aspect of reality in form, if not necessarily in content. Learning occurs by studying the effects of change on one or more factors of the model. Simulations are commonly used to test hypotheses about what happens in a system—often referred to as "what if?" analysis—or to examine best-case/worst-case scenarios.

THEORY A presentation of an idea from a conjectural perspective. Theories are useful because they encourage us to examine behavior and phenomena through a different lens.

TOPICS

The twin goals of providing effective and practical solutions for workforce training and organization development and meeting the educational needs of training and human resource professionals shape Pfeiffer's publishing program. Core topics include the following:

Leadership & Management

Communication & Presentation

Coaching & Mentoring

Training & Development

e-Learning

Teams & Collaboration

OD & Strategic Planning

Human Resources

Consulting